MW01036051

'Another book about Jesus? Dusenbury's book will be worth your time, even in disagreement.'

Joseph H. H. Weiler, Co-Director, Jean Monnet Center for
International and Regional Economic Law and Justice,
New York University School of Law

'An astonishingly erudite example of a decidedly philosophical commentary on the gospels, this book investigates the unsettling suspension of the "power to judge, compel or fight" by Jesus, the mystical judge. Yet, it does more than that. It shows why philosophical investigations of the gospel are still indispensable if we want to understand the notoriously misconceived roots of our Western civilization.'

Johannes Hoff, Professor of Dogmatic Theology,
University of Innsbruck

I JUDGE NO ONE

DAVID LLOYD DUSENBURY

I Judge No One

A Political Life of Jesus

OXFORD
UNIVERSITY PRESS

OXFORD
UNIVERSITY PRESS

Oxford University Press is a department of the
University of Oxford. It furthers the University's objective
of excellence in research, scholarship, and education
by publishing worldwide.

Oxford   New York

Auckland   Cape Town   Dar es Salaam   Hong Kong   Karachi
Kuala Lumpur   Madrid   Melbourne   Mexico City   Nairobi
New Delhi   Shanghai   Taipei   Toronto

With offices in

Argentina   Austria   Brazil   Chile   Czech Republic   France   Greece
Guatemala   Hungary   Italy   Japan   Poland   Portugal   Singapore
South Korea   Switzerland   Thailand   Turkey   Ukraine   Vietnam

Oxford is a registered trade mark of Oxford University Press
in the UK and certain other countries.

Published in the United States of America by
Oxford University Press
198 Madison Avenue, New York, NY 10016

Copyright © David Lloyd Dusenbury 2023

Library of Congress Cataloging-in-Publication Data is available
David Lloyd Dusenbury.
I Judge No One: A Political Life of Jesus.
ISBN: 9780197690512

Printed in the United Kingdom on acid-free paper
by Bell and Bain Ltd, Glasgow

"The just man will have to endure the lash—and finally, after every extremity of suffering, he will be crucified."

– Plato, *Republic*

"The state, or rather, the whole world is in such error that it persecutes good and just men—torturing, condemning, and killing them."

– Lactantius, *Divine Institutes*

For my brother,
Timothy Dusenbury

il miglior fabbro,
the better maker

CONTENTS

CONTENTS

PART ONE

A PLACE TO BEGIN

1

JESUS THE STRANGER

We no longer know how to think about Jesus.

In one of his memorandum books, Ludwig Wittgenstein mentions that he cannot call Jesus *Lord* for the simple reason that he cannot meaningfully "utter the word 'Lord'". However, he remarks: "I could call him 'the paragon', 'God' even—or rather, I can understand it when he is so called."[1]

In *Human, All Too Human*, Friedrich Nietzsche refers to Jesus disarmingly as "the noblest human being".[2] He writes in a later book that "one could, with a degree of license, call Jesus a 'free spirit'".[3] In Nietzsche's lexicon, there is no higher praise.

Immanuel Kant's idea of Jesus is that of "a person whose wisdom, even purer than that of previous philosophers, was as though descended from heaven".[4]

And Benedict de Spinoza makes this arresting confession: "I believe no one has achieved such perfection compared to others as Christ, to whom the decrees of God which lead humankind to salvation were revealed directly." If the legislator Moses met God "face to face", the philosopher Christ knew God "mind to mind".[5] (See fig. 1.)

A book could be written about this sequence of fragments on Jesus—and other texts could be brought forward.[6] But this is not that book. Rather, we can take these fragments as a bare indication that even many of Christianity's harshest critics have held Jesus to be thought-worthy.

If we no longer know how to think about the enigmatic figure who moves through the four gospels, the fault may be ours.

H. S. Reimarus and the Modern Idea of Jesus

One reason for our lack of philosophical interest in Jesus may be confusion. We tend to confuse the person of Jesus with the legacy of Christianity, and to confuse mere denunciation with critique. Nietzsche is clarifying. He finally decided to call *The Antichrist*—his 1888 tirade—a *Curse upon Christianity*, and not a *Critique of Christianity*, as in early drafts.[7]

A curse is not critique. And critique is not the root of any culture.

In a volume of her lectures and conversations, Julia Kristeva suggests that there can be no culture of pure critique. The deepest sources of any culture must be not only interrogated, but—in a highly nuanced way—*believed*. She argues that Christianity "has introduced and continues to diffuse radical innovations ... we have not done taking the measure of", and that we "do not dare recognize ... as 'Christian difference'".[8]

But there is, to my mind, a more specific cause of our philosophical disinterest in Jesus. It is that late modern historians often envision him in the terms described by Anna Della Subin in the first pages of her shimmering book, *Accidental Gods*.[9] Subin writes that "scholars who search for the man-in-history" behind the gospels find Jesus to be immersed in "the politics of his day". He is "a Jewish dissident preacher who posed a radical challenge to the gods and governors of Rome". And this is how Subin fleshes out her modern idea of the Jesus of history:

He practices the rite of baptism as liberation, from sin and from the
bondage of the empire that occupied Jerusalem. Jesus, like many in
his age, warns that ... the current world order, in its oppressions
and injustices, will soon come to an end and the kingdom of the
Israelites will be restored, the message for which he will be arrested
for high treason.[10]

Here, Subin is restating a theory which was first formulated
in secret notebooks kept in the 1760s by a scholar of the high
Enlightenment, Hermann Samuel Reimarus, and only printed a
number of years after his death. (See fig. 2.) What made
Reimarus' theory iconoclastic is not the idea that the Jesus of
history is, in Subin's words, *a Jewish dissident preacher*. He manifestly is that. It is rather the idea that Jesus is *not* a dissident.
According to Reimarus, the historical Jesus held a relatively
orthodox conception of Israel's divinely chosen liberator, or
"Christ" (from the Greek *Christos* or *Messias*, from the Hebrew
Mashiah and Aramaic *Meshiah*).[11]

But Reimarus' Jesus is not a liberating figure. He is himself a
captive of the first-century political imaginary.[12] In Reimarus'
words, Jesus is not "a spiritual deliverer of humankind", but a
hill-country rebel who longed to become the "worldly deliverer
of Israel".[13] His Jesus—the exemplarily modern one—is not a
mystic visionary of a divine kingdom "within you" (*Luke* 17:21),
but a Zealot-style aspirant to sovereignty in a last-days kingdom
of Israel. It is therefore not Jesus' dissent, but rather his violent
sectarian hopes which Subin signals when she says that the historical Jesus *posed a radical challenge to the governors of Rome* and
called for *the kingdom of the Israelites to be restored*. Her twenty-
first-century rendering of Jesus owes much to Reimarus.

Curiously, however, this modern theory of Jesus is one that
Spinoza, Kant and Nietzsche all rejected—as do I—because it makes
the "dialectician out of Nazareth" philosophically uninteresting.[14]

I JUDGE NO ONE

Three Critics of the Modern Idea of Jesus

Reimarus died in Hamburg in 1768. Of course, this means that Spinoza—who died in The Hague in 1677—could not have read his secret writings on Jesus. Spinoza could only have rejected Reimarus' theory before it had been brought to expression, or *avant la lettre* as the French say. And he did. This may be because Spinoza reacted to the image of Jesus that he encountered in *The Three Impostors*, a notorious clandestine text of the seventeenth century.[15] In contrast to the lying, tyrannical Jesus who is portrayed in that anti-Christian (also anti-Judaic, and anti-Islamic) text, Spinoza's Jesus is an unexcelled icon of ethics. In his own words, Jesus was sent "to teach the universal law alone". And what is this *universal law*? Like the Hebrew prophet Isaiah, Jesus condemns hypocrisy and commends "charity towards oneself and one's neighbour".[16] The "whole of Christ's teaching", per Spinoza, inculcates love of God and humankind.[17]

Kant's relation to the hotly contested legacy of Spinoza, or *Spinozismus*, is murky. But whatever we make of that subtle question, it is clear that, like Spinoza, Kant believes that Jesus came *to teach a universal law*. (See fig. 3.) Kant's Jesus is not a Galilean terrorist or a Judaean partisan; nor is he a war-making prophetic legislator like Moses or Muhammad. (Spinoza is struck by the title of one of the lost 'books of Moses' which is cited in *Numbers* 21: "The Book of the Wars of God.")[18] Rather, Jesus is "the first [human] to advocate a pure and compelling religion, one within the grasp of the whole world", precisely because—according to Kant—the religion of Jesus is a "religion of reason".[19] And what is this *religion of reason*? A "moral faith", says Kant, and not a "political faith".[20] It is on this basis that he sharply criticizes Reimarus—and, with him, anyone who wants to make "a political and not a moral concept" of the Christ-idea.[21]

There is no limit to Nietzsche's contempt for Kant and Spinoza.[22] "Anti-nature as instinct", Nietzsche seethes, "German *décadence* as philosophy—*that is Kant!*²³ But our only interest, here, is that Nietzsche nevertheless breaks totally with Reimarus' line of thought. For Nietzsche, Jesus' revolt was not against Rome but "against 'the saints of Israel', against the hierarchy of society". His Jesus is a "holy anarchist". And though Nietzsche concedes that Jesus had a flair for "language that even today would send him to Siberia", and was thus "a political criminal", he denies that Jesus was "conscious" of the political challenge that he personified. In other words, he was an *unconscious* political criminal. "'Resist not evil'", for Nietzsche, is "the deepest word in the Gospels, their key in a certain sense".²⁴

Therefore, Nietzsche's Jesus is—like Kant's and Spinoza's—both a philosophically intriguing figure and a critic of first-century zealotry.

Two Theories of the Political Life of Jesus

For Reimarus, the historical Jesus is nothing but a failed political figure. For him, Jesus' life, sayings, and death are *in essence* political. What Jesus calls a "kingdom of heaven" is a cipher of the theocratic political order he hoped to impose on the "land of Israel".²⁵ The logic of coercion belongs to Jesus' kingdom of heaven, and vice versa. What Jesus brought was, in Kant's words, a "political faith".²⁶

Reimarus' Jesus is a radical from a gentile-heavy statelet to the north—namely, Galilee—who incited a rebellion in Jerusalem.²⁷ The *Realpolitik* drama which is concealed, or half-concealed, in the gospels is that of a failed Galilean coup in the holy city of Roman-controlled Judaea. For Reimarus, Jesus' uprising was too ill conceived to be bloody, but his 'Christ' lost his life and one of the Judaean high priest's slaves lost an ear.²⁸

Kant criticizes Reimarus' theory of Jesus by distinguishing two ideas of the *state*. One he calls *juridico-civil*, the other *ethico-*

civil. A juridico-civil state is one in which humans live together under a system of "juridical laws", all of which are coercive. To belong to such a state is to belong to an ordered system of coercion. An ethico-civil state, however, is one in which humans are united by laws *without* being coerced, which is to say, "under laws of virtue alone".[29]

In a less rebarbative terminology, Kant holds that a "political community" is by definition one that "compels its citizens" in a host of ways. An "ethical community", however, is one that has "freedom from coercion in its very concept". What Kant means is that what he calls "ethical ends" can only be *chosen*. Virtue originates in the *heart*, a place where—Kant stresses—"a human judge cannot penetrate". Only a divine mind can be the judge of human hearts, because human judgments cannot reach "the depths of other beings".[30] This is a Kantian idea which is deeply rooted in the gospels.

For Kant, the Jesus of history hoped to inaugurate an *ethical community*, a new form of order in which, theoretically, all humans could be united by laws *without* coercion. Numerous caveats could be made here, but this new form of order is what Christians call the *church*, and what Kant calls the "invisible church" (giving the phrase an Enlightenment-style meaning).[31] In Reimarus' telling, the Jesus of history hoped to revolutionize the *political community* of first-century Judaea, by installing himself at the summit of an apocalyptic system of coercion.

Reimarus' Jesus failed because his political revolution was crushed, and his political faith was traduced by his cadre of disciples. The gospels, for Reimarus, are a testament to the disciples' final betrayal of Jesus. It is in these writings that they systematically corrupt the memory of Jesus' life and hope.

Kant's Jesus, no less than Reimarus', is revolutionary. But his Jesus did not *ultimately* fail, because an "undeserved yet meritorious death" became the symbol of an ethical revolution,[32] and because the ethical faith of Jesus is still with us. Kant writes that Jesus "brought about" through his life and death "an incalculably great moral good in the world, through a revolution in the human race".[33] At the heart of that revolution is the idea of what Kant calls "a *kingdom* of virtue".[34] And what is a *kingdom of virtue*? It is one which has "freedom from coercion in its very concept".[35] It is a 'kingdom' which must be freely chosen.

Before Jesus, the idea of a *kingdom of virtue*—one which is still contentious—had never been articulated with the force and urgency that we hear in some of the sayings in the four unsigned texts which we call, in keeping with tradition, *Matthew*, *Mark*, *Luke* and *John*.

This book offers a political life of Jesus in the broad and variegated tradition of Spinoza, Kant and Nietzsche. With them, it resists the modern notion that Jesus' life, sayings and death are *in essence* political. Against Reimarus' idea of a political Christ—one which has been revived countless times in the last 250 years—I will try to show

(i) that the modern theory of a *political Christ* is utterly incongruent with the dramatic structure of our earliest texts on the life of Jesus; and

(ii) that something like Kant's theory of an *ethical Jesus*, whatever its limitations, is far more philosophically interesting.

For the divergent philosophical traditions which Nietzsche, Kant and Spinoza represent, the modern idea that Jesus is nothing but a failed, first-century rebel is doubly problematic. It blurs (or destroys) the structure and meaning of our earliest witnesses to the life of Jesus, and it is philosophically inert.[36]

I believe that if the figure of Jesus is to be thought-worthy in future, we must break with the modern tendency to reduce him to his milieus. In the city of his youth (Nazareth), in the tetrarchy to which he legally belonged (Galilee), in the Roman province he visited (Judaea) and in the holy city where he died (Jerusalem), Jesus remained—in Nietzsche's words—a "strange figure" (*fremde Gestalt*).[37] It is this strangeness that shaped his political life, and that led—I will argue—to his death as a political criminal. It is this strangeness, too, that makes Jesus' life intriguing and his sayings still worthy of reflection.

2

"WHAT IS THIS WISDOM?"

In *The Gospel of Thomas*, one of Jesus' disciples says to him: "You are like a wise philosopher (*philosophos*)."[1] Jesus has been a recurring figure in philosophical texts for twenty or twenty-one centuries.[2] From the beginning, his sayings have been seen by certain 'pagans' and Judaeans as "wise"—and, by certain Christians, as transcending the "human tradition" of philosophy (*Colossians* 2:8–9).[3]

A second-century Syrian rhetorician, Tatian, brashly tells the 'pagans' that Christ-belief is "our philosophy".[4] And there have been philosophical commentaries on the gospels since at least the late second century, when an Egyptian Christian philosopher, Clement, wrote a brief, subtle text on a scene in *Mark*.[5]

Nevertheless, the notion that the life and sayings of Jesus are philosophically inspiring might strike many of us as odd. In *Mark*, when provincials hear Jesus speak, they ask: "What is this wisdom (*sophia*) that has been given to him?"[6] And in *Luke*, when he is criticized for keeping bad company, Jesus says: "Wisdom (*sophia*) is vindicated by all her children."[7] Yet there is no mention of philosophy (*philosophia*) in the gospels.[8] Isn't phi-

I JUDGE NO ONE

losophy, then, irrelevant to them? It seems eccentric to fault
Reimarus' theory of Jesus for being philosophically uninteresting
(in chapter 1), if the Galilean rabbi is not originally depicted *as*
philosophically interesting.

But I believe he is. And there seem to be echoes of philosophical sayings in the gospels.

A Saying of Jesus, Dio, and Epictetus

The first scene to which I referred is in *Mark*, where the inhabit-
ants of Nazareth ask where Jesus obtained his wisdom. It ends
with him saying: "A prophet is not without honour, except in his
own country" (*Mark* 6:4). This dictum is attested in the four
canonical gospels and *The Gospel of Thomas*. In *Luke* it reads:
"Truly, I say to you, no prophet is acceptable in his own country"
(*Luke* 4:24).[9] This saying has a double relevance for us.

In the first place, though Jesus here calls himself a prophet—
not a philosopher—something like his saying seems to have
circulated in Graeco-Roman philosophical circles in the first
centuries BCE.[10] Consider that

(i) A Cynic philosopher, Dio of Prusa, says in one of his
Orations: "All the philosophers held that life in their own
country was hard."[11]

(ii) A Stoic philosopher, Epictetus, recollects in one of his
Discourses: "The philosophers counsel us to leave our own
country."[12]

Both Dio's *Orations* and Epictetus' *Discourses* post-date the gospels; yet, both philosophers seem to be referring to a saying that
pre-dates them—and that may, conceivably, pre-date Jesus. This
possibility becomes more intriguing when we note that the sayings of Jesus, Dio and Epictetus all centre upon the same Greek
word for one's native city or country—*patris*.

The disbelief of one's people in the first centuries CE seems to have been a fate shared not only by Hebrew prophets, such as Jesus and John the Baptist, but by many Graeco-Roman philosophers.[13] It is this incredulity which makes a philosopher's life hard and a prophet's life 'without-honour' (*atimos*, says a very Hellenic-sounding Jesus).

But there is more. For Dio and Epictetus both cite this saying in the context of a recurring drama in the history of philosophy.

Epictetus says that "philosophers counsel us to leave our own country" because it is disheartening to hear your fellow-citizens say: "Look! This one is now a 'philosopher', who was formerly such and such."[14] This is structurally very close to the scene in *Mark* (and *Luke*, and *Matthew*). For what are those in Jesus' country saying in this scene?[15] "Is this not the carpenter", they ask, "the son of Mary?" (*Mark* 6:3).[16]

What is more, in *Mark* this is the scene in which Jesus' rejection-drama starts to become a resentment-drama. The Nazarene prophet's return to his own country is not only inglorious—because, in *Mark*'s telling, "he could do no mighty works" there—but also scandalous.[17] There is a darkening of the emotion and a shift in *Mark*'s narrative.[18] Here in *Mark* (as in *Matthew*), we are told that the Nazarenes "took offence at him".[19] This is an offence that has a future. For this resentment-drama ultimately becomes a persecution-drama in Judaea, one that will give rise to *other* resentment- and persecution-dramas in the coming centuries.

But neither the nature nor the dark future of this offence is unique to the gospels. This becomes clear when we turn to Dio's *Orations*. Here we see that a centuries-long history lies behind Dio's statement: "All the philosophers held that life in their own country was hard." We can confine ourselves to two instances:

(i) "[The archaic philosopher] Pythagoras fled from [his native island of] Samos ... and yet, among all other peoples—and especially, I believe, on the shorelines of Italy—he was honoured as a god (*etimato hōs theos*)."[20]

(ii) "[The philosopher Socrates] always lived in his own country, doing whatever seemed best to his fellow-citizens and their laws, [but it is hard to say that he] helped the Athenians ... For even now they are still reproached concerning Socrates, for not having behaved in a just or holy way towards him. And it is said that [the Athenians'] conduct [towards him] is the cause of all their later calamities."[21]

The figures of Pythagoras and Socrates differently illuminate Dio's saying about philosophers' lives being hard in their own countries. Pythagoras is held to be a god in other countries, and Socrates is put to death in his own.[22] But it is the same prodigiousness of intellect or soul which ignites resentment in one's native city and inspires awe in "a strange land".[23] Dio is conscious of a resentment-drama which becomes a persecution-drama (Socrates), if it is not disrupted by flight or exile (Pythagoras).

The structural similarities of Dio's and Jesus' sayings are not merely verbal but also historical.[24] Like Socrates, Jesus is put to death as a subversive in his own holy city; and like Pythagoras, he comes to be honoured by other peoples as a god—or, indeed, as God.

A Saying of Jesus, Aristippus, and Antisthenes

We can glance at one more of Jesus' sayings, one in which he calls himself not a prophet, but a physician (Greek *iatros*, Latin *medicus*).[25] The scene I have in mind is emblematic of his prophetic life; he is at table and he causes a scandal.

Jesus' customs at table and his choice of table companions consistently give offence, and are structuring elements in all four gospels.[26] There is no reason to doubt that this motif is taken from the deepest stratum of first-century memories of Jesus' life.

With that much for context, this is the scene in *Mark* (closely paralleled in *Matthew* and *Luke*):

> As [Levi, a tax collector,] reclined at table in his house, many tax collectors and sinners were reclining at table with Jesus and his disciples; for there were many who followed him.[27]

> And the scribes of the Pharisees, when they saw that Jesus was eating with sinners and tax collectors, said to his disciples, "Why does he eat with tax collectors and sinners?"

> And when Jesus heard it, he said to them, "Those who are strong have no need of a physician, but those who are ill. I have not come to call the righteous, but sinners." (*Mark* 2:15–17)[28]

This image of Jesus as a divinely skilled healer—*Christus medicus*, in later tradition—has a rich history, not only in theology but in art.[29] Yet Jesus' saying about the physician's calling—to visit the sick, and only then to heal them—may also have an intriguing prehistory.[30]

As before, our 'pagan' texts post-date the gospels—yet the sayings in question may conceivably pre-date them. There are two relevant sayings in Diogenes Laertius' *Lives of the Philosophers* (third century CE):[31]

(i) Aristippus moved in Socrates' circle in his youth.[32] He later founded the hedonist tradition of "Cyrenaic" philosophy, which takes its name from a prosperous Greek colony in Africa—Cyrene—which is mentioned in the gospels.[33] We read this in Diogenes Laertius:

> "In reply to one who commented that he always saw philosophers at the doors of the rich, Aristippus said: 'So, too, physicians are in attendance on those who are ill.'"[34]

(ii) Antisthenes moved in Socrates' circle.[35] He founded the "Cynic" philosophy and is said to have asserted, after hearing that Plato had bad-mouthed him, "It is a royal privilege to do good things and hear bad things." This could call to mind one of Jesus' sayings: "Blessed are you when people ... utter all kinds of evil against you falsely."[36] However, the immediately relevant text in Diogenes Laertius is this:

"One day when Antisthenes was criticised for keeping low company, he said: 'And physicians are in attendance on those who are ill, but do not catch the fever themselves.'"[37]

The sayings of Jesus, Aristippus and Antisthenes all assert the right of healers to be surrounded by the sick—and, thus, the right of prophets and philosophers to surround themselves with the morally compromised. Aristippus claims that he has high-minded reasons for calling on the rich.[38]

More interesting is Antisthenes' idea that a philosopher, like a physician, will not be influenced by bad company. In other words, he or she will elude the rule that Paul of Tarsus takes from a lost tragedy by Euripides, or from a lost comedy by Menander: "Bad company corrupts good morals" (*I Corinthians* 15:33).[39]

Like the Cynic and Cyrenaic philosophers, Jesus asserts his right to dine with tainted characters. The gospels' central figure knows that he, like a Graeco-Roman physician, will not be infected by 'those who are ill'; and that he, like a Graeco-Roman philosopher, will not be contaminated by 'sinners'. Whatever prehistory we may imagine for Jesus' saying, it is not *less* philosophical than those attributed to Aristippus and Antisthenes. As this shows, philosophical texts and reasonings are not necessarily foreign to the gospels.

A Subtle Difference

Yet there is a subtle but revealing difference in Jesus' saying. Consider:

(i) Aristippus says: "Physicians are in attendance on those who are ill."

(ii) And Antisthenes says: "Physicians are in attendance ... but do not catch the fever themselves."
(iii) But Jesus says: "Those who are strong have no need of a physician, but those who are ill."

Both Antisthenes and Aristippus make a claim about *the figure of the physician*, which vindicates them by means of that figure. But Jesus, on the other hand, makes a claim about *the needs of those who are ill*. Just like those who are ill need a physician, those who are sinners need Jesus. Why? Because the Son of Man—as he calls himself—has authority to "forgive sins" (*Mark* 2:10).[40]

It is this human need—a need for forgiveness—which seems to justify his eating with violators and infringers of the law. In the gospels, Jesus is not only a figure who calls sinners to repent, but who claims to bring forgiveness.

3

JESUS THE PHILOSOPHER

Forgiveness is one of the irreducible motifs in the gospels which sets them apart from any philosophical corpus in the first centuries of our era. We find this claim in several lines by the visionary poet William Blake—not a historian of religion, yet not a man to disregard. (See fig. 4.)

"There is not one Moral Virtue that Jesus Inculcated but Plato and Cicero did Inculcate before him", Blake writes in one of his late notebooks. "What then did Christ Inculcate?" he asks. "Forgiveness of Sins. This alone is the Gospel and this the Life and Immortality brought to light by Jesus."[1]

What Blake may have meant by *Forgiveness of Sins* is not our question. For us, his opening line is more suggestive. We can read it a second time: "There is not one Moral Virtue that Jesus Inculcated but Plato and Cicero did Inculcate before him." This is meant to provoke; in terms of the history of ideas—contemporary to Blake, and to us—it is eccentric. But it is still illuminating, as Blake invariably is.

For most of their history, the gospels have been read in connection to Graeco-Roman philosophy—Blake's "Plato and

19

Cicero". And, indeed, they may have been *written* with an eye to certain philosophical traditions. It may now seem *outré* to compare a saying of Jesus with a retort by Antisthenes, but this was by no means unheard-of in the second and third centuries CE. In fact, at that time, it was still a novelty for Christians to read the gospels as a "four-formed" tradition (*tetramorph*).[2] When the gospels were still modern, it was not odd for 'pagans' or Christians to compare them to, say, Plato's dialogues.[3] (Though I will write 'pagan' without inverted commas, hereafter, we must remember that it is a derogatory Christian term that post-dates the gospels by centuries. The gospel-writers' basic term for pagans is 'Greeks'.)[4]

A Fragment of the Philosopher Amelius

Most pagan texts on the gospels are "marked by hostility".[5] But there is one highly positive judgement of *John* in a third-century fragment by Amelius Gentilanus, a disciple of the great Egyptian philosopher, Plotinus. In this fragment, Amelius harmonizes the archaic philosophical notion of a divine Word in Heraclitus, and the Word that becomes human in the first lines of *John*. "This was therefore the Word", Amelius writes,

> which exists eternally and according to which what is generated was generated, as Heraclitus, too, would most probably say ... [and the Word] which the Barbarian holds to be ... directed towards God, and to be God. The Barbarian holds that simply everything came into being through this Word; that in it what had been generated grew to be alive and live and have being; and that it fell into the bodies; and that, after it had put on flesh, it appeared as a man ...[6]

It is striking to see Amelius call the writer of *John*, here, "the Barbarian". And yet, the voices in *John* are Judaean—which is to say, not Hellenic—so, for a third-century pagan philosopher, they remain "barbarian".[7] But what is most striking about

Amelius' fragment is just that it shows us a "zealous" Platonist and one of the most impressive "new philosophers" (*neōn philosophōn*) courteously recasting the first verses of *John*.[8]

However rare Amelius' fraternal interpretation of *John* may have been, it could not have been unique. For we later see Augustine of Hippo fuming that some of "those who love Plato have dared to assert that our Lord Jesus Christ has taken all those sayings of his, which they are compelled to admire and praise, from the books of Plato".[9] This seems to point to a pagan theory of the origins of Jesus' sayings—or, of some of them— that we no longer have; a theory in which Platonic philosophy is a discernible influence on Jesus or the gospel-writers.[10]

A brief first-century testimony by a Judaean writer, Justus, demonstrates that Socrates and Plato were not unheard-of in Jesus' native country. And this vivid tradition about Socrates' trial comes to us from, of all places, Tiberias—a Herodian city near "Capernaum by the sea", where Jesus lived after he abandoned Nazareth (*Matthew* 4:13).[11] Further, a gentile city of the Decapolis, Gadara—which Jesus seems to skirt in *Matthew*—is the birthplace of a Cynic philosopher, Meleager.[12] Some have taken this as evidence of a Cynic presence in the gospels' original milieu.[13]

But whatever Jesus or the gospel-writers may, or may not, have drawn from Platonic or Cynic traditions in Galilee and Peraea, Decapolis and Syria, Samaria and Judaea,[14] it is worth remembering that a fourth-century Christian tried to rewrite the gospels in the form of Platonic dialogues—as a Christian historian named Socrates tells us.[15]

Contrast-Imitation: Judaean and Christian

Much modern commentary assumes no imitation of philosophy—or "contrast-imitation"—in the tradition-forming work of the gospel-writers. But Amelius' fragment suggests that

Blake's line about Plato, Cicero, and Jesus might be less of an historical outlier.

It would be bizarre if none of the gospels were written with the intention of vying with the pagan "regime" which was structured at the deepest levels by Graeco-Roman philosophy.[16] And in writing this book, I have come to the believe that *Luke* and *John*, at least, were written with such an intention.[17] But it must be stressed that this neither diminishes nor negates the Jewish provenance of the gospels, which are "documents of Jewish-Christian literature".[18] Indeed, much the same could be said of the *Book of Ben Sira* and certain books of *Maccabees* in Israel, Philo in Egypt, and Flavius Josephus in Rome.[19] They, too, were written in hopes of competing with Graeco-Roman culture, philosophy, and historiography.

The origins of such Judaean contrast-imitation antedate the gospels by centuries. There is a tantalizing scene in Josephus' corpus which he takes from a lost text by one of Aristotle's disciples, Clearchus of Soli. In this scene, which Clearchus seems to have copied from a lost text by Aristotle, it is the Greek master-thinker himself who tells us that he once conversed with a Judaean philosopher. This Judaean "was in the habit of coming down from the [Syrian] highlands to the coast" to talk with cultivated persons. And Aristotle is struck by the intellectual subtlety and rigour of this "Judaean by descent, from Coele-Syria". Perhaps more importantly, he respects "the immense and extraordinary endurance of the Judaean in his mode of life, and his moderation".[20]

If we can trust a third-century CE text by the philosopher Porphyry, it is Aristotle's successor in the Lyceum, Theophrastus, who called the Judaeans "a nation of philosophers" (*philosophoi to genos*).[21]

Much more could be said, but the fruitful confrontation of the Hebraic and Hellenistic traditions precedes the gospels by centuries. Before the Greeks discerned 'Plato' in the gospels,

Hellenistic Judaean savants put forth the idea that there is much 'Moses' in Graeco-Roman philosophy. This is an idea that early Christians *inherited*.[22]

Neither does contrast-imitation compromise the source. To hear echoes, however remote, of a Platonic rule in one of the gospels—say,

(i) "We ought neither to take revenge nor to do harm to any man, not even if we suffer anything from him" (Plato's *Crito*); and

(ii) "You must not resist a man who insults you" (*Matthew* 5:39)

— is not, per se, to make Jesus less Judaean.[23]

Graeco-Roman philosophy belongs to the reception horizon not only of the gospels (certainly of *Luke* and *John*), but also of most first-century Judaean literature. It should not surprise us that a stray saying of Jesus' is paralleled in a letter by Seneca:[24]

(i) "The Lord Jesus ... himself said, 'It is more blessed to give than to receive'." (*Acts* 20:35)

(ii) "Whoever receives a benefit more gladly than he repays it is in error." (Seneca's *Moral Epistles*)[25]

Jesus was put to death like a slave, during Tiberius' reign, in a restive Roman province; Seneca died by his own hand, during Nero's reign, on the heights of the Roman *basileia*. Yet both seem to have honoured, in the very simplest language, the beauty of generosity.

Recent contributions help us to see the gospels as complex works of double contrast-imitation.[26] The gospel-writers seem to imitate, and vie with, both pagan and Judaean traditions. Jesus is a figure whose life and sayings connect him to the legacies of both Hebrew prophecy and pagan philosophy. In *The Gospel of Thomas* he is "like a wise philosopher",[27] and in one of Josephus' histories, too, he is remembered as a "wise man" (*sophos anēr*).[28]

In the gospels and all other first-century texts, the figure of Jesus resembles not a provincial belligerent, but the nameless Judaean philosopher whom Aristotle purportedly met, marked by his "immense and extraordinary endurance" and his "moderation" (*sōphrosunē*).[29]

A Fragment of the Philosopher Hierocles

The first Christ-believers were often felt to be subversive to the regimes in Jerusalem, Rome and other cities in the Roman ecumene (though they insisted they were not). There is a moment in *Acts of the Apostles* when a tribune suspects that the apostle Paul might be connected to an Egyptian insurrectionary who had 4,000 "knife men" (*sicarii*) with him in the desert (*Acts* 21:27–39).[30] But Jesus is not a knife man in *Acts*.

Rather, he is portrayed as one who "went about doing good (*euergetōn*) and curing all who were oppressed by the devil" (*Acts* 10:38). Or, in Erich Auerbach's words—written in exile circa 1942—he went about talking with "the highest and deepest dignity" with "publicans and fallen women, the poor and the sick and children".[31]

In strong contrast to this, we can glance at a surviving fragment from antiquity which vaguely anticipates the modern theory of Jesus as a violent Christ-figure.[32] The fragment's provenance is revealing, and it will help us to retrace the political life of Jesus in the coming chapters.[33]

A Christian philosopher at the court of Constantine I, Firmianus Lactantius, tells us that one of his pagan contemporaries claimed: "Christ himself, when forced out by the Judaeans, gathered a force of 900 men and resorted to brigandage."[34] Though brief, this fragment conveys a provocative image of Jesus. He is a hardened criminal, hated by Judaeans and hostile to Romans.

Why is this fragment's origin revealing? First, there is reason to believe that it emanates from the upper echelons of the

Roman Tetrarchy around the time of a steely suppression of Christianity in the years 303 to 311 CE.[35] Second, there is reason to believe that it was written by a reactionary pagan philosopher, Sossianus Hierocles.[36] Lactantius only divulges that one of the instigators of the Tetrarchy's attack on Christians—this could be Hierocles—made the claim about Jesus having been a marauder with 900 fighters at his back.[37] We can therefore call this text, non-dogmatically, *the Hierocles fragment*.

Significantly, the Hierocles fragment is what French cultural philosopher René Girard would call a "persecution text"—a text written by persecutors to legitimize persecution.[38] The idea that Jesus *resorted to brigandage* seems to justify his crucifixion circa 30 CE—and, obliquely, the suppression of his devotees circa 300 CE.

What the Hierocles fragment reveals is that the marauder-Jesus theory is tied to persecution. And, to my mind, it is a dubious feature of the modern Zealot-Jesus theory that it revives, and reconceives, a slur by pagan intellectuals who agitated for the persecution of Christians in late antiquity.

Another dubious feature of the Hierocles fragment is that its conclusion is philosophically inert and politically deadening: *The convict is guilty.* This seems to be Hierocles' unconscious premise. Because Jesus is a convict, he is guilty. The man who said "all who take the sword will perish" *must* have taken a sword, since he perished on a cross (*Matthew* 26:52). And Jesus' devotees, in turn, *must* be guilty of worshipping "a malefactor and his cross".[39]

A Comment on a Fragment of the Philosopher Cicero

In another vein, Lactantius comments on a fragment of Cicero's *Republic*. "There is a passage in Cicero", he writes in his *Divine Institutes*, "not too far from the truth". In a lost book of the *Republic*, Cicero imagines a dark scenario in which, "in keeping with the feelings of all the citizens", a supremely good man is "harassed and seized, his hands cut off, his eyes gouged out, and he himself is condemned, imprisoned, branded, cast out, impoverished", while the citizens all believe that it is "entirely just that he is in such depths of suffering".[40]

Lactantius sombrely comments that the Roman "state" (*civitas*)—"or rather, the whole world (*orbis ipse totus*)"—is "in such error that it persecutes good and just men as if they were evil and impious—torturing, condemning, and killing them".[41]

One conclusion we could take from Cicero's fragment and Lactantius' comment is that *some convicts are innocent*. But there are greater depths here. For Lactantius is not just granting that some convicts are innocent. He seems to be asserting a subtler and more unnerving truth. The state—or rather, the world— convicts some *because they are innocent*.

Cicero's own head ended up on a spike, but this is not the fate to which Lactantius is referring.[42] Rather, he seems to be reworking one of the most shocking scenes in Plato's *Republic*. In book II, one of Socrates' interlocutors traces out a brutal, hypothetical sequence in which the supremely "just man will have to endure the lash ... and finally, after every extremity of suffering, he will be crucified".[43] In the fourth century BCE, Plato seems to sense—after Socrates is tried, convicted, and put to death in Athens—that there are times when a just person's *justice* makes him or her intolerable.[44]

Plato's word for the 'worst death', in *Republic* II, can denote crucifixion or impalement.[45] And on the night before his crucifixion, Jesus seems to prophetically name the tragic human compulsion to destroy a witness to the truth. He calls it "the authority of darkness" (*Luke* 22:52–53).

For Plato in the fourth century BCE and for Cicero in the first century BCE, Socrates is the icon of a dark history in which the just and wise are convicted *because* of their justice.[46] But for a pagan philosopher such as Epictetus circa 100 CE, it seems that Jesus may have already come to figure in that history. "If you wish to be crucified", Epictetus says in a meditation on Socrates' death, "wait and the cross will come".[47] However we read this sentence by Epictetus, it is clear that for a Christian humanist such as Lactantius, Jesus is "the just one" who, after every extremity of suffering, was crucified.[48]

The Old Idea

The logic of Jesus' political life in Hierocles' ancient fragment, and in Reimarus' modern theory, is plain. He challenged greater powers, *on the terrain of power*, and was crushed.

The logic of Jesus' political life is different in Lactantius' comment on Cicero and in Kant's modern theory. Jesus, like Socrates, challenged *the terrain of human power*. And in being crushed he had, in Kant's words, "the greatest influence on human hearts at that time"—or, Kant adds, "at any time".[49]

The risk taken in this book is a return to the old idea: that it is Jesus' *resistance* to the political which makes his life and death, unexpectedly, redemptive. Jesus can only judge the political world in a world-historical way because he can say, resolutely, "I judge no one" (*John* 8:15).

PART TWO

QUESTIONS ABOUT THE CRUCIFIED

4

JESUS AND THE DESIRE TO DIE

Did Jesus *want* to die? It is not a modern question.

There is a scene in *John* in which Jesus is conversing in the Temple with his disciples and critics.[1] Sensing that his death is near, he interrupts his discourse to say, darkly, to his critics: "I am going away, and ... where I am going, you cannot come." This confuses them, but not readers of *John* who know how the Jesus-tradition unfolds. They murmur to themselves, without putting the question to him: "Will he kill himself?" (*John* 8:21–22).

This is an arresting question.

In Greek, the construction implies a negative. A free translation could read: "Surely he won't kill himself?" This is not insignificant, since the idea of Jesus' suicide seems to be evoked by the gospel-writer in order to be denied. For the most part, this question on the lips of Jesus' critics is a sign of their incomprehension. For the most part—but not entirely. I suspect that in *John* the question—Surely Jesus won't kill himself?—is a real one.

We can see this by glancing at a similar scene in *John*. Again, here Jesus is in the Temple, saying to his hearers that in the near future, "You will search for me, but you will not find me." They begin to ask themselves, but not him: "Surely he doesn't intend to go to the diaspora among the Greeks, and teach the Greeks?" (*John* 7:34–35).

A Greek particle in this question, too, could imply a negative—and, in a strict sense, *John*'s reply to this question would be negative. Jesus never travels to Antioch, say, or Rome; and he never teaches the Greeks.

And yet, later in *John*, we do read that "some Greeks"—meaning, some Hellenized gentiles—come to Jerusalem and tell one of Jesus' innermost circle: "We wish to see Jesus." We note that the disciple they approach is Philip—a Greek name.[2] For reasons the gospel-writer does not disclose, Jesus doesn't meet his gentile inquirers face to face. But he does send them an oracle through Philip and another disciple, Andrew—another Greek name. "Those who love their life lose it." In this way, *John*'s Jesus instructs wisdom-seeking Greeks about life, and death, and "eternal life" (*John* 12:20–25).[3]

Within the arc of *John*'s gospel, then, the question in *John* 7—Surely Jesus doesn't intend to teach the Greeks?—is a real one.[4] So, too, is the question in *John* 8—Surely Jesus won't kill himself?

Whatever else could be said about this question, it touches upon one of *John*'s mystical ideas about the death of Jesus— namely, that he chooses it. "I lay down my life", we hear him say. "No one takes it from me", he stresses, "but I lay it down" (*John* 10:17–18). Doesn't this mean that, according to whoever wrote *John* (and the gospel only calls him "the disciple whom Jesus loved"), Jesus wanted to die?[5]

Nietzsche, Decadence and the Death of Jesus

If Jesus' desire to die is not a modern question, it resurfaces in a striking way in Friedrich Nietzsche's writings. (See fig. 5.) A decade before he began to sign crazed letters to the King of Italy and the Vatican's Secretary of State—"The Crucified"—Nietzsche wrote a paragraph that he titled, "Judicial murders".[6] In it, he notes a weird resemblance between what he calls "the two greatest judicial murders in world history"; he means the deaths of Socrates and Jesus. "In both cases", he writes, "the victim *wanted* to die." And in both cases, the victim bent "the hand of human injustice to thrust the sword into his own breast".[7]

For Nietzsche, in the late nineteenth century, these two deaths constitute the most intellectually charged court-ordered killings in history. But, unlike most commentators on Socrates and Jesus, Nietzsche is obsessed by a pathology of world-negation which he thinks he detects in both figures. It is because of this pathology, he concludes, that both Socrates and Jesus drama-tized their own deaths.

For him, the philosopher's poisoned cup and the prophet's cross are not ultimately court-inflicted punishments but self-chosen denouements.

At first glance, then, Nietzsche's reflection on judicial murder (*Justizmord*) is transformed into a reflection on suicide (*Selbstmord*). Yet Nietzsche attributes both deaths to "the hand of human injustice".[8] Their legal ordeals may have been self-murders, but Nietzsche still believes that the court of 500 citizen-judges who condemned Socrates, and the Roman judge who condemned Jesus, *were not innocent*. The twinned suicides that western cultures (and not only western cultures) sanctify were not *simply* suicides. Whatever the convicts' pathologies—in Nietzsche's telling—they were nevertheless judicial *murders*.

This is interesting.

Nietzsche is one of the rare modern philosophers to reflect on the fact that western cultures stem, symbolically, from the trials and deaths of Socrates and Jesus.[9] He seems to recognize that western cultures are distinctive, in so far as they take their rise from a sequence of legal ordeals in which *innocent figures are condemned*.[10] That western philosophy and theology are both inspired by a legal drama which ends in the same way has rarely been analysed. And yet, it must have had deep and diffuse effects on western history that its drama of truth begins—not once, but twice—with a witness to truth being sentenced to death.[11]

The potency and philosophical intrigue of these deaths is not nullified if, as Nietzsche believes, they both wanted to die. Rather, the question would then become: *Why* did they want to die? Nietzsche's reply is, in a word, decadence.

To Nietzsche's mind, wherever there is a diminution of the will-to-power, there is decadence.[12] As such, he sees both Socrates and Jesus as deniers of the human will-to-power, as icons of European enervation—which is to say, decline. Their deaths are both "symptoms of decay".[13] However much they may differ, both Socrates and Jesus finalized a diminution of will-to-power in their own lives by dramatizing their own deaths—and, finally, they both came to symbolize a culture of declining will-to-power in Europe.

Socrates *wants* to die, Nietzsche stresses, because he wishes to be free of his incurable disease of the spirit.[14] And similarly, Nietzsche's Jesus is a tremendously "interesting *décadent*", a death-seeker who embodies "the thrilling charm of ... the sublime, the sick, and the childish" in first-century Galilee.[15] The gospels are, for him, a treacherous witness to Jesus' sickness. "One cannot read these gospels too cautiously", he warns. "The impression of so much corruption is too strong."[16]

Yet *within* the corrupt and corrupting gospels, the "strange figure" from Nazareth emits a wan yet beautiful light. For he is a prophet of limitless love. And what is love, for Nietzsche? "The *last* possibility of life ..." (His ellipsis.) Love is not a height or a conquest, but the *only* possibility of a life which has become so sensitive, so withdrawn from the world, that it can no longer *resist*.[17] Here, then, is Nietzsche's sketch of Jesus' death in *The Antichrist*:

> This "bringer of glad tidings" died as he lived ... *not* in order to "redeem humanity", but to show how one should live. It is his *practice* that he bequeathed to humanity: his conduct before the judges ... before the accusers and all kinds of slander and scorn—his conduct on the *cross*. He does not resist, he does not defend his rights, he takes no step that would ward off the extreme, on the contrary, *he provokes it* ...[18]

For Nietzsche, Jesus is an icon of death-by-provocation. He wanted to die—but not, like Socrates, to be free of himself. Rather, Jesus contrived his own death to show other humans how they could live in love—"no longer offering resistance, not to anyone".[19]

Socrates contrived his own death because he had lived enough.[20] Jesus contrived his death because he could not love or forgive enough. "He loves *with* those, *in* those, who do him evil."[21] And yet, both killed themselves by provocation—and thus, their self-contrived deaths are alike, for Nietzsche, "an expression of *décadence*".[22]

Kant, Duty and C. F. Bahrdt's Jesus

Nietzsche deemed Kant to be "a *deceitful* Christian".[23] Whatever lies behind this description, there is a momentous note on Jesus' death—or suicide—in Kant's book, *Religion within the Bounds of Mere Reason*.

In the note I have in mind, Kant rejects a now-forgotten theory of Jesus' suicide—a "fanciful fiction", he calls it—aired by a bohemian, proto-Jacobin figure of the high Enlightenment, professor-and-bartender Carl Friedrich Bahrdt, who died in 1792 when Kant was writing this book.[24] (See fig. 6.) In Kant's telling, Bahrdt held that Jesus "*sought* death in order to promote a worthy purpose through a shining and sensational example". His critique? "That would be suicide." Kant elaborates:

> One may indeed dare something at the risk of losing one's life, or even endure death at the hand of another, when one cannot avoid it, without betraying an irremissible duty. But one cannot dispose of oneself and one's life as a means, whatever the end, and thus be the *author* of one's death.[25]

Roughly a century before Nietzsche, Bahrdt argued that Jesus sought his own death. And Kant rejected this argument, not on historical but philosophical grounds.

Kant is writing, he tells us, as a "philosophical researcher of religion".[26] And, for him, Jesus' life can only be *philosophically* meaningful if it ended in an "undeserved yet meritorious death"—as Kant believes it did.[27] For him, no death can be "shining" if it is suicide.

Bahrdt's death-seeking Jesus is therefore one who can be seen to be "betraying [his] irremissible duty" in the last days and hours of his life. No one who contrives to be killed is a moral exemplar—and Kant's Jesus *is* a moral exemplar.[28] For him, Jesus is one "whose wisdom [is] even purer than that of the previous philosophers", such as Socrates.[29] "We cannot think" of Kant's Jesus, *except* as one who was willing,

> not only to execute in person all human duties, and at the same time to spread goodness about him as far wide as possible through teaching and example, but also, though tempted by the greatest temptations, to take upon himself all sufferings, up to the most ignominious death, for the good of the world and even for his enemies.

In brief, Kant's Jesus is "the prototype of humanity".[30] As such, he cannot be thought to be either a death-seeker or a suicide.

Kant rejects Bahrdt's sensationalistic Jesus—and, *mutatis mutandis*, Nietzsche's decadent Jesus—because he is morally compromised, and thus, in Kant's mind, philosophically uninteresting.

JESUS AND THE DESIRE TO DIE

Kant, Morality and H. S. Reimarus' Jesus

Of much deeper and more lasting significance is Kant's critique in the same note of Reimarus (whom we met in chapter 1). More precisely, Kant criticizes a theory of Jesus that he attributes to "the Wölfenbuttel fragmentarist"—a reference which is hopelessly obscure to those of us who are not steeped in the modern literature on Jesus, but which conjured up for Kant and his contemporaries a massive scandal of the 1770s known as the Fragment Controversy (*Fragmentenstreit*).[31]

The eponymous fragments were made by Reimarus in the 1760s and collected and published after his death by a philosopher and dramatist, Gottfried Ephraim Lessing, who was then head of the Ducal Library at Wölfenbuttel, in Saxony. (His predecessor at the Ducal Library was Gottfried Wilhelm Leibniz.) It seems that Kant must have known that Reimarus was the free-thinking "Wölfenbuttel fragmentarist".[32]

The notoriety of this fragment-writer is due to his Jesus being in no sense "a spiritual deliverer of humankind".[33] Rather, in the days before his death, so Reimarus writes, the Jesus of the synoptic gospels—as *Matthew*, *Mark* and *Luke* are called—enters the holy city and:

> lays aside his gentleness, begins a disturbance, and commits acts of violence, like one who suddenly considers himself possessed of worldly power. He overturns the tables of the moneychangers, takes a scourge and drives the buyers and sellers and dealers in doves into the outer court of the Temple ... Early on the following day he delivers a sharp harangue against those Pharisees and scribes who sit on the seat of Moses ... He then publicly declares himself to be the Christ, and that he alone is their Lord and master. He abuses the Pharisees and learned Scribes ... calling them "hypocrites, who close the gates of the kingdom of Heaven, who devour widows' houses, who are blind guides, fools, whited sepulchres, murderers of the prophets, serpents, and a generation of vipers" ... Now is not this

inciting the people to rebellion? Is not this stirring them up against the government?[34]

For Reimarus and certain other theorists, a close reading of Jesus' last days in the canonical gospels discloses the repressed and encrypted memories of a failed insurgency in Jerusalem.

Jesus' desire to die is less decisive in Reimarus' theory than in Bahrdt's—or later, in Nietzsche's—but it is still detectable in his willingness to "*stake* his life" (Kant's stress) for what is "a political though illegal purpose, and not a moral one". And what is this illegal purpose in the Wölfenbuttel fragments? "That of over-throwing the rule of the priests", writes Kant, "in order to estab-lish himself in their place with supreme temporal power".[35]

Though Kant concedes that "one may indeed dare something at the risk of losing one's life", he seems contemptuous of Reimarus' claim that "the teacher of the Gospel" would have risked his life for a *coup d'état*.[36] Such a Jesus is of no philosophi-cal interest since his crushed revolution would be provincial, his refuted hopes sectarian, and his suppressed uprising banal. But if Kant seems bored by Reimarus' novel theory, he is not finished with it. For he then offers this striking historical argument:

> In opposition to [Reimarus' theory] stands the admonition, "Do this in remembrance of me", which [Jesus] gave to his disciples at the Last Supper, when he had already given up the hope of attaining any [political] power. This admonition, if intended as the remembrance of a worldly design which had come to nothing, would have been an offensive exhortation, such as to provoke ill-will against its origina-tor, and hence self-defeating.[37]

Kant's idea seems to be that Jesus' ritualization of his own death, on the night before he was crucified, needs—and has—a positive meaning. The remembrance of Jesus' death with bread and wine is not the remembrance of a botched political coup, but of a sublime moral deed. We learn of this rite in a letter Paul wrote circa 53 CE. "This is my body", says Paul's Jesus, "which is for you" (*I Corinthians* 11:23–26). The death of Jesus—whatever we may choose to make of it—seems to appear, the first time we encounter it in writing, as *a gift*.

For Kant, this founding rite of Christ-belief is only conceivable if the revolution that Jesus headed was not political, but moral. He continues:

> The remembrance [of Jesus' death] could just as well refer to the failure of a very good and purely moral design of the Master, namely, to bring about in his own lifetime a *public* revolution (in religion), by overthrowing a morally repressive ceremonial faith and the authority of its priests [in Judaea] ... and we may indeed even now regret that the design did not succeed. However, it was not in vain, for after the Master's death it gave way to a religious transformation that quietly spread everywhere, though in the midst of great sufferings.[38]

For Reimarus, the humble meal that commemorates Jesus' death can only be a ritualization of failure. Kant dismisses this idea—but isn't it a ritualization of failure for him, too? He tells us plainly that Jesus' "design did not succeed". Isn't it therefore necessary to conclude that his prophetic life failed? And that the Lord's Supper is, for Kant, nothing but a giving-of-thanks (Greek *eucharistia*) for defeat?

It is not.

But to see why it is not, we must turn from Kant's note on Jesus' death—contra Bahrdt and Reimarus—to part II of his text, "The Philosophical Doctrine of Religion". For it is here, in part II of *Religion within the Bounds of Mere Reason*, that he asks whether Jesus' life was a failure, and determines that it was *and was not*. This double-reply, which Kant does not think is an evasion, is made possible by his claim that Jesus' hope is ultimately not political. For Reimarus, Jesus is *only* a failure; but for Kant, Jesus is a *political* failure and a *moral* victor.

Turned differently, Kant's Jesus is a *physical* failure and a *legal* victor. This is because his death itself "was the manifestation of the good principle" in human history—that is to say, of "humanity in its moral perfection".

For Kant, then, the Lord's Supper becomes a rite which honours Jesus' *physical* failure as a *legal* victory. In remembering the death of Jesus, Christians can remember a *political* failure who became the *moral* exemplar.[39]

Further, Kant's idea that the hope of Jesus is ultimately moral permits him to make two more double-replies. First, he is able to assert that Jesus' *moral* design—namely, to revolutionize religious culture—failed in first-century Judaea, but went on to succeed in the Roman ecumene and beyond. Like Jesus' life, then, his moral design *was and was not* a failure—and it is precisely in a grander sense that it was not.[40] Second, Jesus was *willing* to die for the "good principle", as Kant calls it, yet without *wanting* to die.

But if Kant is right, and Jesus is not a deluded fanatic or a death-seeking decadent—if he died *without* wanting to die—this raises a very different question. Was Jesus a coward?

This question, too, is not modern.

5

JESUS AND THE HORROR OF DEATH

"There is an atheism in Christianity", says Maurice Merleau-Ponty in one of his 1950s lecture courses at the Collège de France. (See fig. 7.) How can the French philosopher claim this? Because Christianity is the "religion of God made man", he continues, "where Christ dies, abandoned by God".[1]

In this part of his lecture course, Merleau-Ponty is commenting on philosophical, not biblical texts. Yet the moment of godlessness or divine desertion to which he is referring, in the gospels—and thus, in the anguished core of Christian history—can be identified. It is the moment of Jesus' death in *Mark*, which is copied, with minor changes, by *Matthew* (but not by *Luke*).[2]

In *Mark* 15, which is the first surviving depiction of Jesus' death (according to a stable consensus), the dying man's final cry on a Roman gibbet—on which he hangs, gasping, for many hours in the bright light of morning and through an abnormal gloom—comes in two phases.[3] First, he cries out in his Semitic mother tongue, Aramaic. His cry is a question, taken from the Hebrew *Psalms*, which *Mark* transliterates from Jesus' Aramaic and then translates into Greek. "My God, my God, why have you

41

deserted me?" A little later, the gospel-writer tells us that Jesus let out a wordless cry, or sigh, or death rattle—and breathed his last (*Mark* 15:34–37).

Remarkably, Jesus' despairing question and inarticulate cry are the last we hear from his lips in *Mark*. For though this gospel ends with a prelude to the resurrection, Jesus is never shown in *Mark* in his post-mortem glory, comforting his devotees and urging them on as in *Matthew, Luke* and *John*.

To be sure, the received text of *Mark*, or *textus receptus*, contains scenes in which Jesus appears in a deathless state. But there is a strong consensus that all the verses in *Mark* which depict him after his return to life—the gospel's traditional, longer endings—were added by other hands or taken from later documents, and stitched onto *Mark*'s abrupt and nervy conclusion.[4] Which seems to have been this: "Mary Magdalene, Mary the mother of James, and Salome ... fled from [Jesus' empty] tomb, for trembling and confusion had come upon them. And they said nothing to anyone, for they were terrified" (*Mark* 16:1–8).

Once we realize that the terror-struck yet portentous silence of Mary Magdalene, another Mary, and Salome brings *Mark* to its original conclusion, it is clear that Jesus' cry on the cross is the last we hear from him in the first gospel to be written.[5]

Twenty centuries later, for Merleau-Ponty, it is what we might call the godlessness of the real that shines through these final scenes. Desertion by God is so total, on Merleau-Ponty's reading of the sacred page, that it is not only humans who come to feel that they are deserted by God. In *Mark*, even the Son of God comes to feel that he is deserted by God.[6] Which is perhaps to say that, for Merleau-Ponty, *even God is deserted by God in the end*. In this picture—which is certainly not *Mark*'s—the desolation of the divine is absolute.

But if Merleau-Ponty's reading of *Mark*'s death-scene is late modern, the question of Jesus' anguish beforehand and all-too-human desolation on the cross is not. The early modern philos-opher-mystic-mathematician, Blaise Pascal, queries in one of his notebooks: "Why do the gospel-writers make Jesus weak in his agony?"[7] (See fig. 8.) And there is some reason to believe that the writers of *Matthew*, *Luke* and *John* may have asked them-selves much the same question about *Mark*.

"Remove This Cup from Me!"

Mark's Jesus may be the most tumultuous in the canonical gos-pels. *Matthew* seems to subtly quiet Jesus' passions, and they are further quietened in *Luke* and *John*—though it is in *John* that we read, "Jesus wept", and in *Luke* that he exudes "great drops of blood".[8]

The tendency to calm Jesus' passions seems to be observable from early in the synoptic tradition (*Mark*, *Matthew* and *Luke*). For instance, in *Mark* we read that Jesus gazed "with anger" at his critics and felt "grieved by their hardness of heart" (*Mark* 3:5). In the parallel texts of *Matthew* and *Luke*, this double-recollection of his grief and anger has been omitted.[9] And this tendency is perhaps most meaningful in the four gospels' narra-tives of Jesus' betrayal and capture, trials and death—in his Passion. We can see this by glancing at the night before his death in *Mark*.

If there is in *John*, and in Nietzsche's idea of Jesus, a sort of cold-blooded death-drive which impels him towards his painful fate; there seems to be in *Mark*, and in Merleau-Ponty's idea of the Passion, a mounting terror in Jesus as he nears what he senses will be a very hard death. Merleau-Ponty may like the godforsaken realism of Jesus' desolation in *Mark*, but it may have troubled early Christian commentators—and it certainly offended the gospels' early critics.

One critic alleged that Christians had altered "the original text of the gospel three or four times" in order to "deny difficulties in face of criticism".[10] Whatever we make of that allegation, it is not unreasonable to conclude that the earliest reactions to *Mark* may have led the other gospel-writers—*Matthew*, and more so, *Luke* and *John*—to render *Mark*'s Passion less passionate.

One thing is certain. No one in *Mark* thinks that Jesus is plotting his own demise. Rather, on the night before his death, in the first gospel to be written, we read this:

> [Jesus] began to be greatly distressed and troubled. And he said to [his disciples], "My soul is very sorrowful, even to death ..."
>
> And going a little farther [from his disciples, in a place called Gethsemane], he fell on the ground and prayed that, if it were possible, the hour might pass from him.
>
> And he said, "*Abba*, Father, all things are possible for you. Remove this cup from me! Yet not what I will, but what you will." (*Mark* 14:33–36)

This is not the place to analyse the parallel scenes of Jesus' agony in *Matthew* and *Luke*. It suffices to say that in *Matthew*, Jesus' first prayer that "the hour might pass" is omitted; and in *Luke*, this prayer is omitted along with the moment in which Jesus is "distressed and troubled", saying to his disciples that his "soul is very sorrowful".[11]

In *John*, Jesus seems to renounce *Mark*'s death-averting prayer—namely, "Remove this cup from me!" To be sure, he still confesses in *John* that his soul is troubled. But he says this in the context of an oracle that he gives to "some Greeks", through Philip and Andrew, in which he warns that "unless a grain of wheat falls into the earth and dies, it remains alone". It is therefore reasonable that *John*'s Jesus then says to himself, as if in soliloquy: "What shall I say, 'Father, save me *from* this hour?' No! For this purpose I have come *to* this hour" (*John* 12:20–27).[12]

In *John*, the *Sturm und Drang* of *Mark*'s Jesus seems to have given place to a philosopher's tranquillity in the face of death.

JESUS AND THE HORROR OF DEATH

The first gospel's Jesus falls to the ground and pleads to be saved from his hour. The last gospel's Jesus is ready to fall into the earth, like a grain of wheat, and die.[13]

"Loud Laments and Wailings"

If *Mark*'s death scene commends itself to Merleau-Ponty, *Matthew*'s death scene—based on *Mark*'s—disgusts a second-century philosopher named Celsus. In his acid critique of a brazen new faith, *The True Word* or *True Discourse* (*Alēthēs Logos* in Greek), Celsus asks those who worship Jesus:

> Do you [criticize Graeco-Roman myths and yet] think that ... the ending of *your* tragedy is to be regarded as noble and convincing? [Jesus'] cry from the impaling-stake when he was breathing his last? And the earth's shuddering, and the darkness?[14]

Though all of the synoptics mention the darkness, it is clear from "the earth's shuddering" that Celsus is referencing *Matthew*.[15]

What matters most for us is the intensity of Celsus' disdain for Jesus' last words on "the impaling-stake". The philosopher seems to have in mind the desperate question that *Matthew* takes from *Mark* and, ultimately, from *Psalm 22*: "My God, my God, why have you deserted me?"[16] The pagan finds this sort of shattered melancholy at the end of one's life to be unworthy of any enlightened person, much less an incarnate deity.

Though Celsus seems to have been the first programmatic critic of the gospels' historicity, his objection to Jesus' final cry is not that it is historically dubious. It is *philosophically* suspect. This is because, for a second-century pagan, horror in the face of death is not a mark of brave disillusionment but of ignorance, guilt and low-mindedness. And the Passion seems, to Celsus, to be a low-spirited affair.

"What fine action did Jesus do like a god?" the philosopher asks. "Did he despise men's opposition and laugh and mock at the disaster that befell him?"[17] No, Jesus never mocked his tormenters. Nor did he joke about his wounds or make light of his death. "What does [Jesus] say while his body is being crucified?" Celsus prods. "Was his blood like 'ichor such as flows in the veins of the blessed gods'?"[18] He seems to be alluding, here, to a legendary remark by Alexander of Macedon, who is said to have pointed to one of his own red-gushing wounds and said something like: This isn't the golden fluid that flows in the veins of gods![19]

Celsus takes no interest in the fact that, in *Matthew*'s passion, the accused man is noted for his sangfroid. Jesus' pagan judge is struck by the provincial holy man's cool taciturnity (*Matthew* 27:14; *Mark* 15:5). Yet it is true, nevertheless, that the conclusion of Jesus' death scene is loud and tormented.

Though Celsus' demolition of the gospels is filled with hauteur, it resists a crude, class-based reading. For he knows that a slave, no less than a world-conqueror, can look down on his or her own sufferings. "What about Epictetus?" he asks. He is thinking of a story in which the Stoic philosopher, from whom we heard in chapter 2, is still a slave. "When his master was twisting his leg", in Celsus' telling,

> He smiled gently, and calmly said: "You are breaking it." And when his master had broken it, he said: "Did I not tell you that you were breaking it?" What comparable saying did your god utter while he was being punished?[20]

On Celsus' reading of *Matthew*, the Stoics' slave manifestly outshines the Christians' god.

In Platonic circles and beyond, Socrates was held to be an icon of justice and illumination because he could gently laugh in his final moments. His last words in Plato's death-scene dialogue,

Phaedo, are not only devout and clever, but light-hearted. Socrates tells one of his friends that, because he is departing this life, a sacrifice is due to Aesculapius, the god of healing. "Do not neglect it", whispers Socrates.[21]

The contrast with Jesus' death is stark. Immersed in his dark night of the soul, the Galilean convict noisily grieves that his God has not remembered him. In Pascal's words, he can "no longer contain his overwhelming pain (*douleur excessive*)".[22] And for Celsus, this is simply not how a god, or a good human, dies.

The pagan philosopher is shocked, too, that unheroic behaviour is portrayed not only on the day of, but on the night before, Jesus' death. Relentlessly, he asks second-century Christians: "Why ... does [Jesus] utter loud laments and wailings, and pray that he may avoid the fear of death, saying something like this, 'O Father, if this cup could pass by me'?"[23] Celsus is here referring to—and shortening, and rhetorically heightening—a prayer on the night before Jesus' death recorded in all of the synoptics (but not *John*): "My Father, if it be possible, let this cup pass from me. Nevertheless, not as I will but as you will" (*Matthew* 26:39).

Later the same night, uniquely in *Matthew*, we read that Jesus utters a more compressed prayer: "My Father, if this [cup] cannot pass unless I drink it—your will be done" (*Matthew* 26:42).

The difference in tone between the first-century gospel and its critics in later centuries is marked. *Matthew*'s Jesus is not a Nietzschean decadent—he wants to live. But neither is he a Celsan antihero—he is willing to die. Celsus seems to wilfully read what he calls "fear of death" into *Matthew*'s Passion-narrative.[24] For, though Jesus could seem to betray "signs of fear" in *Matthew*, "the word 'fear' does not occur" in any of the canonical depictions of his last hours, as Runar Thorsteinsson has noted.[25] In other words, Jesus' fear is not *present* in the gospels' Passion narratives; it must be—or rather, can be—inferred. The inner source—and thus, the meaning—of Jesus' anguish is not given in the text. It is a matter of speculation or of imagination.

I JUDGE NO ONE

"Piety and Greatness of Soul"

Celsus' contempt is palpable. For this second-century philoso-pher, Jesus is a man who "wandered about most shamefully in the sight of all men" until he was "dishonourably arrested and punished to his utter disgrace".[26] There is nothing more to his Jesus, and this seems to distort his reading of the gospels. Of course, I am not the first to have noticed this.

The fragmentary copy of Celsus' *True Word* that has come down to us is scattered throughout a monumental critique of it, *Against Celsus*, written by a third-century Egyptian Christian philosopher, Origen (a name that means "born of Horus", Egypt's falcon-headed deity). In hundreds of closely reasoned pages, Origen tries to demonstrate that Celsus is an unreliable reader of the gospels and critic of the Christian hope.

For instance, in *Against Celsus* book II, Origen extracts this question from the pagan's text: "Why ... does [Jesus] utter loud laments and wailings, and pray that he may avoid the fear of death, saying something like this, 'O Father, if this cup could pass by me'?"[27]

It is hard to deny the rhetorical force of Celsus' question. It is structured by recognizable moments in the gospels—namely, by Jesus' prayer that God might spare him, and by his final cry on the cross. Yet Origen tries to show that the force of this question is sophistic, or merely rhetorical. The Christian philosopher alleges that the pagan philosopher had failed to respect:

> the honesty of the writers of the gospels, who could have been silent on these matters, but were not ...

> But Celsus attacks the words of the gospels by embellishing and quoting the text incorrectly. No statement is to be found [in the gospels] that Jesus *uttered wailings*.

> And he alters the original text: "Father, if it be possible, let this cup pass from me."

> And he does not quote the saying which at once shows Jesus' piety towards his Father and his greatness of soul ... "Nevertheless, not as I will but as you will" [*Matthew* 26:39].

> Celsus pretends, too, not to have read of the willing obedience of Jesus to the will of his Father concerning the sufferings to which he was condemned, which is made clear by the words: "If this cannot pass from me except I drink it, your will be done" [*Matthew* 26:42].[28]

What Origen does not note is that *Luke* and *John* do seem to write the despair out of Jesus' last words.[29] The later gospel-writers are, if not silent, then *muted* on certain moments in *Mark*'s and *Matthew*'s Passions that deeply offend Celsus—and that, no doubt, troubled other early readers.

Origen's other objections to Celsus' question are more convincing.[30] For it is true that Jesus is never portrayed in the gospels as unmanly in his suffering—which is what Celsus seems to imply when he censures him for "loud ... wailings".[31] On the contrary, Jesus' silence is what is most striking throughout his ordeal. The Son of Man may voice his inner anguish *to God* before he is captured, and he may cry out *to God* just before he dies; but in most of the Passion-scenes in *Matthew* (and *Mark*), he neither speaks nor cries out in pain.[32]

It is exactly this, Jesus' silence, which inspires a subtle vein of speculation in some early Christian circles that eludes Celsus' critique—but that differs, too, from the dogmas of the second-century "Great Church", as the philosopher calls it.[33] Both Celsus and Origen know that there are circles of Christ-devotees who call themselves, or could be called, Gnostics (from the Greek *gnōsis*, 'knowledge').[34] Origen deplores the "strange new ideas" of Gnostics, which "do not harmonize with the traditional doctrines received from Jesus".[35] However that may be, one of the things that marked Gnostic thought is the notion that Jesus did not suffer during his judicial torture and crucifixion.

In the second-century *Gospel of Peter*, for instance, we read that when Jesus was pinned to the cross he, "held his peace as he felt no pain" (or, perhaps, "as if he felt no pain").[36] Other, more elaborate texts could be cited.[37] My only point here is that this radically different line of thought, however problematic it might be, is closer to *the letter of the gospels' Passion narratives* than is Celsus' "laments and wailings".[38]

Apart from Jesus' despairing question—which is uttered to God, not those watching him die—his hours on the cross are remembered by the gospel-writers as a time in which he is oppressively silent. This silence takes its meaning, in a narrative sense, from the conclusion of Jesus' prayer in the hours *before* his ordeal. That is, from the part of Jesus' prayer that Celsus suppresses: "Your will be done" (*Matthew* 26:42).

It is in these words, which are uttered to God, that Origen sees what he calls Jesus' "greatness of soul" and "obedience ... to the will of his Father".[39] And it is striking that we see a similar greatness of soul, a similar form of obedience, in one of Epictetus' first-century *Discourses*, in which Socrates says, just before his death: "If so it is pleasing to God, so let it be."[40]

But Jesus' behaviour on the night before his crucifixion raises a further question: Did he know, *before* his capture, that he was facing a hard death in Jerusalem?

6

JESUS AND THE PRESENTIMENT OF DEATH

There is a visceral, meaning-charged scene that comes to us from Josephus, a first-century CE historian. He seems to have taken it from a lost book by Hecataeus of Abdera, from the fourth century BCE.[1] Whatever its origins, the scene I have in mind is set somewhere in the Red Sea littoral, and occurs sometime after Alexander of Macedon's lightning-bolt conquests and early death in 323 BCE.[2]

The troops of a Ptolemaic ruler are marching in formation towards the Red Sea. The main formation is Greek infantry, flanked by a cohort of mounted Judaean archers.[3] Hecataeus introduces one of these horsemen, a Judaean fighter by the name of Mosollamos. Even the Greek troops concede that Mosollamos is the Ptolemy's finest archer, though he is a "barbarian"—meaning, a non-Hellene.[4]

As the scene opens, Mosollamos notices that the Ptolemy's infantry formation is beginning to blur and loosen, and that the whole column is marching fitfully. The troops keep halting to gaze at a gentile omen-reader who has his eyes trained on the sky. A bird is hovering over the formation.[5] Displeased by this, the archer approaches the seer to ask why he is disrupting the troops' progress. Hecataeus then tells us:

> The diviner pointed out the bird to him and said that, if it stayed there, it was expedient for everyone to wait; if it flew off and went forwards, to march on; and if it went backwards, to retreat. Mosollamos said nothing but drew his bow, fired, hit the bird, and killed it.[6]

No reader of Homer's *Iliad* could fail to predict the effect of this spectacular act of slaughter. The seer and the Ptolemy's Greek troops are enraged. Hecataeus tells us that they swarm Mosollamos and curse him for felling the bird.[7]

According to archaic Greeks, a bird in flight is a message-bearer of the gods. The course of a bird's flight, when skilfully interpreted, can attune us to otherwise imperceptible stirrings of numinous beings, to the wind-like movements and intentions of deathless gods.[8] To kill an omen-bearing bird is therefore to destroy a heaven-sent entity.[9] In the eyes of the Ptolemy's Greek troops, Mosollamos' bloodshed is not only senseless, but sacrilegious.

In the story, the Judaean archer is unperturbed. He takes the bloodied bird in his hands and urges them to face what its death implies. This is Mosollamos, speaking to his gentile comrades:

> How could this thing give us any saving information about our journey, when it couldn't foresee its own well-being? For if it had been able to know the future, it would not have come to this spot for fear that it be shot and killed![10]

The archer's question is a real one. How *could* a divinely inspired beast fail to foresee its imminent death? And why *would* a heaven-sent creature not forestall its own doom? For Mosollamos, the answer is clear.

The Death of a Bird in Mid-Flight

The death of Jesus, like the death of Mosollamos' bird, is attested by Josephus. In a notorious paragraph of his *Judaean*

Antiquities, Josephus states that a first-century Roman prefect sentenced Jesus to death after he had been charged by the Temple aristocracy.[11] I am intrigued by the way in which Jesus' death seems to resemble that of the bird brought down in Hecataeus' fragment.

"How could this thing give us any saving (*sōtērian*) information", asks Mosollamos, "when it couldn't foresee its own well-being?"[12] Like the archer, but with reference to Jesus, it is reasonable for us to ask: How could a prophet not foresee his own grisly fate?[13]

Because this is a reasonable question, it is not a new one. Indeed, just this question was formulated by Celsus, whom we have met, and who asks in *The True Word*—his lost, second-century critique of Christianity:

> Who—whether god, or daemon, or sensible man—if he foreknew that such things [as Jesus' capture, torture, and crucifixion] would happen to him, would not avoid them if at least he could do so, instead of meeting with just the events which he had foreseen?[14]

Who, indeed? Yet if the gospels are taken as read, we could reply—Jesus. For, the gospels all differently stress that Jesus *did* foresee his death.

All the synoptic gospels show Jesus warning his disciples that he will "suffer many things" and will ultimately "be killed" in Jerusalem.[15] More graphically, in *John*, Jesus predicts that he will be "lifted up from the earth". A gloss by the gospel-writer, or one of his editors, points out that Jesus said this "to indicate the kind of death he was to die" (*John* 12:32–33).

In literary terms, the question for readers of the gospels is not whether Jesus could "know the future" (in Mosollamos' words); but rather why he did not slip his death-trap in Jerusalem, "for fear of being killed" (again, in Mosollamos' words).[16] Differently put, the question created by the gospel-writers is not whether Jesus "foreknew that such things would happen to him" (in

Celsus' words); but rather why he did not "avoid them" instead of undergoing "the events which he had foreseen" (again, in Celsus' words).[17]

"I Knew It"

Naturally, it is possible to treat Jesus' predictions of his death as pious fictions. In this line of thought any such sayings were either concocted by Christ-believers or were heavily redacted after the fact. In either case, they reflect the *memory* of Jesus' death and early Christ-believers' reasonings concerning that memory. The extent to which such theories are supported by close readings or critical reconstructions of the gospel texts lies beyond the limits of this book.

On a conceptual plane, however, I want to register a certain discontent with the unconscious or half-conscious drift of both theories. The imperative to 'demythologize' the gospels still controls much commentary; but this imperative is too often taken as a licence to banalize the sacred page.

Life is mysterious—or, as Louise Glück puts it, "very weird ... very filled with dreams".[18] Regardless of what one may believe in the gospel-writers' narratives, it is unreasonable—I think—to read them in a way that fails to reckon with the fact that *Jesus' life is more mysterious than most.*

Of course, a modern commentator can object *a priori* to the idea that, say, Jesus restored to life a dead boy outside the Galilean settlement of Nain (*Luke* 7:11–17).[19] But we should not forget that Jesus is a man to whom such deeds were irreversibly attributed—and not only by his disciples. Josephus, for instance, seems to remember Jesus as a man who "did marvellous things" (*paradoxōn ergōn poiētēs*).[20]

My concern is that such a methodology may, in rushing to disavow his divinity, diminish his humanity. Whatever else Jesus is or is not, the gospels convincingly portray him as a man of startling intensity and acuity. And any plausible reading must reckon with this.

There are grounds in secular literature, and in life, for believing that a premonition of one's death may be an integrally human form of cognition. To grant that this form of cognition is rare, or uncanny, is not to grant that it is mythic. Many forms of natural cognition are rare, and human cognition is *per se* uncanny. And finally, Jesus' predictions of death touch upon "only human matters"—to draw upon one of Spinoza's comments on Hebrew prophecy—"not beyond the limits of human understanding except in being in the future".[21] It therefore seems to me, in a real sense, *uncritical* to strip Jesus of his presentiments of death.[22]

The first-century philosopher, Seneca, writes that "the wise man knows all the things that are in store for him. Whatever happens, he says: 'I knew it'".[23] For Seneca, this sort of prescience is not a mark of prophecy or divinity but of concentration and clarity—in a word, sagacity. And whatever we may question or reject in the gospels, it seems discourteous to deny that the man who gave us the phrase "signs of the times" is sagacious.[24]

"Spare Pharion!"

To render this more concrete, we could recall a tradition concerning another first-century life. Apollonius of Tyana was a Pythagorean philosopher to whom Jesus was sometimes compared in late antiquity.

The incident takes place in Egypt. Apollonius sees twelve thugs or rebels (Greek *lēstai*) being led out of Alexandria to be beheaded in a pit, and he declares that one of them "has been falsely accused and will be set free". Apollonius urges the executioners to kill this innocent man last, and distracts them with a long-winded discourse until, after eight convicts have been finished off, a messenger gallops up shouting, "Spare Pharion!" Needless to say, Pharion is the convict whose innocence Apollonius had intuited.[25]

This scene is inexplicable—and thus is doubtful. It may be purely fictional. But it is not, in the context of Philostratus' *Life of Apollonius*, totally unbelievable. To confirm this, it is only necessary to glance at a scene from a modern life. Charles Sanders Peirce was a path-breaking logician of the early twentieth century. (See fig. 9.) Peirce described an episode in his own life which uncannily resembles Apollonius' perception of the one innocent convict.

Peirce once relied on an inarticulable sense of *recognition* to identify, on sight, the one *guilty* man in a line-up of innocents. (Apollonius' story is more redemptive.) Peirce had never laid eyes on the man whom he nevertheless judged to be responsible for the theft of some of his property. To repeat, Peirce is a modern logician of the first rank, and his detection of the 'guilty party', on the strength of sheer intuition, was later corroborated by an investigation.[26] What is more, this episode seems to have given rise to Peirce's theory of 'abduction'—and, thereby, to have influenced semiotic theory in the late twentieth century.

As Peirce's bizarre feat indicates, it *can be* uncritical for historians to treat inexplicable scenes as *necessarily* implausible.

That said, a feat of 'prophetic' recognition is far more credible in the context of Apollonius' life than of most others. It is necessary to make a concrete determination regarding *lives*. Some human lives are *prodigious*. For me, the prodigiousness of Apollonius' life is confirmed by the fact that even the more hardheaded chroniclers of late antiquity wrote of Apollonius with a certain reverence.[27]

I believe that the life of Jesus positively towers over the lives of his late modern commentators, including my own. Personally, I take it to be a mark of banal thinking—rather than a critical

JESUS AND THE PRESENTIMENT OF DEATH

finding—when this datum, *the prodigiousness of Jesus*, is buried by theories that deny his premonitions of death.

It must be reiterated that this line of reasoning turns upon a concrete determination. One must decide whether Jesus seems to be the sort of man who could have sensed his fate and braced himself to meet it. This is the image that emerges in the gospels. It is moreover reflected in the core of Josephus' Testimony. And it is an idea that may offer us less tortured interpretations of some of the canonical material.

The Prodigiousness of Jesus

The idea of prodigiousness is linked, conceptually and historically, to the idea of divinity, but the former by no means entails the latter. On the contrary, the 'Euhemerist' forms of religious critique, which thrived in antiquity, centred upon this link. The Homeric gods, according to Euhemerus in the fourth century BCE, were nothing but mystified images of archaic cities' most impressive humans.

'Euhemerist' critique of the Graeco-Roman gods has a strong reception in early Christian philosophy, which is why reading a second-century Christian like Clement of Alexandria can feel eerily like reading Nietzsche. This is Clement to second-century pagans:

> By now, even your myths have grown old ... Where is Zeus? ... He has grown old ... See, the myth is stripped bare! ... Search for your Zeus. Do not scour heaven, but earth! Callimachus the Cretan, in whose land Zeus lies buried, will tell you where his tomb is ... Yes, Zeus is dead![28]

For Clement, the highest pagan god can die because he is merely the enhaloed memory of a towering archaic Hellene.[29] And the basic concept of 'Euhemerist' critique is that theology is prodigious anthropology. This echoes—and perhaps refines—

57

a nineteenth-century cliché distilled from Ludwig Feuerbach's philosophy.

Returning to the gospels, a Christian would hold that Jesus was prodigious because he is divine. Thus, an early-fourth-century Palestinian bishop can reason that Jesus "must have had some extraordinary power beyond that of other men—for how else could he have attracted many Jews and Greeks?"[30] And a late-fourth-century Syrian bishop can assert that Jesus' nature must be "more novel" than that of other humans.[31] In contrast, a 'Euhemerist' reader of the gospels would conclude that Jesus is divine, in Christian doctrine, because he was prodigious. But what both would reject—and what I, too, reject—is a modern tendency to portray Jesus as unoriginal and uninspired.

"The Realism of the Gospels"

A distinguished historian of Roman law, Aldo Schiavone, has advanced a naturalistic theory of Jesus' premonitions.[32] Where 'post-diction' theories make the Galilean a passive, imperceptive victim of hostile political forces, Schiavone sees him as a commanding presence. He therefore seeks to salvage more of the narrative arc of the gospels without having recourse to the tenet of Jesus' divinity.

According to Schiavone, Jesus is the decisive figure in his Passion. And in literary terms, the Passion narratives begin when Jesus begins to foreshadow his death. Schiavone therefore holds that Jesus predicted his crucifixion. He finds this idea convincing in what we could call formal terms. A sharply delineated sense of fate seems, to him, to cohere with the human figure of Jesus that is drawn in the gospels.

Schiavone's theory is a precise inverse of theories that treat Jesus' premonitions as *post eventum* fabrications. He conjectures that Jesus must have steered his disciples (including Judas

Iscariot, his betrayer), his Judaean accusers (a featureless chorus in the gospels), and finally his Roman interrogator (the sceptical prefect, Pilate) towards the grim fulfilment of his own prophetic utterances.[33] In other words, Jesus contrived the crucifixion. Or, to recall Nietzsche's image, he seized "the hand of human injustice to thrust the sword into his own breast".[34]

Jesus' premonitory sayings are still, in a sense, fabricated—but they are not fabricated *post eventum*. Rather, Schiavone suggests that they are fabricated *ante eventum*. Jesus is a prophet who chooses to be killed, and then chooses his killers. "I lay down my life", as he says in the fourth gospel. "No one takes it from me, but I lay it down" (*John* 10:17–18).

This saying in *John* invites critique. It requires only the most rudimentary critical move to assert that it is not Jesus who speaks in a *logion* like this, but the gospel-writer or his community. Yet this critical move is one that Schiavone is not inclined to make. He is markedly open to what he calls, "the original 'realism' of the narrative".[35]

Similarly, it is "the realism of the gospels" that excites Auerbach in his rich mid-century book, *Mimesis*.[36] According to him, it is the gospel-writers' literary combination of "the lowest with the highest", in "the Christian drama of redemption", that "created an entirely new kind of sublimity".[37]

To be sure, there are moments in the Passion narratives that Schiavone, like most philologists and historians, deems unhistorical. Of a highly charged cluster of verses in *Matthew* in which Pilate rinses his hands to show that he is not culpable for Jesus' death, Schiavone writes: "Not a single word of this can be believed."[38] But he is more impressed by the inner force and logic of the Passion narratives than by the modern reconstructions.

Schiavone is a cool-headed legal historian, and he seeks to read the gospels, he says, "without obligations".[39] It is the texts that lead him—and Nietzsche before him—to hazard his thesis that Jesus sentenced himself to the cross and then convinced a Roman prefect to formalize that sentence. "It is [Jesus], in the end, who judges", he concludes, "not the prefect".[40]

This forcefully returns us to the second question, in Mosollamos' words: Why is there no "fear of being killed" in this depiction of Jesus?[41] Or, in Celsus' words: Why did Jesus choose to endure "the events which he had foreseen"?[42] This we could follow with a new question: Why did Jesus not only contrive his own death, but contrive to be *crucified*—the most degrading form of punishment in the first-century world?

"A Necessary Death"

We remember from this chapter's opening scene that the Judaean archer Mosollamos demythologized the omen-reader's bird by killing it. But Jesus' death seems to defy the archer's logic. His death is at the core of the Christian mystery—and, despite the realism of the material, it is his death that *mythologizes* Jesus.

This is presumably because Jesus' death is not only predicted by him, but—in a vague yet decisive sense—*chosen* by him. The gospels make it clear that Jesus sensed, before he went to Jerusalem to celebrate the Passover, that he would be killed there. By choosing to enter the holy city, he chose to die.

What is more, the gospels indicate that Jesus sensed he would die by crucifixion, a Roman punishment—rather than by stoning, a Judaean one. It has been conjectured that Jesus *wanted* to be stoned by the Judaean rulers and was horrified to suffer "a meaningless execution by crucifixion at the hands of the Romans".[43] The gospels, however, suggest—and Schiavone seems to accept—that Jesus' death on a gentile cross had a dense and immanent sense *for him*.

"For Jesus", in Schiavone's words, "death became the transfiguration of love". Here he has in mind a saying of Jesus' in the fourth gospel. "No one has greater love than this, to lay down one's life for one's friends" (*John* 15:13). It is because of this transfiguration, Schiavone reasons—because death becomes, for Jesus, a cipher of supreme love—that the cross becomes, for him, "a necessary death".[44]

There is nothing incredible in this reconstruction. On the contrary, there is much reason to believe that Jesus might have embraced his death, if not as a decadent's obsession (à la Nietzsche), then as a demonstration of his love (à la Schiavone). Further, it is a validation of his prophetic calling; for Jesus' contemporary, John the Baptist, was put to death by Herod Antipas for his outspokenness—as were other prophets and martyrs of Israel before him.[45] On the night before his death in *John*, Jesus says, "I have spoken openly (*parrhēsia lelalēka*) to the world" (*John* 18:20). In his late seminars, Michel Foucault convincingly renders this Greek word, *parrhēsia*, as "fearless speech".[46] And it has never been uncommon for fearless speakers to be martyrs.

The idea of dying for truth is by no means unique to the prophetic calling in Judaean history.[47] Jesus' rough contemporary, Apollonius—whom we met in this chapter—says that it is "proper for the wise (*sophois*) to die for the sake of their beliefs".[48] For him, Socrates is exemplary of this fate.[49] And the Christian philosopher Origen, in his reply to Celsus, writes:

> Socrates knew that if he drank the hemlock he would die, and [he knew that] he could have escaped the guard and avoided suffering any of this. But he chose the course that seemed to him reasonable, thinking that it was better for him to die in accordance with the principles of his philosophy than to live in contradiction to them.[50]

Socrates is neither the first nor the last philosopher to die for his calling. There is a neglected genre of *martyr philosophers* in Hellenistic and post-Hellenistic literature.[51] And in the gospels, Jesus sternly warns his hearers that he will not be the last to die for his 'code'—the laws and mysteries of the kingdom of God. To this day, global history is brutally fulfilling that prophecy.[52] Origen makes this connection in his retort to Celsus:

> Why is it amazing if, although Jesus knew the things which would happen, he did not avoid them, but met with just the events which he had foreseen? ... Many of our contemporaries who have known that if they confessed Christianity they would die, while if they denied they would be set free and regain their possessions, have despised life and willingly chosen death for the sake of religion.[53]

Part of the gospels' power and intrigue—which makes many, in our century, still willing to die for their religion—is that they transmute every question about the crucifixion into a single, controlling question about the Crucified: Who is he?

PART THREE

A CERTAIN JESUS

7

"A GOD WHO WAS CONDEMNED"

By the time of Constantine "the Greatest", as the Roman Senate styled him, Jesus' death seems to have been known as the Passion (Greek *pathos*, Latin *passio*).[1] And to this day, the Passion is an inexhaustible sequence of scenes, gestures and sayings. In it, Jesus is a sorrowful man who glistens with sweat "as drops of blood" in a dark garden.[2] He is a friendless man who receives the kiss of death from one he calls "friend".[3] A prisoner who "turns and looks" at the follower who is renouncing him. He is the half-dead mendicant who says of his killers, "They know not what they do". The numen who assures a remorseful criminal, "Today you will be with me in Paradise".[4] The corpse into which a Roman pike is thrust, on a gibbet-hill called Skull.[5] And the son that history's most venerated mother— Maria in Greek, Mariyam in Aramaic—timelessly gazes on and grieves.[6] (See fig. 10.)

What is the truth of this sequence?

One philosopher concludes that "Christian faith holds that those who are able to look on the crucifixion and live, to accept that the traumatic truth of human history is a tortured body, might just have a chance of new life".[7] This is one way to describe what Christians believe. If nothing else, it calls to mind Paul of Tarsus' idea of "newness of life" (*kainotēti zōēs* in Greek) in his letter to Rome.[8]

Whatever we believe, it is imperative to note that the sayings, gestures, and scenes just catalogued only come to us from the gospels. This does not necessarily mean that they are unhistorical. There is reason to believe, say, that Judas' kiss (or some other duplicitous gesture), like Peter's disavowal of Jesus (on the night before his death), is rooted in the very earliest Christian memories. But before we try to retrace his life within them, it seems right for us to ask how the life of Jesus is recollected outside the gospels.

Pascal is right to comment in his *Pensées* that Jesus lived "in such obscurity (according to what the world calls obscurity) that historians writing of important matters of state hardly noticed him".[9] Auerbach, too, stresses that Jesus' death is "nothing but a provincial incident".[10] It is precisely because of this that it is remarkable that the death of an impoverished Galilean rabbi is mentioned in a certain number of non-Christian texts in the first centuries CE.[11]

"New Laws": Mara bar Sarapion

The first non-Christian notice of Jesus' death may be preserved in *The Letter of Mara bar Sarapion*, a Syrian pagan philosopher's letter to his son.[12] But Mara's *Letter*, which was recovered in the nineteenth century in a single seventh-century manuscript, is vexingly hard to date.[13]

One eminent historian, Fergus Millar, suggests that *Mara's Letter* is a first-century text, written as early as 72 or 73 CE.[14] This dating would make it the earliest pagan text to mention Jesus' execution. In it, Mara offers a philosophical reflection on the Passion which may be roughly contemporary with the gospels' Passion narratives.[15]

This first-century dating is contested, however.[16] Mara's allusion to the fall of Jerusalem and other catastrophes might have been occasioned by the second Judaean revolt of 132 to 135, and not the first revolt of 66 to 73 CE.[17] But whether Mara's *Letter* is dated to the first or second century, it is a pagan philosophical text, composed in Syriac, in which Jesus' death seems to be remembered.[18]

Anticipating Nietzsche by as much as 1,800 years, Mara links the deaths of Socrates and Jesus. Unlike Nietzsche, he sees their deaths as belonging to an august history of philosopher-martyrs. This ancient Syrian philosopher believes that it is culpable human error which led to the executions of Pythagoras, Socrates, and Jesus—and the ruination of the cities that put them to death. Here is the text in question:

> What else can we say, when wise men are forcibly dragged by the hands of tyrants, and their wisdom is taken captive by slander, and they are oppressed in their intelligence without defence? For what benefit did the Athenians derive from the slaying of Socrates? For they received the retribution for it in the form of famine and plague. Or the people of Samos from the burning of Pythagoras? For in one hour their entire country was covered with sand. Or the Judaeans [from the slaying] of their wise king? For from that very time their sovereignty was taken away. For God rightly exacted retribution on behalf of the wisdom of these three. For the Athenians starved to death, and the people of Samos were covered by the sea without remedy, and the Judaeans, massacred and chased from their kingdom, are scattered through every land. Socrates did not die, because of Plato; nor yet Pythagoras, because of the statue of Hera; nor did the wise king, because of the new laws that he gave.[19]

Mara's brief meditation on the deaths of Pythagoras, Socrates, and Jesus is ultimately redemptive. For he tells his son that, despite a confusing tradition about Pythagoras' death-by-fire, the spirit of Pythagorean thought is honoured, in some way, by the great Samian shrine to the goddess Hera. And despite the poisoned cup that killed him, "Socrates did not die"; rather his wisdom lives on in Plato's dialogues. And despite Jesus' passing, he is still present in the observance of "the new laws that he gave". What Mara calls *new laws*, here, we would now call Syrian Christianity—a rich and long-suffering tradition.[20]

That Mara's *wise king* is Jesus is suggested by his claim that Judaeans were punished after his death, by the destruction of Jerusalem, just as Athenians were punished after Socrates' death, and so on. There is nothing untoward about this notion of "divine nemesis", per se.[21] In chapter 2, we glimpsed the pagan conviction in Dio of Prusa's *Orations* that Socrates' death is "the cause" of the Athenians' later misfortunes. Similarly, Josephus tells us that many Judaeans interpreted Herod Antipas' humiliating defeat in 36 CE, by a Nabatean king, as divine retribution for the murder of John the Baptist.[22]

The notion that Jerusalem incurs its ruin in 70 CE, by Jesus' death in the year 30 or so, is rooted in the gospels and many early Christian traditions. It is worth noting, however, that in *Matthew* and *Luke*, Jesus' lament for Jerusalem is *not* only occasioned by his sense that he will be killed there. Rather, it seems that in Jesus' mind, his holy city is doomed because "killing the prophets" is a *recurring* drama in that city. His death belongs to a history of Hebrew prophet-martyrs.[23]

This must be stressed.

For a first- or second-century pagan philosopher such as Mara, 'killing the philosophers' is a recurring drama, which crescendos in the gods' destruction of Mediterranean cities. And for a first-century dissident rabbi such as Jesus, 'killing the prophets' is a recurring drama which includes himself, and which calls down God's judgement on Judaean cities.[24]

Beyond this, there seems to be a recognizably Syrian physiog-
nomy to Mara's Jesus. We catch this by glancing at a later text by
the dazzling Syrian satirist, Lucian of Samosata.

"New Mysteries": Lucian of Samosata

Writing circa 180, Lucian contemptuously refers to Jesus as "the
man who was crucified in Palestine because he introduced new
mysteries (*kainēn ... teletēn*) into the world".[25] Note that Jesus'
crime, here, is *innovation* (Greek *kainotomia*). The gospels do not
list innovation as one of the crimes with which he is charged.
However, Socrates is accused of introducing "new divinities"
(*kaina daimonia*) in the Athenian temple-state—and in the first
pages of *Mark*, Jesus is credited with a "new teaching" (*didachē
kainē*).[26] Like Mara, Lucian seems to constellate the deaths of
Socrates and Jesus.[27]

What is more, Lucian—like Mara—seems to perceive Jesus as
a sort of lawgiver. He writes the following about second-century
Syrian Christians:

> Their first lawgiver persuaded them that they are all brothers of one
> another after they have transgressed once for all by denying the
> Greek gods and by worshipping that crucified sophist himself and
> living under his laws. Therefore, they despise all things indiscrimi-
> nately and hold them to be common property.[28]

Jesus is not named, here, but Lucian refers to Christians in the
lines before and after this.[29] His "crucified sophist"—which is to
say, *not* a philosopher—is certainly Jesus.[30] And it is striking
that he takes Syrian Christians' choice to hold property in common—an early practice which is dramatized in *Acts of the
Apostles*—to be a mark of what both he and Mara call the *laws*
that Jesus gave.

For Lucian in the late second century, Jesus is a *crucified sophist* and the *first lawgiver* of the Christians. For Mara in the late
first or early second century, he is a *wise king* who was errone-

ously killed, but not before he had promulgated *new laws*. This is interesting, and there is much more that could be said.

For our present purposes, though, note only this. Mara attributes Jesus' death to Judaeans and fails to mention the cross. Lucian mentions the crucifixion and fails to note any Judaean role. This slight Syrian archive suggests that pagan intellectuals of Roman Syria had come to know, by the late second century CE, that Jesus had been put to death—like Socrates—as a political criminal. But it is not clear *who put him to death*. Mara has no doubt it is Judaeans, and Lucian is sure it is Romans.

When Mara's and Lucian's brief lines on Jesus are read in conjunction, we might suspect that both Judaeans and Romans had a hand in the death of this *new lawgiver*.

"Executed by Pilatus": Tacitus

Early Roman mentions of Jesus are scant, but we can relate them in interesting ways to our Syrian notices. The pagan historian Tacitus settles the question of who sentenced Jesus. "In the reign of Tiberius", he writes, Jesus was "executed ... by the procurator Pontius Pilatus".[31] Jesus' condemnation is now attributed to *Pilate*, and this graphs onto what we read in numerous early Christian texts. Tertullian of Carthage writes in Latin that Jesus was "crucified under Pontius Pilate"; Marcellus of Ancyra copies a Greek liturgical formula in which Jesus is "crucified under Pontius Pilate", and so on.[32]

It is significant, too, that Tacitus refers to Pilate's convict as *Christ* (Latin *Christus*), and not as *Jesus*. This is a point of commonality in the early Roman texts on Jesus.[33]

"In Honour of Christ": Pliny

In Pliny the Younger's letters, we find several charming ones to his friend Tacitus. But Pliny's most-cited letter is one he sent to

Trajan from a remote province on the Black Sea which he governed for a couple of years in the early second century. Pliny informs Trajan that the Christians in his province "come together before dawn on a fixed day"—surely the first day of the week—"to chant songs ... in honour of Christ, as if to a god (*quasi deo*)".[34] For Pliny, then—as for Tacitus—Jesus bears a Latin title, *Christus*.

This is logical, since the Romans sentenced Jesus as a messianic 'king'—in Latin, a *Christus*. (That said, the word does not figure in Pilate's interrogation or sentencing of Jesus in the gospels). It is only by keeping in mind Tacitus' *Christus*, crucified by Pilate, and Pliny's *Christus*, reverenced as a god, that we can turn to the third early Roman text on Jesus, by Suetonius.

"A New Superstition": Suetonius

I have mentioned that Pliny and Tacitus were friends. So, too, were Pliny and Suetonius. If Tacitus and Pliny refer to Jesus as *Christus*, then Suetonius should, too. And he seems to—nearly. For, in his life of Claudius, Suetonius writes: "Since the Judaeans [in Rome] were always making disturbances because of the instigator Chrestus (*impulsore Chresto*), he"—Claudius—"expelled them from Rome."[35]

Is Suetonius' *Chrestus* the *Christus* referred to by his friends, Tacitus and Pliny? There is a considerable literature on this question.

On the one hand, Suetonius' *Chrestus* might be Jesus. For a Christ-related expulsion of Judaeans from Rome, circa 49 CE, is recollected in *Acts of the Apostles*: "Claudius ... ordered all the Judaeans to leave Rome" (*Acts* 18:2).[36] What is more, Tertullian notes that Roman bureaucrats tended to soften the Greek-derived *Christian* into a Latin-sounding *Chrestian* (Latin *Christianus, Chrestianus*).[37]

ONE

On the other hand, Suetonius' *Chrestus* might not be Jesus. Nothing in Suetonius' syntax indicates that this man is twenty years dead, executed "during the reign of Tiberius".[38] What is more, Suetonius seems *not* to be one of the Roman elites who soften Greek vowels into Latin. For in his life of Nero, Suetonius writes that Christians—*not* Chrestians—are in the grip of "a new and malignant superstition".[39]

The meaning of Suetonius' text is therefore unclear.[40] His brief mention of *Chrestus* may, or may not, be an early pagan witness to Pilate's convict *Christus*. Nonetheless, Suetonius' text reveals that the name *Chrestus*—which *might* be taken to refer to Jesus—was a cause of unrest in many Judaean circles in Rome by 50 CE. And by 65 CE, the name *Christiani*—which *some* Roman bureaucrats pronounced *Chrestiani*—was stigmatized and semi-criminalized as a "new ... superstition" (*superstitionis novae*).[41]

By the first years of the second century CE, then, in the most rarefied circles of the Roman ecumene, the name or names *Christus–Chrestus* seem to have designated a man crucified in Judaea by Pilate (Tacitus), a man reverenced in Asia as a god (Pliny), and a man identified in Rome as a cause of unrest in Judaean circles (Suetonius).

Glancing back at our Syrian texts we can ask: What are Christians thought to have derived from Jesus? Mara talks of laws, Lucian of mysteries and Suetonius of a superstition. There is one eye-catching commonality, however. The laws are *new* for Mara, the mysteries are *new* for Lucian, and the superstition is *new* for Suetonius. "The man who was crucified in Palestine", as Lucian calls him, seems to be the figure of something new.[42]

Judaean Voices

According to the Syrian philosopher Mara, Judaeans were held responsible by God (or the gods) for Jesus' death, and we may suppose that this death took place in their renowned temple-city, Jerusalem. Yet none of the texts cited thus far is from a Judaean hand.

We will come to a Judaean text momentarily—by coming to the Judaeo-Roman historian, Josephus. But a Judaean consciousness of Jesus is not restricted to Judaean authors.

A couple of second-century texts come to mind—one by a Christian, the other by a pagan—which likely contain very early Judaean traditions about Jesus. Now, the Judaean voice in both texts is transmitted by a non-Judaean author. It would be unforgiveable to fail to reckon with that fact. Yet in both cases, recent scholarship urges us to hear that voice *as* Judaean, and there are signs that the Judaean personae in these texts are not mere fabrications. They may rather be neglected sources of authentic Judaean thought and rhetoric.[43]

"A Galilean Deceiver": Justin's Judaean

The first text I have in mind is Justin the Philosopher's *Dialogue with Trypho the Judaean* from the second century CE. Justin is a Christian; his interlocutor is not. But, according to Justin, Judaean polemicists claimed in his day that

> a godless (*atheos*) and lawless heresy had sprung from one Jesus, a Galilean deceiver, whom we crucified, but his disciples stole by night from the tomb, where he was laid when unfastened from the cross, and now deceive men by asserting that he has risen from the dead and ascended to heaven.[44]

Wherever this sentence originated, it is shocking for us to hear a 'Judaean' speak of "Jesus ... whom we crucified". Crucifixion is a Roman, not a Judaean form of punishment. It is strange, too, because Justin holds that Jesus was put to death "under Pontius Pilate".[45]

Remarkably, this incrimination of Judaeans—which will have dark consequences in European history—seems to be a trope of Judaean self-incrimination.[46] What could strike us as being an anti-*Judaean* trope might well be an anti-*Christian* trope. Other anti-Christian and anti-Judaean tropes have proved to be convertible.[47] But, in sum: Justin *might* be copying out, here, a second-century Judaean claim regarding Jesus' Galilean roots, crucifixion and tomb-drama.

"We Punished the Man": Celsus' Judaean

The second text I have in mind is Celsus' *True Word*. One of the marks of this philosopher's brilliance is his choice of a mouth-piece. Though himself a pagan, Celsus calculates that his attack on Christian faith, circa 180 CE, will be most devastating if it is conducted by a Judaean. Yet since Celsus' text only survives in the pages of a counter-attack by Origen—*Against Celsus*—this Judaean is not only trapped within a pagan text. He is trapped within a pagan text *which is trapped within a Christian text*. This double-entrapment must be noted. And Origen dismisses this Judaean as "imaginary", but he *might not* be a fictitious persona.[48] There are signs that he might be a conduit of real Judaean claims about Jesus in the second century CE.[49]

"*We* punished the man", says Celsus in his Judaean's voice.[50] The philosopher says also in his own voice that Jesus "was punished *by the Judaeans*".[51] And again, Celsus has his Judaean say: "*We* convicted him and condemned him and decided that he should be punished."[52] The insistence on a Judaean conviction and punishment of Jesus could hardly be more categorical. And there is no reason, that I can tell, why Celsus would want to diminish the Roman hand in his death. This may, then, be a polemical claim emanating from Judaean circles in the first or second century CE.

"A GOD WHO WAS CONDEMNED"

This picture of Jesus' death is complicated by a fragment in which Celsus' Judaean says to the Christians: "The one who condemned [Jesus] did not even suffer any such fate as that of Pentheus by going mad or being torn in pieces."[53] This can only be a reference to Pilate. And if this jab is drawn from a lost Judaean source, it is a rare Judaean recollection of Pilate's sentencing of Jesus.[54]

However that may be, Celsus is a pagan philosopher who draws upon a Judaean source or concocts a Judaean persona. His *True Word* is thus neither a pagan nor a Judaean text; it is both. And this makes it highly suggestive that it seems to recollect a Judaean *and* a Roman condemnation of Jesus. Jesus "was punished by the *Judaeans*", and the "one who condemned him" was a *Roman*.[55] The most notorious reference to Jesus' death seems to confirm this double-condemnation.

"A Wise Man": Josephus in Greek

Josephus' Testimony, or *Testimonium Flavianum*, is found in a huge book composed circa 90 CE for the Roman elites, by a Jerusalem native with political ties to Galilee. Not entirely unlike Celsus' text, Josephus' *Judaean Antiquities* are neither Judaean nor pagan, but both. It is in a singularly Judaeo-Roman history that Jesus seems to be charged by Judaeans and crucified by a Roman.

Now, the integrity of Josephus' Testimony has been doubted since the sixteenth century. It seems clear that a Christian hand, or hands, corrupted the received text.[56] To my mind, however, this Testimony was credibly restored in the nineteenth century.[57] And this is a modern reconstruction of what Josephus may be thought to have written in Greek:

> At about this time lived Jesus, a wise man. He did marvellous (or strange) things, a teacher of those who receive the truth (or novelties) with pleasure. He attracted many Judaeans and many of the

75

Hellenes. Upon an indictment brought by the leading men among us, Pilate sentenced him to the cross. But those who had loved him from the very first did not cease to do so, and to this very day the brotherhood of the Christians, named after him, has not died out.[58]

But this text is not only known to us in Greek.

"A Wise Man": Josephus in Arabic

There is an Arabic version of Josephus' Testimony in the *Universal History* by Agapius of Manbij, a Syrian bishop of the tenth century. Intriguingly, in Agapius' medieval chronicle, the death of Jesus is linked to the history of philosophy. For he tells us that he had "found in many books of the philosophers that they refer to the day of crucifixion of Christ (*al-Masīḥ*), and that they marvel at it".[59]

Who are the philosophers in question?

First, Agapius cites a text which he ascribes to a second-century pagan compiler, Phlegon of Tralles. We read in this fragment of Phlegon that, on the day of Jesus' death, "the sun was darkened and there was night for nine hours; the stars appeared ... and strange things happened".[60]

Second, Agapius cites someone whose name is illegible in its medieval Arabic transliteration. Ursinus? Orosius? It is impossible to say.[61] Yet this obscure "philosopher", as the bishop calls him, remarks that "the sun was darkened ... and many terrifying things are stated to have happened in the country of the Hebrews" on the day of the crucifixion.[62]

Third in this sequence is "Josephus (*Yūsīfūs*) the Hebrew".[63] Though Josephus does not comment on "the *day* of the crucifixion of Christ", he tells us much about Jesus' life and death. Namely, here, in his Arabic Testimony:

At this time there was a wise man who was called Jesus. His conduct was good, and he was known to be virtuous. And many people from among the Judaeans and the other nations became his disciples.

Pilate condemned him to be crucified and to die. But those who had become his disciples did not abandon his discipleship. They reported that he had appeared to them three days after his crucifixion, and that he was alive. Accordingly, he was perhaps the Christ, concerning whom the prophets have recounted wonders.[64]

We notice that in Josephus' Arabic Testimony, there is no Judaean charge behind the Roman trial and conviction of Jesus.[65] In this, it differs not only from the gospels and Josephus' Greek Testimony, but from the 'Judaean' traditions in early texts by Justin (a Christian) and Celsus (a pagan). What is more important for us is that, in this Arabic Testimony:

(i)   Jesus is called a "wise man" (as in the Greek Testimony);
(ii)   Jesus' disciples are drawn "from among the Judaeans and the other nations" (as in the Greek Testimony); and
(iii) although Jesus is "known to be virtuous", Pilate condemns him to the cross (as in the Greek Testimony).

In both the Greek and Arabic traditions of Josephus' Testimony—as in Mara's Syriac *Letter*—Jesus belongs to a sombre history in which "the whole world ... persecutes good and just men as if they were evil and impious—torturing, condemning, and killing them".[66]

Conclusions

In Syrian, Roman, and Judaean texts of the first centuries CE, the depictions of Jesus are divided. For Mara, he is a philosopher—for Lucian, a sophist. For Pliny, he is a sort of numen—for Tacitus, a dead convict. For Josephus, a wise man—and for the Judaean in Justin's dialogue, a deceiver.[67] Even the pagan deities seem divided. "The gods have pronounced Christ to have been most holy and immortal", says Porphyry of Tyre in *Philosophy from Oracles*.[68] And there is backing for this in surviving oracular fragments. The night-goddess Hecate seems to have regarded Christ as "a supremely righteous man", though she warns that Christians are "hated by the gods". In contrast to this, Apollo mocks the one he calls "a god who died deluded". For him, Jesus is an impious man who was "condemned by just judges" and compelled "to die cruelly by the worst of deaths".[69]

What are we to make of this man whom a god calls *deluded* and a goddess calls *supremely righteous*, and who everyone knows suffered *the worst of deaths*? We can begin by asking where he lived, and under whose jurisdiction he died so cruelly.

8

JURISDICTIONS AND *DRAMATIS PERSONAE*

The Passion is remembered less in this century, in Europe and the Near East, than at any other time in the last thousand years, and the cultural memory of Christianity seems to be dimming in the Americas. It may be useful, then, to introduce the jurisdictions and *dramatis personae* that structure the political life of Jesus. They determine much in "the milieu in which this strange figure moved".[1]

The Temple-State of Judaea

In the autumn of 63 BCE, during the consulship of the philosopher Cicero, Jerusalem fell to Rome.[2] We read that when Rome's troops streamed into the Temple, the priests of Israel continued serenely to circle the altar. A massacre commenced. Josephus says that many of the priests were "butchered in the act of pouring libations and burning incense, putting the divine offerings before their own salvation".[3]

To the horror of Judaeans, the gentile Pompey strode into the Temple's holiest place and inspected the nation's *arcana*—a gleaming candelabrum, a heap of spices and a mass of "sacred currency".[4]

Pompey did not lay a hand on Israel's *arcana*, and Josephus tells us that that he restored the high priesthood to Hyrcanus II, who had held it before Pompey arrived.[5] This is how the history of Roman Judaea begins—with Hyrcanus II, a high priest, governing the Judaean temple-state as a client-ruler of Rome.[6]

Throughout Jesus' life, Jerusalem is the holy city of Judaea.[7] And throughout his life, Judaea is *cultically* ruled by a hereditary caste of priests, one of whom reigns as the high priest.[8] This high priest makes no claim, however, to *monarchical* rule. For, beginning in 6 CE and lasting till 41 CE, Judaea was an imperial province of Rome.[9] This means that Judaea fell under the control of a Roman prefect who lived in a palace in the coastal city of Caesarea Maritima.

Note that this centre of the Roman presence in Judaea is named for the object of a first-century cultus, the divinized Caesars.[10] There are toponyms in the gospels—such as Caesarea Philippi in *Mark*, and the Sea of Tiberias in *John*—which alert us to a symbolic presence of the Caesars, and their cultus, in Jesus' native Galilee.[11]

Since Judaea's high priest remained in Jerusalem, it became customary for the Roman prefect to reside there during Israel's high holy days. This is the situation during the last week of Jesus' natural life. This is why he is interrogated by the highest office-holder in the *Judaean* temple-state, Joseph Caiaphas, and of the *Roman* temple-state in Judaea, Pontius Pilate.[12]

Why this insistence on calling Rome and Roman Judaea *temple-states*? The Judaean polity was centred on the Temple precincts in Jerusalem and culminated in the office of the high priest. This centrality of the sacrificial cult in Judaea is clear; but Rome has acquired a veneer of 'secularity' in modern historiography. Though this is not entirely without reason, it is deceptive.[13] The emperors were themselves the Roman polity's high priests (Latin *pontifices maximi*), and even in Judaea, sacrifice lay at the core of Roman politics.

To be sure, the emperor-cult was not enforced in Judaea, but every morning and evening sacrifices were offered in the Jerusalem Temple, "for Caesar and the Roman nation". The daily immolation seems to have consisted of an ox and two lambs.[14] According to Josephus, Judaea's catastrophic war with Rome began when a zealot-priest banned the imperial sacrifice in Jerusalem.[15]

As this indicates, both Judaea and Rome were temple-states. Jesus, however, did not belong in either.

The Tetrarchy of Galilee

In terms of maternal descent, ritual and creed, Jesus was a Judaean. And in terms of Roman law, he was a non-citizen (Latin *peregrinus*). However, he was not merely a non-citizen, for he was recognized by Rome as belonging to a statelet, Galilee.[16]

In terms of Roman jurisdiction, then, Jesus was a Galilean. And unlike Judaea, Galilee was not a Roman province, but a client state. Its ruler, Herod Antipas, was a scion of the Herodian line and reigned 4 BCE to 39 CE.[17] His father, Herod I, was named "King of the Judaeans" by the Roman Senate in 40 BCE. It was he who restored Jerusalem's Temple.[18] In this book, *Herod* refers to this "younger Herod", and not his father.

It is worth noting that many familial murders and other heartless acts structure the Herodian dynasty. In the words of one late ancient chronicler, the dynasty's shadows are "darker than any in tragic drama".[19] And some of those shadows loom, vaguely, in the gospels.

Rome—Judaea—Galilee

Galilee was not a Roman province. The importance of this fact has been sharply stated by one Roman legal historian. "In none of the four gospels is there the slightest indication that Jesus felt any personal hostility to the Romans." What is more, "as a Galilean he was not subject to Roman domination or to the hated Roman tax".[20] It is erroneous to blur the Roman governance of Judaea into the Herodian governance of Galilee. And the gospels place Jesus, for most of his prophetic life, in the settlements and desert places of Galilee, Samaria, Decapolis and Peraea, to the north and east of "the Judaean land" (*tēn Ioudaian gēn—John* 3:22).

It bears repeating that Jesus is a Judaean in terms of maternal descent, ritual and creed. When he and his cohort, the Twelve, are near the settlement of Sychar in Samaria, the woman he converses with can tell that he is a Judaean (*John* 4:5–9). But in terms of jurisdiction, Jesus and his cohort are *not* Judaean. In Judaea's holy city, he is "Jesus the Galilean" (*Matthew* 26:69).[21] And in one heated scene in the fourth gospel, he is even called "a Samaritan" (*John* 8:48).[22] This territorial and political sense of the term 'Judaean' must be held in mind when reading the gospels.

The term *Judaei* came to be attached to the ritual and confessional identity of premodern Europe's most considerable non-Christian minority. And in modern Europe the word *Jew* took on a malevolently racialized sense, especially in the nineteenth and twentieth centuries. Both senses are deceptive within Jesus' milieu, which is to say, in the gospels.

This is because there are no 'Christians' in the gospels. The term is first invented in Syria, decades after Jesus' death.[23] And also, Jesus' circles—and the gospels—seem to be marked by critiques of racialized theology. In the first lines of *John*, for instance, we read that the divine Word "illuminates every human" (*phōtizei panta anthrōpon*), and that children of God are born "not of blood, nor of the will of the flesh, nor of a husband's will" (*John* 1:9, 13).[24] This is a bold renunciation of any racialized idea of divine belonging, and it is written—how could we forget?—by a 'Judaean' by descent, who is a 'Christian'.

In the gospels, one of the most basic meanings of *Judaean* is simply, *pertaining to the Roman province of Judaea*. This is important because, for most of Jesus' prophetic life, he skirts Judaea. The synoptic gospels—*Matthew, Mark* and *Luke*—show Jesus only entering Judaea once during his prophetic life. And this precipitates his death. In *John* he enters Judaea a number of times to celebrate the high holy days; but still, his prophetic life is centred in Galilee and Samaria. In strictly jurisdictional and territorial terms, these were not *Judaean*.

There in a decisive scene in *John* in which Jesus says: "Let us return to Judaea." His disciples—all of whom are cultic and ethnic Judaeans—say: "But, rabbi, the Judaeans were just trying to stone you!" When they realize that Jesus cannot be deterred, Thomas—the iconic doubter—says: "Let us go [to Judaea] to die with him!" (*John* 11:7–8, 16). The idea that 'the Judaeans' (*hoi Ioudaioi*) in *John* are a racialized 'entity' to which Jesus, or his disciples, are hostile seems to me indefensible. Rather, what this conversation reveals is that one of the determining senses of the word 'Judaea', hence 'Judaeans', in all four gospels is this: Roman Judaea is a jurisdiction in which Jesus cannot survive.[25]

Herod the Galilean Tetrarch

Herod Antipas seems to have died, not in one of the gleaming new-built cities of Galilee and Peraea, but in a remote settlement of Roman Gaul, after Caligula stripped him of his title and forced him into exile.[26] Roughly a half-decade before this, according to *Luke*, Herod questioned Jesus on the morning of his death. Fergus Millar concludes that there is "no inherent improbability" in this tradition.[27] But regardless of whether we believe that Jesus and Herod Antipas met, there is no reason to doubt *Matthew*'s claim that the tetrarch had heard "the rumour of Jesus" (*tēn akoēn Iēsou*—*Matthew* 14:1).[28] And there is no reason to doubt that that Herod looms large in Jesus' political life.

Herodian dynasts had a gross habit of marrying their nieces, and their brothers' wives—and Herod Antipas' feat is to have done both, in marrying his second wife, Herodias.[29] He is notorious for this illicit marriage to the wife of his brother, Philip, in the synoptic gospels—or one of his half-brothers, in Josephus.[30] And it may be this scandal which incites Jesus' hard sayings on divorce and adultery.[31] John the Baptist publicly condemns the marriage, sealing his fate. For both Josephus and the synoptic tradition identify Herod as the one who imprisons John, and then has him beheaded.[32]

It is John's imprisonment which seems to induce Jesus to begin proclaiming a divine kingdom or empire (Greek *basileia*) which differs radically from Rome, from the Roman province of Judaea, and from the tetrarchy of Galilee and Peraea (*Mark* 1:14–15).[33] Further, John's death in captivity seems to have deeply troubled Jesus (*Mark* 6:17–29), convincing him that Israel's first-century prophets—like many of their forbears— would suffer violence (*Mark* 9:11–13).

Herod seems to have put John to death in one of his fortress palaces, Machaerus, in the hills that encircle the Dead Sea.[34] And it is interesting that both *Mark* and *Matthew* tell us that he is reluctant to kill the prophet, and feels "grieved"—in *Mark*, "deeply grieved". But his wife Herodias, and her unnamed daughter (Salome?), force his hand after the "young girl" dances for him and Galilee's nobility at his birthday party (Greek *genesia*, Latin *natalis*).[35]

It is this dance of Herodias' daughter which fascinates not only *Mark*'s seedy tetrarch but a huge number of nineteenth-century artists.[36] René Girard criticizes this cult of Salome, noting that in *Mark*'s gospel—unlike the modern imaginary—"Herodias's daughter is a child". She is not described by the gospel-writer as a *korē* ("girl"), but a *korasion* ("young girl" or "girl-child"). She is certainly not a seducer, and "has no desire to formulate" in John's death scene in *Mark*. It is Herod's wife, not her daughter, who has in mind the shocking gift that Herod is sorry to have to give—John's head "on a dish" (*Mark* 6:24–26). This macabre touch—that the prophet's head should be set, during a banquet, on a plate—is the child's only contribution. "Herodias had mentioned the head", as Girard notes, "but not the dish".[37]

Premodern commentators differ on the question of Herod's grief. Is it genuine? One medieval glossator notes the link to Pilate's 'grief', in the gospels, before he crucifies Jesus. "Herod's sorrow", reads his gloss, "was like Pilate's repentance".[38]

But what matters most for us is that the tetrarch of Galilee and Peraea is a prophet-killer. The beheading of John the Baptist is a structuring moment in *Matthew*, *Mark* and *Luke*—and Jesus' premonitions of his own death are doubtless heightened by the beheading of the man who had baptized him.[39]

Caiaphas the Judaean Pontiff

There is not much information in Josephus or in the gospels about Joseph Caiaphas, who seems to have reigned for nearly twenty years as the high priest of Judaea.[40] Josephus only relates that he was made high priest by the prefect Valerius Gratus in the year 18, and that he was deposed by the legate Vitellius in the year 36.[41] We infer that Caiaphas was high priest throughout the prefectship of Pontius Pilate (26 to 36 CE). And from this we can judge that he must have been "no mean politician".[42] Every morning and evening of his pontificate, oxen and lambs will have been sacrificed in the Temple—perhaps by Caiaphas himself—with prayers for Caesar and the Roman *imperium*.[43]

Three other facts are salient. First, Caiaphas' most hallowed high-priestly accoutrements were held by the Roman prefect, and only released before the holiest days of Israel's year.[44] Second, only the high priest had the authority in Jerusalem to convene the Sanhedrin—a high council of seventy priests and legists. Finally, there is reason to believe that, during this time, Caiaphas had the power (*de facto*), but not the authority (*de jure*) to put the Sanhedrin's convicts to death. His supreme jurisdiction, or what Roman law calls "the right of the sword" (*ius gladii*), is dubious. There is no modern consensus as to whether he could have lawfully executed Jesus without Pilate's sentence.

Pilate the Roman Prefect

"Jesus?" asks a soft, hulking man with fine features and vacant eyes, "I do not recall him". This is how Anatole France's urbane 1892 fiction, "The Procurator of Judaea", ends. On the cusp of the twentieth century, France fantasizes that Pilate, having crucified "a young Galilean seer" for "I know not what crime", then condemned him to a sort of *damnatio memoriae*, as the Romans called punishment-by-oblivion.[45]

In 1961, a limestone block was uncovered at Caesarea in Israel, which bears this inscription:

[PO]NTIVS PILATVS

[PRAEF]ECTVS IVDA[EA]E

The text is lacunar, but no one disputes that it reads:

PONTIUS PILATE

PREFECT OF JUDAEA[46]

The block on which this wording is carved seems to have been fitted into a structure built by Pilate in honour of Caesar. The structure may have been a temple on the coast of Roman Judaea to the then reigning "son of a god" (*divi filius*), Tiberius Caesar.[47]

This inscription places several things out of doubt. A man named Pontius Pilate held high office in Roman Judaea; his title was prefect (Latin *praefectus*, Greek *eparchos*); and his prefectship fell during the reign of Tiberius. One Roman writer (Tacitus), two Judaean writers (Philo and Josephus) and a host of Christian writers confirm this. And his dates in the province are commonly held to be 26 to 36 (or 37) CE.[48]

Remarkably, his presence in Judaea may have found new material confirmation in the course of a dig at one of Herod Antipas' fortress palaces, in a desert south of Jerusalem.[49] Here, a slight copper alloy ring was itemized[50] with a cache of other bronze objects and first-century Judaean coins. It revealed a non-linear Greek inscription that is taken to read:

PILATO[U]

The Herodium excavators take this to mean:

OF PILATE

Although it is unlikely that he would have worn such a ring himself, our Roman prefect is the only *Pilate* currently on record.[51] The current idea seems to be that this ring may have belonged to a functionary or slave.

By the early second century, however, this name is only attested in connection with Jesus. Writing circa 115, as we have seen, Tacitus mentions that Jesus—or, as Tacitus calls him, Christ—suffered the extreme punishment by Pilate's sentence.[52] This is the prefect's only mention in Tacitus' *Histories* and *Annals*. And judging by extant Roman histories, Pilate's only significance in the history of empire lies in the fact that he crucified Jesus.

It is different when we turn to the extant histories written by Judaean elites. Both Philo and Josephus identify Pilate as a prefect, or procurator, of Judaea during Tiberius' reign.[53] This, too, is what we read in *Luke*. During "the reign of Emperor Tiberius ... Pontius Pilate was governor of Judaea" (*Luke* 3:1).

Philo's recollection of Pilate appears in a fiercely political text titled *Embassy to Gaius*. It is a damning depiction, but Philo is furious. The emperor Gaius "Caligula" had threatened to place a "colossal statue" of himself in the "inner sanctum" of the Jerusalem Temple.[54] It is in this context that the great philosopher calls Pilate to mind. Philo's *Embassy* is dated circa 40, perhaps just three years after Pilate's removal. The Judaean philosopher is therefore writing what we might call a history of the present. Philo's Roman is "hard-headed and cruel", and his prefectship is notorious for its corruption, illegality and brutality.[55]

In Josephus, and in the gospels, the tone is cooler. Josephus senses that Pilate is basically hostile to "the laws of the Judaeans". Yet his Pilate "marvels", too, at "the intensity of their devotion to the laws".[56] Both aspects of Pilate—his hostility to Judaean laws, and his capacity for awe—are glimpsed in the gospels' Passion narratives, towards which we are ultimately making our way.

9

JUDAEAN PHILOSOPHIES
AND CONFUSED JUDGES

In 53 CE—roughly twenty years after Jesus' death—a high-born boy in Jerusalem decided to acquaint himself with the three most prominent "sects" in Judaea and Galilee. Or so he tells us in his memoir, *Life of Josephus*.[1] In *The Judaean War*, Josephus calls the same sects "philosophies"—a term that I prefer.[2] But though his terminology differs, he consistently identifies the three mid-century movements in Galilee and Judaea as the Pharisee, the Sadducee and the Essene.[3]

Josephus tells us that he engaged in all three between the ages of sixteen and nineteen, before finally choosing to be a Pharisee. He tells his pagan readers that this Judaean philosophy is not unlike first-century Stoicism.[4] What could this mean? Perhaps we could say that Pharisaic thought is a "*savoir-faire* of living" (*peri bion technē*). And that where a Stoic must strive "in every circumstance" to hold himself, or herself, "in a state of accord with nature", a Pharisee must strive in every circumstance to act in accordance with Mosaic law.[5]

Josephus returns on a number of occasions to his Pharisee–Sadducee–Essene triad, but it is significant that he rarely confines himself to it. In his *Life*, for instance, Josephus tells us that, after his immersion in the three Judaean philosophies, he made himself the disciple of an ascetic named Bannus, who lived in the desert and only wore "such clothing as the trees provide".[6]

When Josephus comes to write about Judaea in the decade after his time with Bannus, circa 66, he formally introduces a fourth philosophy.[7] This fourth Judaean philosophy seems not to have been salient during Josephus' youth (circa 53–56), and he nervously states that it has "nothing in common" with the other three.[8] He later concedes, however, that it is close to Pharisaic thought.[9] This new philosophy seems to have roots in a counter-Roman insurgency mounted in the year 6 CE by Judas the Galilean. It differs from the other philosophies in that it is fanatically committed to eradicating the Roman presence in Galilee and Judaea.[10]

Pharisees and Sadducees figure prominently in the gospels. Essenes and Zealots are never mentioned, but they have come to the fore in much of the modern New Testament literature. There is an immense body of writing on Jesus and the Essenes; and there is a centuries-old fixation on certain verses, where we read that one of Jesus' cohort is "Simon, who was called the Zealot" (*Luke* 6:15; *Acts* 1:13).[11] As one legal historian dryly remarks, this only proves that Jesus and his disciples were *not* Zealots; for the appellation would be meaningless in a circle of Zealots.[12] More to my point, Simon's appellation is attached to the disciple himself, and not to a zealotic "philosophy", which seems not to have been conspicuous during Jesus' prophetic life.[13]

There can be no pretence, here, of doing justice to the first century's four Judaean philosophies. But without a vague sense of the two philosophies which figure in the gospels—Pharisee and Sadducee—and the other two which have come to the fore in much of the modern literature—Essene and Zealot—many scenes in Jesus' political life will be impossible to decode.

JUDAEAN PHILOSOPHIES AND CONFUSED JUDGES

"Purity Broke into Israel"

The term 'Pharisee' in the gospels denotes a strong tradition of Judaic thought and practice in Jerusalem and other Judaean cities.[14] The Pharisees emerged in the Hellenistic period out of a new, urban class of "petty bourgeois". A saying in the Talmud has it that "purity broke into Israel" when the Pharisees formed their *habūrā*, or circles of "comrades" who committed to practice Levitical purity in daily life.[15] This meant, for instance, that a level of purity kept at table by priests in the Temple precincts must be imitated in a Pharisaic home.[16] Such a commitment of course called for a tremendous, centuries-long task of legal reasoning and counter-reasoning.

Pharisees derived the authority for their legal reasonings from an elaborate, notionally unbroken chain of transmission that reached back to "the fathers"—and, indeed, to Moses.[17] Though Jesus concedes that such reasoning has a certain real authority (*Matthew* 23:2–3), he is nevertheless a severe critic (*Matthew* 23:4–5).

The hostility between Jesus and Pharisees is by no means categorical in the gospels, but it is palpable. His characteristic refrains, "I say to you" (*Mark* 2:11), and "Truly I tell you" (*Mark* 3:28), were clearly felt—and may have been meant—as an affront to Pharisaic thought. In one of the first scenes of *Mark*, we are told that Jesus spoke "as one having authority, and not as the scribes".[18]

The gospels portray Jesus as the heir of the "God-loving prophets", as Eusebius calls them.[19] He is rumoured in Galilee to be "a prophet like one of the prophets of old" (*Mark* 6:15), and it is wholly in line with the prophetic tradition that he is remembered as a searing critic of Judaea's scribal culture—or that, in Spinoza's words, he "convicts the Pharisees of obstinacy and ignorance".[20] It is perfectly clear in *Matthew*, for instance, that his hostility to aspects of the Pharisaic mentality is inherited from John the Baptist (*Matthew* 3:7–9).

But Jesus did not only dispute with Pharisees; he also dined with them (*Luke* 7:36, 11:37, 14:1).[21] We read in *Luke* that when he was at table in a Pharisee's house, "they were watching him closely". This captures a sense of unease that pervades many of the scenes in Jesus' life.[22] Although Pharisaic hostility to Jesus is strongly attested in the gospels, it is not they who captured him in the holy city. And it is only in *John* that the Pharisees figure in a Passion narrative (*John* 18:3).

"More Heartless than Other Judaeans"

"The origin of the Sadducees", writes Günter Stemberger, "must be considered to be unknown". Even the meaning of their name is doubtful.[23] But several facts stand out. They left no writings, which puts them at the mercy of their critics. The gospels contain the earliest mention of Sadducees, where they represent a landed priestly caste.[24] To be a Sadducee is to belong to Judaea's hereditary aristocracy.[25] And due to their unique connection to the Temple, their philosophy is rooted in Jerusalem.[26]

The Sadducees distrusted Pharisaic legal reasoning, and they denied the resurrection of the dead.[27] According to Josephus, they were "more heartless than any of the other Judaeans ... when they [sat] in judgement".[28] And it was Sadducees—not Pharisees—who arrested Jesus, questioned him, and conveyed him to Pilate for sentencing.[29] What is more, it seems that Sadducees remained "ardent persecutors" of Christ-believers in Jerusalem in the decades following Jesus' death.[30]

The Schismatics and Rebels

The Essenes and Zealots do not figure in the gospels. I can only say of them, here, that Jesus' prophetic call for "repentance"

(*metanoia*)—a change of mind, a change of life—may be antici-
pated by the Essenes.[31] But Jesus' seminomadic life, his seeming
unconcern with ritual purity, his refusal to judge, and his radical
sayings on love, form a stark contrast with the Essenes. "Look",
say Jesus' critics, "a drunkard! A friend of ... sinners!" (*Luke* 7:34;
Matthew 11:19). No one ever accused the Essenes—or indeed,
John the Baptist—of drunkenness or slumming.[32] In this context, Jesus cannot be mistaken for an Essene.[33]

While it is not certain that a zealotic philosophy had formed
in Galilee or Judaea during Jesus' prophetic life; it seems clear
that zealotic impulses were in the air. We have already seen that
one of Jesus' inner circle was called a "Zealot", and we will see in
a later chapter that on one occasion Jesus is himself called a
"Zealot".[34] And yet, in the lines of *Matthew* and *Luke* that I have
just quoted ("drunkard" and "friend of sinners"), Jesus' critics
also say: "Look! ... A friend of tax collectors!" (*Luke* 7:34;
Matthew 11:19). No one ever accused the Zealots of fraternizing
with tax collectors.

Josephus informs us that the Zealots menaced, brutalized, and
murdered Judaeans who could be accused of *consenting to pay* a
Roman tax.[35] In his words, the fanatics were known for:

> threatening death to those [Judaeans] who submitted to the Roman
> *imperium* ... Dividing themselves by cohorts in the countryside, they
> both plundered the homes of the powerful and did away with them.
> And they set the villages ablaze, so that all Judaea was being filled
> up with their madness.[36]

There is simply no comparable rhetoric or violence in the gospels. In this context, Jesus cannot be mistaken for a Zealot. And
the most discerning historians recognize this. "Jesus is no Zealot
or enemy of Rome."[37] It is a discredit to modern historiography
that the Zealot-Jesus theory is still with us, 250 years after
Reimarus' fragments were published by Lessing.

For it is the gospel-writers who place Jesus, in collective memory, in the presence of a criminal named Barabbas: "The man who had been put in prison for insurrection and murder" (*Luke* 23:25). The gospel-writer's description is cool and exact: Barabbas has been convicted by the Romans for inciting rebellion and taking human life (Greek *stasin kai phonon*; Latin *seditionem et homicidium*).[38] There is therefore a lexicon, in *Luke–Acts*, for zealotry—and the writer of *Luke–Acts* is not unnerved by it, because he knows that it fails to describe the form-of-life of Jesus and his cohort.

The same could be said of Josephus. His Jesus is "a teacher of those who receive the truth with pleasure".[39]

And who are the imitators of Judas the Galilean? Josephus calls them "knifers"—*sicarii*, hated for "murdering people by day and in the heart of the city". Their tactic was this: "Mingling with the mob and concealing small daggers under their clothes, with these they ... stab[bed] their foes." And what was the effect of this form of rebellion? The Judaeans, Josephus tells us, started to "scrutinize their foes from a distance", and "there was no trust even among approaching friends".[40]

The contrast with Jesus is stark. "Love your enemies", he says in *Luke*. "Do good to those who hate you, bless those who curse you, pray for those who abuse you." This is an absolute renunciation of the terroristic logic of cutthroats—and of the subtler cruelties that Jesus seems to recognize in certain forms of civility.[41]

Harold Bloom is right to conclude that the merciless philosophy of Judaean rebels is "totally against [Jesus'] nature".[42]

But though the gospels—and the coming chapters—cannot be read without a vague sense of the Judaean "philosophies", Jesus is not put to death by a Judaean philosophy. Rather he is brought face to face, in his last hours, with Judaean and gentile judges. And in the gospels, neither his gentile nor his Judaean judges seem entirely certain what to make of him. Their confusion, I believe, is historically credible—and revealing.

"Who Is This Young Man?"

"Who is this young man", asks a priest in the 430s CE, "who confused Pontius Pilate?"[43] The priest's name is Quodvultdeus (Latin for "What-God-Wills"), and his sermon is preached at a dead-of-night vigil in the catholic basilica of Carthage.

There is now an ocean of literature—reverential and hostile, critical and uncritical—whose deepest question is the same: Who is Jesus? This book will not resolve that question, for the simple reason that it is irresolvable. But Quodvultdeus' question is useful in that it draws our eye to a moment in the gospels—namely, *the confusion of Pontius Pilate*.

The first thing to note is that when Quodvultdeus says that Jesus is the "young man" who "confused" Pilate (Latin *turbavit*), he is not merely lifting material from the gospels. Quodvultdeus is glossing them, and restating what he has read in them. The Latin verb which he uses—*turbare*, to "disturb or confuse"—is not found in the canonical Passion narratives. Even in the early Latin versions of the gospels, we see that Pilate "marvelled" at Jesus (*mirari*), and that he is "terrified" by a rumour that Jesus is the Son of God (*timere*).[44]

Of the four gospels, only *Luke* says nothing about Pilate's mood during his interrogation of Jesus. Yet even from *Luke*, Quodvultdeus could have inferred that Pilate was disquieted. For instance, when Pilate urges Jesus to tell him whether he is a king—or, more precisely, "King of the Judaeans"—the reply is only: "You say so" (*Luke* 23:3). One legal commentator deems this to be "no different" from a refusal to testify.[45] That seems dogmatic. It might be more precise to say that Jesus' reply is, as Quodvultdeus intuits, a *confusing* one.

Luke dramatizes Pilate's confusion by having him say to the Temple elites: "I have examined him in your presence and have not found this man guilty of any of your charges against him"

(*Luke* 23:14). It develops in the next verse: "Neither has Herod" (*Luke* 23:14–15). Neither Herod nor Pilate have found Jesus guilty of the charges brought by the Temple aristocracy.

Quodvultdeus asks in the 430s: "Who is this young man ... who *confused* Pontius Pilate?"[46] And, we can now add, this young man who confused *Herod Antipas*?

Now, *Luke's* tetrarch and prefect are both depraved rulers. The gospel-writer shows Herod plotting Jesus' death (*Luke* 13:31), and Pilate sentencing him to death (*Luke* 23:24). The tendency of modern criticism is to ask: What could induce a gospel-writer to make brutal and immoral rulers declare a man innocent—hours before they kill him? Theories are rife, often positing biases or repressed memories to explain the action. It seems to me uncritical to seek factors which lie beyond the horizons of the gospels before we demonstrate that the logic of the texts is not hiding in plain sight.

Quodvultdeus' question is more piercing, and more arresting. And like him, we can ask: What *young man* could induce brutal and immoral rulers to declare him innocent—hours before they kill him?

The African priest's question suggests *his* reply—which is mine, too: *Confusion*. I believe that it is Jesus' confusion of rulers which illuminates the structure, and the inner logic, of the Passion narratives.

In the following chapters, we will reconstruct Jesus' political life in light of his trials—and, more precisely, in light of the *confusion* of his judges. It is this confusion at the end of his political life which leads us to a new question: Is there something at the very beginning which might clarify his judges' doubts and hesitations at the end?

PART FOUR

THE POLITICAL TEMPTATIONS OF CHRIST

10

JESUS AMONG THE BELIEVERS

In *Matthew*, *Mark* and *Luke*, Jesus' prophetic life begins after he is baptized by an ascetic preacher, John, and tempted by the accusatory spirit, Satan. There is a parallel to be observed here. After Jesus is baptized, he is blessed by "a voice from heaven" which calls him the "Son, the Beloved" of God.[1] The revelation that Jesus is uniquely blessed leads to a drama in which he is uniquely tempted.

The temptation narrative in *Mark* is, in one commentator's phrase, "astonishingly obscure".[2] In the first gospel to be written, we read only that Jesus "was in the wilderness forty days", during which time he is surrounded by wild beasts and angels of light and "tempted by Satan" (*Mark* 1:13). That this temptation drama might concern Jesus' authority is suggested by the first scenes of his prophetic life in *Mark*.[3] The early theme of his authority crests at the end of *Mark* 2, in Jesus' breath-taking claims that he brings "new wine" to Israel (*Mark* 2:18–22), and that he is "lord of the sabbath day" (*Mark* 2:23–28). Yet ultimately, the Marcan temptation motif culminates in his trial and death.[4] In *Mark*, Jesus' prophetic life begins and ends with a solitary ordeal.

Matthew and *Luke* narrate a sequence of three temptations. The closeness of their narratives might suggest a common origin in a conjectural gospel that scholars call *Q*, from the German *Quelle* ("source").[5] In the first of the sequence, Jesus is tempted to abuse his authority in Nature.[6] "If you are the Son of God", says the devil, "command these stones to become loaves of bread". Jesus refuses, though both gospels tell us that he is famished (*Matthew* 4:2–3; *Luke* 4:2–3).

In the second temptation (third for *Luke*), Jesus is tempted to flaunt his authority in Israel. Here, the devil perches him "on the pinnacle of the Temple", saying: "If you are the Son of God, throw yourself down." Again, Jesus refuses (*Matthew* 4:5–7; *Luke* 4:9–12).

And in his third temptation (second for *Luke*), Jesus is tempted to corrupt his authority in the World. For the devil now sets him on "a very high mountain", laying out before him "all the kingdoms of the World", and saying: "To you I will give their glory and all this authority ... if you will worship me." Jesus refuses (*Matthew* 4:8–10; *Luke* 4:5–8).

Both *Matthew* and *Luke* tell us that "the devil left" him after this third temptation (*Matthew* 4:11; *Luke* 4:13). But in *Luke*, there is a highly suggestive structural note. "The devil", says *Luke*, "departed from him *until an opportune time*". Jesus' third temptation in the desert—whether in *Luke*'s ordering (the Temple), or in *Matthew*'s (the World)—is not his last temptation.[7] It is not clear from later mentions of 'the devil' in *Luke* when, or whether, his temptations of Jesus recommence. This raises an interesting question: Is *Luke*'s note an empty literary gesture? Or does it offer a way of understanding the dramatic structure of *Luke*'s gospel? Or even, of the entire collection of gospels? I believe it may.

This claim is influenced by a twentieth-century Göttingen professor, Joachim Jeremias, who concluded that Jesus' temptation drama forms a unity. His prophetic life can only begin after he resists the temptation to incite a palace-torching, throat-slitting, Jerusalem-liberating rebellion.[8] For Jeremias and other commentators, Jesus' spectral ordeal in the desert is the first moment in the gospels which dramatizes the gospel-writers' conviction that he is "no Zealot".[9] But it is not the last.

On this reading, Jesus' temptation reveals a deep and abiding conflict in his life as it is remembered in the gospels. And I suggest this conflict gives rise to three questions:

(i) Will Jesus compel believers?
(ii) Will he punish lawbreakers?
(iii) Will he resist rulers?

Throughout the gospels Jesus provokes confusion, not only among his critics and judges, but among his disciples. This seems to arise from the fact that he assumes unheard-of authority. And yet he decouples this authority from the power to judge, compel or fight—the power that makes political order possible. The kingdom of God is a manifestation of power (*Mark* 9:1), yet it cannot be realized by the normal mechanisms of human power (legislation, punishment, war).

In other words, Jesus seems to announce the presence of a politically hopeless kingdom whose authority is only felt by, and whose power is only realized in, those who live in hope of a kingdom to come. It seems that Jesus' technical term for this confusion, this outrage, is "scandal" (Greek *skandalon*).[10] And the scandal of Jesus' prophetic life is that he vested himself with authority as the king of a *heavenly* kingdom.

What Jesus meant by this is that he lived in Galilee and Judaea as the prophetic legislator of a divine kingdom, renouncing all coercive power in the present world-age.[11] Jesus seems to have claimed that his total renunciation of coercive power in this world-age secured his authority in the "age to come". This renunciation culminated in his torments on the cross, and is why, as Pascal puts it, Jesus "had to die" (*devait périr*).[12]

A Human Temptation Drama

It is not clear from references to 'Satan' and 'the devil' when Jesus' temptations recommence following his temptation drama in the wilderness. The later scenes of Jesus' temptation can be isolated, however, by tracing references to *temptation*, rather than *the tempter*.

Unless I am mistaken, Jesus' *human* tempters—in all four gospels—seek to lure him, much like 'the devil' in the wilderness, to express his authority in coercive power. Or, recalling our three questions, Jesus' human tempters urge him to *become a judge, a king or a rebel*. From the first days of his prophetic life, in the desert wilds encircling Galilee, to the last days of his natural life, in the gardens and Temple courts—and on the gibbet-hill—of Judaea, the Jesus of the canonical gospels resists this temptation.

The whole of this drama could be called *the political temptations of Christ*. And since it is *Luke* who hints at the later temptations of Jesus, we can begin with a scene in *Luke* 12 which becomes important in late medieval and early modern political philosophy.[13]

"Others, Tempting, Asked Him"

There is much talk of Satan in *Luke* 11, since Jesus' exorcistic authority is attributed by his critics to Satan himself.[14] Jesus brushes off this charge as politically incoherent. "Every kingdom divided against itself becomes a desert", he says.

There is also a mention, in this context, of temptation. While some called Jesus a sorcerer, others, "to tempt him (*pei-*

razontes), kept demanding from him a sign from heaven" (*Luke* 11:16–17). Renderings differ, but it is worth noting that in the Vulgate this last phrase reads, *alii* tentantes *signum de caelo quaerebant ab eo*; which is translated, "others, *tempting*, asked of him a sign from heaven".[15] Only *Luke* narrates this temptation. A sign is demanded—a form of Nature-temptation which could, perhaps, remind us of his temptation in the wilderness, the demand to transmute rocks into bread (*Luke* 4:3–4). As before, so now, he refuses.

The Greek terms for temptation are not reintroduced at the close of *Luke* 11, but the theme is still present. Jesus' critics "began to be very hostile towards him", writes *Luke*, "and to cross-examine him about many things, lying in wait for him, to catch him in something he might say" (*Luke* 11:53–54). Here, *Luke* calls Jesus' interlocutors "lawyers" (Greek *nomikoi*, Latin *legis periti*). On a dryly secular register, "Woe to you lawyers!", may be the least scandalous saying of Jesus (*Luke* 11:46).

It is in this context that *Luke* tells us that "the crowd gathered by the thousands" to hear Jesus' sayings.

Jesus warns his inner circle against one of the Judaean philosophies—the Pharisaic—because Pharisees are "lying in wait" for him at the end of *Luke* 11. He urges believers not to "fear those who kill the body, and after that can do nothing more". This "nothing more" is heard, too, in a question that the philosopher Epictetus poses in his first-century *Discourses*: "What tyrant ... or what courts of law are any longer formidable to those who have ... set at naught the body?"[16] This may be the closest we have to a definition by Jesus, or by first-century philosophers, of what we would now call the *secular*.

Human authority in this world-age (Greek *aiōn*, Latin *saeculum*) is confined to the life of the body. Jesus tells his disciples: "When they bring you before ... the authorities, do not be concerned about how you are to defend yourselves" (*Luke* 12:11–12).

This is because there is a divine authority which is *unconfined* by the body (*Luke* 12:4–5).

"Who Set Me to Be a Judge?"

Chapters 11 and 12 of *Luke* are replete with legal-political themes, dicta and images. It is here we read how:

> Someone in the crowd said to Jesus, "Teacher, tell my brother to divide the inheritance with me".
>
> But Jesus said to him, "Friend, who set me to be a judge or divider over you?"
>
> And he said to them, "Take care! Be on your guard against all kinds of greed; for one's life does not consist in the abundance of possessions." (*Luke* 12:13–14)

Jesus' claim that human "life" (Greek *zōē*) is not a matter of possessions, or a thing that humans ultimately *possess*, is in keeping with his earlier division of authority (*Luke* 12:4–5). There is authority over the body and tangible, heritable, fungible things—the life of the body; and there is authority over human life itself—the soul, which gives life to the body.[17] Jesus seems to be a legislator of the life of the soul, and his sayings in *Luke* 12 seem to call his hearers to a kingdom of the soul and a future body.

But one of the most fateful questions in *Luke* is this: "Who set me to be a *judge or divider* over you?" (*Luke* 12:14). At first glance it seems that Jesus is merely denying that he is a divider. But this is not how *Luke* interprets this question. For later in chapter 12, Jesus disillusions his hearers. "Do you think I have come to bring peace?" he asks. "No, I tell you, but rather division!" (*Luke* 12:51).[18]

The scene in which Jesus is asked to "divide the inheritance" must turn on some secret hinge. "Friend, who set me to be a divider over you?" (*Luke* 12:13–14), he replies. "I have come to bring ... division", he says (*Luke* 12:51); but he has not come to bring *that kind of division*. What is happening, here?[19] And what is the temptation that Jesus is resisting?

"Who Set You to Be a Judge?"

To clarify, we must glance at the second book in the New Testament's diptych narrative, *Luke* and *Acts of the Apostles*.[20] In the scene I have in mind, a Christ-believer named Stephen is on trial for his life in Jerusalem. The trial ends in his death. Stephen is portrayed by the writer of *Luke–Acts* as the first Christ-believer to be martyred. But what matters, here, is this eye-catching passage in Stephen's stylized apology:

> When Moses was forty years old, it came into his heart to visit his relatives, the Israelites ... [One] day he came to some of them as they were quarrelling and tried to reconcile them, saying, "Men, you are brothers: why do you wrong each other?"
>
> But the man who was wronging his neighbour pushed Moses aside, saying, "Who set you to be a ruler and a judge over us?" (*Acts* 7:23–27)

There is a reprise of this scene in Stephen's apology. The insolent question to Israel's prophetic legislator is remembered a second time: "Who set you to be a ruler and a judge over us?" (*Acts* 7:35).[21]

This question in *Acts* 7 is identical to *Exodus* 2 in the hallowed Greek translation of the Hebrew scriptures by "The Seventy", the Septuagint.[22] The writer of *Luke–Acts* conscientiously transcribes, more than once, a sentence from *Exodus*' life of Moses in the Septuagint's Greek.[23] It is certain, then, that he knows that text in which the authority of Moses is questioned—and, by being questioned, is denied.

This is surely the key to our scene in *Luke* 12, where the same question is asked with only the slightest variations. But in *Luke*, the questioner is Jesus. Where it is a critic of Moses who says, "Who set *you*?", it is now Jesus himself who says, "Who set *me*?". Where Moses' critic denies that he is a judge "over *us*", Jesus denies that he is a judge "over *you*".

The dramatic logic of this scene is architectonic, I think, not only in *Luke* but in the canonical gospels. For in *Exodus*, Moses' political authority is repudiated by *a disbeliever's* question. But in *Luke*, Jesus' political authority is repudiated by *his own* question: "Who set me to be a judge or divider over you?" (*Luke* 12:13–14).

So Jesus reveals that though he is, like Moses, a prophetic *liberator* of Israel (*Luke* 4:16–21), he is not a liberator like Moses—or, in later centuries, like Muhammad.[24] And though he is, like Moses, a prophetic *legislator* of Israel (*Luke* 4:31–32), the law of the gospels is not like the law of Moses—or, in later centuries, like that of Muhammad. This is because Moses—or Muhammad—and his law judge the *body* and constitute a body *politic*. Jesus and his law judge only the *soul* in this world-age, and thus constitute a *mystical* body.[25]

"You Stood by Me in My Temptations"

In the same chapter of *Luke* in which Jesus says that we should not "fear those who kill the body", he reveals that he is *not* one of those who "kill the body". He is not a *political* judge or divider. Yet he exhorts the multitude in this cluster of sayings to "fear him who ... has authority to cast into Gehenna", the realm of the miserable dead (*Luke* 12:4–5). And in many other sayings, Jesus envisions himself as a *mystical* judge and a *mystical* divider.[26] His time to perfectly judge will, according to *Luke's* gospel, come.

This is what Jesus says to his cadre of twelve disciples on the last night of his natural life:

> You are those who have stood by me *in my temptations*, and I confer
> on you, just as my Father has conferred on me, a kingdom, so that
> you may eat and drink at my table *in my kingdom*, and you will sit on
> thrones judging the twelve tribes of Israel. (*Luke* 22:28–30)

The formal linkage, here, of Jesus' *temptations* and his *kingdom*—and, thus, of his *disciples'* temptations and *their* kingdom—is not an empty formality. It is, I believe, a concrete link.[27]

In *Luke*, a post-historical kingdom is conferred on Jesus *because* he has renounced—"in an instant"—the corrupt and corrupting authority which darkens "all the kingdoms of the World" (*Luke* 4:5–8). It is *because* Jesus resists this political temptation that he says he will inherit—with his disciples—a post-historical kingdom. It is *because* Jesus mocks the idea that he is "a judge or divider" in this world-age, that he will be Judge and Divider in a world-age to come (*Luke* 12:13–14). This, I think, is the political drama—the drama of *political temptation*—which structures *Luke's* gospel.

Similar reconstructions in *Matthew* and *Mark* could be sketched since the synoptic gospels all mark the beginning of his prophetic life with a baptism and a period in the wilderness. In the gospel of *John*, however, there is no depiction of Jesus' baptism or his temptation by Satan. Is this temptation drama—*the political temptation*—lacking in the fourth gospel?

11

JESUS AMONG THE LAWBREAKERS

One of Jesus' most arresting sayings in *John* is: "I judge no one" (*John* 8:15). Yet he seems to contradict this, saying: "I judge, and my judgement is just" (*John* 5:30). And later in the fourth gospel, he assures his disciples: "I have much to say ... and much to judge" (*John* 8:26). Most ominously, perhaps, he stresses that his life and death symbolize—or actualize—"the judgement of the world" (*John* 12:31).

This dark saying regarding "the judgement of the world" is illuminated by a comment made by *John* or one of his editors. We read that Jesus said this "to indicate the kind of death he was to die" (*John* 12:33). What this means is that, within the fourth gospel, Jesus' death on a Roman gibbet symbolizes—or actualizes—a mystical judgement of what John calls "the World". Jesus is believed to have overcome "the *ruler* of this World" at that time and place—Jerusalem's gibbet-hill—at which his life was snuffed out by rulers of this world, or in less mystical terms, by the rulers of Roman Judaea. And who is the world's occult 'ruler'? In Kant's cold formula: "Self-interest [is] the God of this world."[1] However we may define it, what matters here is just that

Jesus' death constitutes a *judgement* within the literary horizons of the fourth gospel.

How are we to interpret the fact that the one who says in *John* 5, "I judge", then says in *John* 8, "I judge no one"?[2] How could a man who brazenly contradicts himself be, as *John* intones, the divine Word? "In the beginning was the Word"—is *John*'s sublime beginning—"and the Word was with God, and the Word was God" (*John* 1:1). Or as the philosopher Amelius writes in his fragment on *John*, the Word "exists eternally" and through it, all that "is generated was generated".[3] How could this Word nullify itself in a matter of pages?

This is not a new problem for us. Without blurring the Christ-ideas of *John* and *Luke*, we remember from chapter 10 that within the confines of *Luke* 12, Jesus mocks the idea that he is a divider on earth—and then warns that he is on earth to bring division. In the third gospel, there is no contradiction. Jesus is not called to divide politically (or juridically), but mystically. So, too, in the fourth gospel, there is no contradiction. Jesus is not a political judge—and this is what he means when he says: "I judge no one" (*John* 8:15); but he is a mystical judge—and this is the reason why one who never judges gravely warns: "I judge" (*John* 5:30).

This may be why the Incident of the Adulteress, or *Pericope Adulterae*, is in the gospel of *John*.

"A Very Early Tradition"

This pericope (scene or sayings-cluster) in *John* 8 is held to be non-Johannine.[4] It is not present in most Greek manuscripts before the year 900 (with one exception being the fifth-century Codex Bezae), and it is not treated in the Greek commentary tradition before the year 1100 or so. The text-critics' verdict is that it "must be judged to be an intrusion into the fourth gospel" and treated as "a piece of floating tradition".[5] In one cluster of eleven-century manuscripts, for instance, it has 'floated' from the middle of *John* to the end of *Luke*.[6]

Though its origins are irrecoverable, the Incident of the Adulteress stems from "a very early tradition".[7] It circulated in Syrian churches in the second century CE, and it is best attested in the Latin tradition.[8] Jerome translated it into Latin for his so-called Vulgate, and Augustine preached on it in his *Homilies on the Gospel of John*. What matters for us is not that this pericope is from the hand of the writer of *John*, but rather, that it *belongs* in the canonical gospel of *John*. And to my mind, it does.[9]

One reason why the Incident of the Adulteress belongs in *John* is that the fourth gospel takes no notice of Jesus' temptation in the wilderness after he is baptized "beyond the Jordan" (allusively, in *John* 1:28–37). There is no quasi-legal ordeal, as in the synoptics, which shows Jesus resisting the temptation to become a political Christ.[10]

On the contrary, in one of *John*'s opening scenes, one of Jesus' disciples says to him: "You are the King of Israel" (*John* 1:49). This is a regal acclamation. And later in *John*, the gospel-writer depicts a "vast crowd" acclaiming Jesus as "the Lord—the King of Israel" (*John* 12:12–13).[11] In a first-century milieu, scenes like this are politically efficacious. A multitude that acclaims a king *makes* a king.[12] And in *John*'s gospel, there can be no doubt that Jesus is a king.

How can a *king* say, "I judge no one" (*John* 8:15)?

It seems hard to reconcile Jesus' non-judgement with the image of a king in the Hebrew scriptures. "Inspired decisions are on the lips of a king"—according to one saying ascribed to Israel's philosopher-king, Solomon—"his mouth does not sin *in judgement*" (*Proverbs* 16:10). But I believe that the Incident of the Adulteress is *John*'s temptation drama—and that, in its unfolding of Jesus' *non-judgement*, we hear his "inspired decision", and we see that "his mouth does not sin in judgement".

I JUDGE NO ONE

"What Do You Say?"

In *John* 8, a woman's life is placed in Jesus' hands—and there is hard evidence, here, of the motif of temptation. For this pericope contains one of only two occurrences, in *John*, of the Greek verb for 'tempt' (*peirazō*).[13] The dramatic structure of this temptation drama—the scenic and symbolic control—is consummate:

> Early in the morning Jesus came again to the Temple. All the people came to him, and he sat down and began to teach them.
>
> The scribes and the Pharisees brought a woman who had been caught in adultery. Making her stand before all of them, they said to him, "Teacher, this woman was caught in the very act of committing adultery. Now in the law Moses commanded us to stone such women. Now what do you say?"
>
> They said this *to tempt him* (Greek *peirazontes auton*; Latin *temptantes eum*), so that they might have some legal charge to bring against him.
>
> Jesus bent down and wrote with his finger on the ground.
>
> When they kept on questioning him, he straightened up and said to them, "Let anyone among you who is without sin be the first to cast a stone at her."
>
> And once again he bent down and wrote on the ground.
>
> When they heard it, they went away, one by one, beginning with the elders; and Jesus was left alone with the woman standing before him.
>
> Jesus straightened up and said to her, "Woman, where are they? Has no one condemned you?"
>
> She said, "No one, lord."
>
> "Neither do I condemn you. Go your way, and from now on do not sin again." (*John* 8:2–11)

The first thing to note is that this temptation is framed by Judaean law—not Roman law. The legal charge that Jesus is in peril of is a Judaean one—namely, that of subverting the divine law-code of "the truly sacred Moses", as a second-century Egyptian Christian philosopher calls him.[14] The question put to Jesus—Now what do you say?—is a lure for him to cancel a Mosaic statute.

But there is also a temptation for Jesus to implicate himself in the machinery of Judaean law and politics. In effect, Jesus cannot release a woman caught in the act (*in flagrante delicto*) without committing blasphemy, and he cannot condemn her without becoming a punisher of the body—and a political Christ.

Hostile observation of Jesus by the "the scribes and the Pharisees" is noted in much the same language in the synoptic gospels.[15] In *Mark*, for instance, certain Pharisees 'tempt' Jesus by asking him: "Is it legal for a man to divorce his wife?" (*Mark* 10:2). There are numerous "legal episodes" of this sort in the gospels.[16] And read with sufficient care, most of Jesus' healing narratives have a legal aspect—they occur on the sabbath day, they render a person ceremonially pure, and so on.[17] Nevertheless, the Incident of the Adulteress is one of only two scenes in the gospels in which Jesus is formally requested to *render a judgement*. The other is in *Luke* 12 (the topic of chapter 10).

Yet the unique scene in *John* 8 should not be read in isolation. Wherever it may have originated, its original *location* in the gospel collection is in chapter 8 of *John*. And this means that Jesus' non-judgement of a condemned woman can be read in light of a later scene of judgement in *John*'s gospel. Namely that in *John* 19, where the prefect of Judea takes a seat with ritual intent on his "judge's chair", and then sentences Jesus to be crucified (*John* 19:13, 16).[18] The penultimate scene of Jesus' natural life, in the fourth gospel, is a legal ordeal in which an innocent man is condemned to death by a *guilty judge*. In dramatic terms, *John* 8 is the inverse. Here, a guilty woman is *not* condemned by a uniquely *innocent judge*.[19]

There is no hint in the received text that the woman set before Jesus is falsely accused. The charge brought is that she has been trapped "in the very act" (*John* 8:4)—or, in one commentator's gloss, *in coitu*.[20] The text introduces this charge without comment (*John* 8:3). Further, there is no sign that Jesus doubts her guilt. On the contrary, he says to her, in parting: "Do not sin again" (*John* 8:11). This implies her guilt.

It is striking, further, that there is no sign that Jesus doubts his *right* to judge. He is seated on a 'judge's chair' when the pericope opens, and he seems to remain seated throughout the ordeal, even when he bends to write—more than once, and with his finger—in the dirt.[21]

"He Bent Down and Wrote"

Before we ask what Jesus wrote in the dirt, we should pause to note a couple of curious parallels which are rarely noted.[22] For the fact *that* Jesus writes is immensely suggestive.

(i) Like Socrates, Jesus is not a writer. In both cases, however, there is one exception to the rule. Socrates traces geometric figures in the dirt, in Plato's dialogue *Meno*, on behalf of a slave-boy who (per Socrates) has an immortal soul.[23] And Jesus writes in the dust, in *John*, during the ordeal of a woman he refuses to condemn.[24]

(ii) Like Pilate, Jesus writes during a trial. The only place in the gospels where Jesus writes is in *John* 8, and the trial of Jesus in *John* 19 is the only place in the gospels where Pilate writes. "What I have written", says the guilty judge, "I have written" (*John* 19:19–22). But what the innocent judge may have written, we are not told.

We can nevertheless ask: What did Jesus write in the dirt during the adulteress' ordeal?

"Nothing certain can be stated", according to Cornelius à Lapide's baroque *Great Commentary*.[25] This is true. Yet J. D. M. Derrett reminds us that "writing *with the finger* was symbolic of divine 'legislation'" in Hebrew culture.[26] Patristic commentators had already made this connection. And Derrett reconstructs the dramatic logic of Jesus' leaning down to write, not once but twice, with his finger, in this way:

> The effect of his writing, and pausing after writing, was to produce from those in a position to watch him an insistence upon his *giving his sentence* ... What he wrote was not unintelligible, but it did not satisfy them. This need not mean that it was irrelevant ... It made them more anxious than ever to hear *what he would say*.[27]

"Has No One Condemned You?"

And what did Jesus say? Of course, this is the question that marks the centre of the pericope. "The law Moses commanded us to stone such women", say the hardliners. "*Now what do you say?*" (*John* 8:5). After he writes in the dirt—and before he *resumes* writing in the dirt—Jesus lifts his head to say to them: "Let anyone among you who is without sin be the first to cast a stone at her" (*John* 8:7). This is Jesus' sentence—and it is, in George Steiner's phrase, a "radiant challenge".[28]

Is it a *judicial* sentence that Jesus utters? In a novel sense, yes. For the lawbreaker figures in Jesus' sentence. Yet the sentence which he pronounces is only *obliquely* concerned with the one who is to be punished for her crime. The subject of Jesus' sentence is not the lawbreaker, but rather her would-be punishers. Her executioners, says Jesus, must be wholly innocent before the punishment sanctioned by Moses can be meted out—beginning with the first, who 'legitimates' the cascading violence of a stoning. The pitiless enforcers of Mosaic law must be flawless observers of that law—and this, Jesus claims, no one is.

"Did not Moses give you a law?" Jesus seems to taunt the scribes and lawyers in *John* before he asserts: "Yet *none of you keeps the law*" (*John* 7:19). The line is uniquely Johannine, but this seems to be a primitive Christian claim.

(i) In *Acts* 7, Stephen says to his Judaean judges: "You are the ones that received the law ... yet *you have not kept it*" (*Acts* 7:52–53).

(ii) "In passing judgement on another you condemn yourself", Paul writes, "because you, the judge, are doing the very same things" (*Romans* 2:1).[29]

Returning with this in mind to the scene in *John*, we notice that it is the same Greek word—*oudeis*—that figures in *John* 7 and 8, where Jesus says first, "*None* of you keeps the law" (*John* 7:19), and then, "Has *no one* condemned you?" (*John* 8:10). It is his prophetic utterance in *John* 7 which foreshadows his juridical utterance in *John* 8. And it is *because* no Judaean—and, *a fortiori*, no human—keeps the divine law that, when Jesus says, "Let anyone who is without sin be the first to cast a stone", he can be certain that he will then be able ask the adulteress: "Has no one condemned you?"

Since no one observes the divine law, and flawless observance of the law is Jesus'—novel—condition for the enforcement of that law in this world-age, the effect is clear. *No one can enforce the Mosaic law.* Derrett concludes that "no one *wanted her* to be stoned under the conditions pointed out by Jesus".[30] But this sort of psychological formulation, it seems to me, blunts the force of Jesus' judgement. The legal effect of Jesus' utterance is far more radical. In theological terms, no one *could permit her to be stoned* under the conditions that Jesus' sentence lays down.

Arthur Schopenhauer's comment on "the striking indulgence that the Saviour in the Gospels shows to the adulteress" is astute. According to Schopenhauer, Jesus "presupposes the *same guilt* in everyone present".[31] How could that be? Well, the saying is uniquely Matthaean—but it *is* Jesus who says that "whoever looks at a woman with lustful desire has already committed adultery with her in his heart" (*Matthew* 5:28).[32] There is a meaningful sense—one that both first-century rabbis and philosophers would recognize—in which Jesus sees the *same guilt* in this woman and her would-be punishers.[33]

The Incident of the Adulteress evokes questions of immense subtlety and obscurity. The brutal penalty of stoning is not remotely unique to Mosaic law. As we read in one early modern humanistic commentary, lapidation was a common penalty for infidelity in antiquity.[34] Tragically, it is not unheard-of today.[35] But if the archaic penalty is formally upheld by Jesus, in the juridical phase of the pericope—*its enforcement is universally, and permanently, suspended by him*—because:

(i) Jesus asserts it as an *a priori* certainty that the enforcers of divine law cannot be wholly innocent (in *John* 7), before

(ii) Jesus promulgates a juridical principle according to which the enforcers of divine law must be wholly innocent (in *John* 8).

"Neither Do I"

The pericope, however, does not end in its juridical phase—the phase in which the lawbreaker is encircled by her accusers and facing Jesus. Nor does the pericope end with Jesus' question to the lawbreaker—"Woman, where are they?"—after her *soi-disant* judges and executioners have recused themselves, "one by one", withdrawing from the circle or half-circle of men who constituted a sort of lynch-court in the vicinity of the Temple (*John* 8:10).

On my reading, the juridical phase of the scene ends when the lawbreaker replies to Jesus' question—"Woman, where are they?" In reply, she utters the very word, "no one" (Greek *oudeis*, Latin *nemo*), that has saved her life.

I am thinking, of course, of Jesus' dictum: "*No one ...* keeps the law" (*John* 7:19). For when Jesus sharpens his question to her, saying: "Has *no one* condemned you?" She is content to echo him, with heart-breaking simplicity: "No one, lord" (*John* 8:10–11).

In the juridical phase of the pericope, Jesus promulgates a new juridical principle—namely, that in a divine-law regime, *the guilty cannot punish the guilty*. The woman before Jesus is guilty—and her would-be punishers, who have withdrawn from her, are guilty. Therefore, although she must be punished (Moses' statute)—*she must not be punished* (Jesus' sentence).

The juridical drama of this pericope is centred on Jesus' novel judicial sentence. But the scene's dramatic logic transcends its juridical moment. For once the quorum of Mosaic accusers has dissolved, two figures remain within the forensic circle—the law-breaker, and her judge. (See fig. 11.) Or, as Augustine beautifully put it, *misera* and *misericordia*—"misery" and "compassion".[36]

Jesus' tempters—her accusers—have withdrawn. They have recused themselves, but *Jesus has not recused himself*. There is no indication here, or in the other gospels, that Jesus sees *himself* as unworthy to judge. On the contrary, it is *as* one who is competent to judge—to punish, and to release—that Jesus says to her: "Neither do I condemn you. Go your way, and from now on *do not sin again*" (*John* 8:11).

"I Judge No One"

The greatest revelation in this pericope is not that Jesus saves the adulteress' life and bans the stoning of women in the name of divine law. The greatest revelation occurs once the adulteress, who stays with Jesus in the forensic circle, has stated *not* her innocence but the absence of her judges.

Having judged the lawbreaker's judges without punishing their bodies or denying her crime, Jesus now declines to punish her body. "Neither do I condemn you", he says, "Go your way".

JESUS AMONG THE LAWBREAKERS

In *John*, as in the synoptic gospels, Jesus resists the temptation to become a political Christ. Or, rather, the politics of Christ involve a *re-conception of the political* which is shown by Jesus' *refusal to punish a lawbreaker*.

In this scene, Jesus asserts a mystical right to judge—and renounces a political will to judge. In other words, Jesus reveals what he means when he says, "I judge" (as in *John* 5:30), and when he says, "I judge no one" (as in *John* 8:15). For he not only judges the lawbreaker in this pericope, but *her judges*—and yet *no one is punished by Jesus*. Her accusers are 'convicted' in a mystical sense, but not a political one. Hearing his sentence, they remove themselves from the forensic circle.[37]

In the synoptic gospels, however, Jesus' re-conception of the political is most clearly seen in his refusal to resist the Roman emperors—*and* his refusal to imitate them. Which brings us to his refusal, not only to be a judge and a punisher, but a rebel in the banal sense of the word.

12

JESUS AMONG THE RULERS

It is in a glaringly political temptation scene that one of Jesus' best-remembered sayings is uttered: "Hand back to Caesar the things that are Caesar's, and to God the things that are God's."[1] Twenty-one centuries on, the line feels clichéd. But the reaction of Jesus' first hearers to this saying, in all the synoptic gospels, is the same. In *Mark*, we read that "they marvelled at him". In *Matthew*, "when they heard this, they marvelled". And in *Luke*, "marvelling at his answer they became silent".[2]

It is not uncommon for *Matthew* and *Luke* to refashion the material they take from *Mark*. Here, however, both retain the Greek root-word that *Mark* attaches to this saying—*thaumazein*, "to marvel, to be amazed". It is necessary for us to ask, then: What is so marvellous, in the gospels' original milieus, about Jesus' saying?

"Why Are You Tempting Me?"

First, we read the pericope—here, in *Mark*'s incredibly controlled telling:

I JUDGE NO ONE

> The chief priests, the scribes, and the elders [of Judaea] ... sent to Jesus some Pharisees, and some of Herod's partisans (*tōn Hērōdianōn*), to trap him in what he said.
>
> And they came and said to him, "Teacher, we know that you are honest, and show deference to no one ... Is it legal to pay census-taxes (*kēnson*) to Caesar, or not? Should we pay them, or should we not?"
>
> But knowing their hypocrisy, he said to them, "Why are you tempting me (Greek *me peirazete*, Latin *me temptantis*)? Bring me a denarius and let me see it." And they brought one.
>
> Then he said to them, "Whose image is this, and whose inscription?" They replied, "Caesar's".
>
> Jesus said to them, "Hand back to Caesar the things that are Caesar's, and to God the things that are God's."
>
> And they marvelled at him. (*Mark* 11:27, 12:13–17)[3]

The political forces which collude in Jesus' death are all present, or half-present, in this scene. We note the presence of Herod—or his partisans—in the Marcan text (*Mark* 12:13). The Herodian dynasty's men are also noted in the Matthaean version of this scene (*Matthew* 22:16). The significance is that, while Jesus' trial before Herod is uniquely Lucan, both *Mark* and *Matthew* implicate the Galilean tetrarch in the conspiracy to kill Jesus.

There is no mention of Herodians in *Luke*'s version of this scene, but *Luke* tells us that Jesus' tempters are conspiring "to deliver him up to the authority and power of the governor" (*Luke* 20:20). He means Pilate, of course, and this gloss heightens Pilate's guilt in *Luke–Acts*. This foreshadowing in *Luke* 20 makes it impossible to doubt that Jesus is crucified by the authority and power of Rome.

To tabulate our early findings, then—for *Mark* and *Matthew*, this temptation scene implicates Herod and his functionaries; for *Luke*, it implicates Pilate and his imperial power. But the

Pharisees and Judaea's Temple aristocracy are implicated in all the synoptic versions.[4] For, it is the Sadducees—Judaea's ruling caste—who deploy the Pharisees and Herodians in hopes of incriminating the Galilean rabbi (*Mark* 11:27, 12:13).

"Is it Legal to Pay Census-Taxes?"

In the temptation scene of *John* 8, Jesus is in peril from Judaean law. There, he renders the 'Mosaic' legal regime inoperative without debasing its divine origins. In this synoptic temptation scene, Jesus is only obliquely at risk from the 'Mosaic' legal culture. Judaean hardliners condemned the Roman tax on political-theological grounds.

Zealots deemed it criminal—in terms of divine law—for Judaeans to comply with the Roman levy. In fact, Josephus tells us that one of the heads of the Zealot insurgency, Judas the Galilean, castigated those who were willing "to put up with paying taxes to Romans". He reasoned that, by paying the census-tax, they had "tolerate[d] mortal masters, after God".[5] A later Zealot states that the God of Israel is the only "true and just lord of humankind". This is the defining Zealot doctrine.[6]

The hardliners in Jesus' milieu hold that "only God is their lord". Zealots are known for a willingness to die, *and kill*, rather than "confess that Caesar is lord".[7] It is in the willingness to kill that they differ from early Christ-believers, who were also willing to die rather than utter the Roman formula, *Kurios Kaisar*.[8] To pay the Roman census-tax is, on the Zealots' logic, to make that confession. To deal in Roman coin is thus to deny "the solitary rule of God".[9]

Another 'Mosaic' aspect of the scene is that a denarius would have borne the 'idolatrous' image of a Roman emperor.[10] Because of this, one relevant contrast to Jesus' inspection of a denarius comes from the Jerusalem Talmud, where we read that one of the revered jurists of Israel is called "Most Holy" because he "never gazed upon the face of a coin in his entire life".[11] Zealots, too, are said to have shunned image-bearing currencies, holding that "one must not carry or see ... an image".[12] But Jesus not only tells his tempters to bring him a Roman coin; he then says, "Let me see it" (*Mark* 12:15). It is clear from this that Jesus is not concerned to be seen as 'Most Holy' by the hardliners in Jerusalem.[13]

Nevertheless, the primary threat to Jesus in this pericope comes from Roman law and its enforcers. This is perhaps hinted at by a marked concentration of Latin terms in this pericope. *Matthew*'s description of the conspiracy behind this scene, where we read in Greek that Pharisees "took counsel" (*symboulion elabon*), suggests a borrowing from Latin (*consilium capere*).[14] Then, the Greek term for "census-tax" (*kēnsos*) is a mere transcription of the Latin (*census*). Finally, the presence of the name 'Caesar' (*Kaisar*) marks an intrusion, in the synoptic tradition, of the cultic nomenclature of Rome (*Caesar Augustus*).[15]

The significance of this is clearest in *Luke*. For the next (and last) time that Caesar is mentioned in *Luke* is during Jesus' Roman trial, when he is denounced for "forbidding us to pay taxes to Caesar", and for "saying that he himself is Christ, *a king*". It is on hearing this that Pilate turns to Jesus and puts the question to him: "Are you the King of the Judaeans?" To which Jesus replies: "You say so" (*Luke* 23:2–3). The reason for this reply lies in the pericope of the census-tax.

"The Mystery of the Kingdom"

There is a link between paying taxes to Caesar and Jesus' claim to kingship, as suggested later by *Luke*'s formulation of the charges against him (*Luke* 23:2). A Zealot-style king will necessarily forbid Judaeans to "pay taxes to Romans".[16] Jesus is hailed as a king in the gospels, and he is crucified by Pilate as a Zealot-style king. But what the pericope of the census-tax reveals is that, bizarrely, Jesus is a Galilean king *who permits Judaeans to pay the Caesar's census-tax.*

Once this pericope is reckoned with, it becomes unnecessary to posit a pro-Roman, or anti-Judaean, tendency in the synoptic Passion narratives. Pilate is unconvinced by the charges against Jesus because he refuses to utter the Zealot creed regarding "the solitary rule of God".[17] And Pilate is *confused* because Jesus *also* refuses to deny that he is a king.

But where is his kingdom? In a scene that comes after his temptations in the desert, in both *Matthew* and *Mark*, he begins to preach that "the kingdom of God has come near".[18] This is the first word of his prophetic life. The kingdom of God is not only *near*, however—it is also *obscure*. This is suggested by a scene in which Jesus tells his disciples, in all the synoptic gospels, that he will reveal to them—and *only* to them—what he calls "the mystery (*to mystērion*) of the kingdom of God".[19]

This mystery is illuminated by a contrast Jesus makes between the divine kingdom (Greek *basileia*) and all human kingdoms. Such kingdoms are controlled by the anxieties of this world-age (Greek *aiōn*, Latin *saeculum*), the lure of wealth and "the desire for other things" (*Mark* 4:11, 19). The divine kingdom is mysterious because it, like the natural world, generates new life "of itself" (Greek *automatos*). Jesus says that those who live for this kingdom *do not know how* it generates new life. In one rendering of that last, critical phrase—he says that they are "all unknowing" how the kingdom survives and advances (*Mark* 4:26–28).[20]

This is not the place to delve further into the question of what this 'mystery' represents in the gospels—much less in the New Testament, where we read of the "mysteries of God", the "mystery of faith", the "economy of the mystery", and so on.[21] In the pericope of the census-tax, Jesus tells his tempters to "hand back ... to God the things that are God's" (*Mark* 12:17), and in this context we can infer that 'the kingdom of God' is a mystical order in which the things that are God's are given to him.

But what belongs to God? The Zealots' reply would be that there is nothing that does not belong to God. Jesus' hearers marvel at him precisely because this is not what he says. Rather, he clearly asserts that there are things which belong to Caesar. And the reason we can be sure of this reading is that this is not the only pericope in which Jesus asserts that *there are things which are not God's*.

One such scene is crucial for us, because it is formally linked to Jesus' satanic temptations. In both *Mark* and *Matthew*, there is a moment in which Jesus says to Peter, one of his cohort of Twelve:

(i) "Get behind me, Satan!" (*Mark* 8:33; *Matthew* 16:23)

This is an echo of what Jesus says to Satan himself in *Matthew* (but not in *Mark*):

(ii) "Away with you, Satan!" (*Matthew* 4:10)

The temptation which ends this way is the temptation to "world domination".[22] But what ties *that* to Jesus' rebuke of Peter? And what ties *both* to the census-tax?

"The Things of Humankind"

When Jesus calls Peter 'Satan', it is because a disciple has just rebuked his rabbi for saying that he will suffer death in Jerusalem. For Peter, this is unthinkable, and Jesus reveals *why*. "You are not setting your mind on the things of God (*ta tou theou*)", he tells him, "but on the things of humankind (*ta tōn anthrōpōn*)".[23]

In the gospels, the things of God—and "the mystery of the kingdom of God"—contain the suffering and death of Jesus.[24] The things of humankind, Jesus concedes, deny the possibility of that suffering and death.

What is of immense interest is that the formulation and structure of Jesus' reply to Peter matches his reply to his tempters regarding the census-tax. "Hand back to Caesar", he says there, "the things that are Caesar's (*ta Kaisaros*), and to God the things that are God's (*ta tou theou*)".[25]

Jesus' hearers marvel because he is intimating, here, a division that is twenty-one centuries in the making, for us, but that even his disciples had not begun to fathom. The revelation is that, with Jesus, "the things that are God's" begin to receive and observe different laws.[26]

"God and Currency"

Jesus' rebuke to Peter is common to *Mark* and *Matthew* but lacking in *Luke*. There is another relevant Jesus tradition which is common to *Matthew* and *Luke* but lacking in *Mark*. Here, in different contexts but identical words, Jesus says: "You cannot serve God and Currency"—or, perhaps, "God and Property", or "God and Possessions".[27] In the original, the lordship of God is contrasted with a lordship of Mammon (Greek *mamōnas*), an echo of Jesus' Aramaic which resists translation.

Mammon certainly denotes a dark and complex sphere of acquisition, consumption and exchange. In its Lucan context, this saying is connected to money and the "love of money" (*Luke* 16:14). And it is worth noting, in passing:

(i) that Josephus praises first-century Essenes for being "despisers of wealth" and practitioners of a Platonic-style communism;[28] and

(ii) that Seneca instructs one of his first-century contemporaries that money cannot bring us near to God, because "God has no money".[29]

In a first-century setting, Jesus' extreme resistance to money-culture is both 'prophetic' and 'philosophical'.[30] And so it remains in later centuries. For instance, a fiercely anti-Christian third-century philosopher, Porphyry, states that "a lover of wealth must be unrighteous, and an unrighteous person is impious towards God ... [and] all humans".[31]

More interesting for us is the bare fact that Jesus contrasts the whole domain of Currency, Property and Possession with the lordship of God. Though the saying, "You cannot serve God and Currency", is not present in *Mark*, it would not be out of place in that gospel.[32] For, in all the synoptics, it is legal to pay the census-tax because 'Caesar' and 'Mammon'—the logic of exchange and the jurisdiction of money—are not claimed for God.

There is another irony in this scene, since the denarius that Jesus inspected bore the mark of a quasi-divine monarch—"Tiberius, son of a god (*divi filius*)". Unlike the Zealots, Jesus seems not to have seen the deity-invoking inscription or Tiberius' image as a threat. For Jesus, these are not a *cause* of idolatry, but a warning. Whatever image or lack of image, inscription or lack of inscription, that the means of exchange may bear—for Jesus, they are instruments of Mammon.

In all the synoptics, the means of exchange seek to subjugate *that which cannot be exchanged* to a logic of exchange. And what is 'that which cannot be exchanged'? This is, for Jesus, virtually the definition of a human soul or life. "For what will it profit a human", he asks in all the synoptics, "to gain the whole world and forfeit their soul?"[33] And in *Mark* and *Matthew*, he clarifies: "Indeed, what can a human *give in exchange* for their soul?"[34] The answer is, of course, nothing. In the gospels a human's life, or soul, is the unexchangeable.

"Give the Coin to Caesar"

What is intimated in all the contrastive sayings that we have glanced at in this chapter, centring on the pericope of the census-tax, is that Jesus boldly differentiates between a realm of exchange and *a realm of the unexchangeable*. The former belongs to humankind—or Commerce, or Caesar—and the latter belongs to God.

The first surviving commentary on *Mark*, apparently a seventh-century composition, offers a brilliant gloss. This nameless commentator, for centuries thought to be Jerome, says that Jesus replied to his tempters, "who were holding the image of Caesar, 'Give the coin to Caesar, as you are *forced to* (Latin *coactum*), but give yourselves *freely* (*libenter*) to God'".[35]

Jesus imposes no necessity on his Judaean hearers to resist Caesar. Unlike the Zealots, he gives them freedom to act as they are 'forced to' within the realm of exchange. Zealots, on the contrary, brutalized Judaeans who complied with the Roman tax-laws.[36] Yet Jesus urges his hearers to use this freedom *within* the realm of exchange, to cultivate a freedom *from* it. This is the kingdom of God, a realm in which humans hand back to God what only God can give—the human soul. And this handing back to God cannot be forced; it can only be done freely, out of love.

The freedom not to *resist* Caesar, in the synoptic gospels, generates a freedom not to *imitate* him. And this is not only suggested by the pericope of the census-tax. There is a crucial scene in *Matthew*, *Mark* and *Luke* which will return us to the confusion of Jesus' judges and bring Part Four to its conclusion.

"The Kings of the Gentiles"

Towards the end of his life—or, in *Luke*, on the night before his death—Jesus is asked to settle a post-historical suit. Two of his disciples—or, in *Matthew*, the disciples' mother—want him to elevate them to the highest places in his future kingdom. As with the two brothers in *Luke* 12, Jesus refuses to settle this question of inheritance.[37]

What matters here is not Jesus' refusal, but the saying that comes after it. This is *Mark*:

> You know that among the gentiles those whom they recognize as their rulers lord it over them, and their great ones (*hoi megaloi*) are tyrants over them. But it is not so among you. (*Mark* 10:42–43)

And this is *Luke*:

> The kings of the gentiles (*hoi basileis tōn ethnōn*) lord it over them, and those in authority over them are called benefactors. But not so with you. Rather, the greatest among you must become like the youngest, and the leader like one who serves. (*Luke* 22:25–26)

This saying seems to perfect Jesus' striking, and epoch-making, contrast of 'kingdoms'. In the first days after his baptism, he resists the temptation to rule like a warlord. Throughout his prophetic life, he refuses to act as a judge, a punisher or a rebel. And on the last night of his natural life, according to *Luke*, he contrasts the kingdom of God and the kingdoms of humankind.

Many in first-century Galilee and Judaea feared monetary- and levy-contamination by 'the gentiles' (*ta ethnē*), but Jesus warns that the source of contamination is deeper, and older, than money. It is the archaic temptation to "lord it over" others (*Mark* 10:42; *Matthew* 20:25). The way to resist this temptation, he says, is not to kill Romans and 'contaminated' Judaeans, but to "become as the youngest" (*Luke* 18:26).

PART FIVE

THE POLITICS OF JESUS

13

REALPOLITIK AND THE
TRANSCENDENT KINGDOM

In contemporary terms, Jesus seems to be a realist. There is only one sort of politics represented in any of his sayings—and that is, I think, *Realpolitik*.

We will recall his hard-headed remarks on the "great ones" (*hoi megaloi*), the so-called "benefactors" of the first-century ecumene.[1] With astonishing brevity, he reveals the vast and complex institution of benefaction to be a corrupt power-game.[2] And in *John*, Jesus seems to abolish this game on the night before his death, saying to the Twelve, "I do not call you servants (*doulous*) any longer ... but I have called you friends (*philous*)" (*John* 15:15). What we call the church seems to begin, in *John*, as a circle of those who are formally recognized as Jesus' friends.[3]

Throughout the gospels, Jesus' sayings seem to reflect a near-total sense of disillusionment with the machinery of human government—which he reveals to be, *inter alia*, a machinery of judgement. We can see this by glancing at how he speaks of officeholders in the synoptic gospels.

I JUDGE NO ONE

Jesus the Realist

Jesus' God–Caesar contrast seems to me to be replicated in a series of rhetorical questions about John the Baptist. In *Matthew*, the context is John's arrest by Herod Antipas. "What did you go out into the wilderness to look at?" Jesus asks his hearers. "Someone dressed in soft robes? Look, those who wear soft robes are in the houses of kings. A prophet?"[4]

The last question's implied answer is clear. There are no prophets in the houses of kings—or, said differently, the houses of kings are where there are no prophets. What is more, wherever there *are* prophets—Jesus continues—they have "suffered violence".[5]

It is clear in the synoptics that Jesus has a special contempt for Herod—in part, because of his hand in John's death. Nevertheless, his questions seem to imply a broader judgement. All that prophets can expect from those who live in 'the houses of kings' is to 'suffer violence'. There is something terribly sad about Jesus' description of John's death in *Mark*. "They did to him", he says, "whatever they pleased" (*Mark* 9:13). This is one of Jesus' recurring themes, and it foreshadows his own trial and death. He firmly believes that the Son of Man must, like the Baptist, "suffer many things and be treated with contempt" (*Mark* 9:12; *Matthew* 17:12).

Yet the captivity and murder of John is not the only *Realpolitik* drama on which Jesus comments. Indeed, there seems to be a density of political 'reality' in his self-chosen and self-mastered narrative form—the "parable", or "dark saying" (Greek *parabolē*).[6] The form is "perfectly bounded yet limitless"; and this is the form which "initiate[s] the disciple", as Steiner sees, "in the method of Jesus".[7]

Much more could be said about the "enigmatics" of the parables. But it is certainly not meaningless that there is a 'facticity' of political and criminal life behind many of them.[8] They seek to initiate hearers and readers into higher realities by means of brief fictions, or true-crime allegories of fraud (*Luke* 16:1–9), extortion (*Matthew* 18:28–30), theft (*Mark* 3:27), brutality (*Luke* 10:30), cruelty (*Luke* 20:12), castration (*Matthew* 19:12), torture (*Matthew* 18:34), murder (*Matthew* 22:5–6), incarceration (*Luke* 12:58) and crucifixion (*Mark* 8:34). Human life is like a questionable labour contract (*Matthew* 20:1–15) or a wasted inheritance (*Luke* 15:12–13). The end of history is like a nocturnal break-in (*Luke* 12:39) or a proto-capitalist financial reckoning (*Matthew* 25:14–30).

There is no hint of what we could call political romanticism.[9] Jesus refers to a king going to battle, for instance, in *Luke* 14. Any such king, he says, will consider "whether he is able with ten thousand to oppose the one who comes against him with twenty thousand". If not, he reasons, "he sends a delegation and asks for the terms of peace" (*Luke* 14:31–32). This is political calculation at its purest.

Again, in *Luke* 18, Jesus refers us to a judge "in a certain city". This is, I think, the only parable in which a judge is the protagonist; and the judicial forms conjured up suggest that Jesus has in mind a Judaean, Samaritan or Idumaean judge—not a Roman. Twice in this brief narrative, Jesus tells us that this judge has "no fear of God or respect for humans". When the man finally consents to hear a poor woman's complaint, it is *only* "so that", he says to himself, "she may not wear me out" (*Luke* 18:2–5). This is judicial, and proto-bureaucratic, reason at its lowest.

Jesus' hard-headed king and low-minded judge only appear in *Luke*. The political realism they imply could perhaps be dismissed, except that it corresponds to the political consciousness we glimpse elsewhere, in a non-parabolic saying. This is Jesus:

When you go with your accuser before a magistrate, on the way make an effort to settle the case—or you may be dragged before the judge, and the judge hand you over to the officer, and the officer throw you in prison. I tell you, you will never get out until you have paid the very last cent. (*Luke* 12:56–59; compare *Matthew* 5:25–26)

Jesus' reasoning, here, hardly differs from that of the Hellenistic king he conjures in *Luke* 14. The law-courts are menacing, labyrinthine and merciless. So he urges his hearers to "interpret the present time" and "judge for yourselves (*aph' heautōn*) what is right".

"That Kingdom Cannot Stand"

Is there any sign in *Mark* of Jesus' political realism? There is. For, in *Mark* 3—with parallels in *Matthew* and *Luke*—Jesus formulates what may be the most basic principle of all *Realpolitik*.

  (i) "If a kingdom is divided against itself, that kingdom cannot stand." (*Mark* 3:24)
 (ii) "Every kingdom divided against itself is laid waste." (*Matthew* 12:25)
(iii) "Every kingdom divided against itself becomes a desert." (*Luke* 11:17)

Ironically, it is this intuition which informs Jean-Jacques Rousseau's repudiation of the Christian political legacy in his pre-revolutionary treatise, *On the Social Contract*. According to Rousseau, it is Christianity that 'divides kingdoms' by splitting the archaic temple-state.[10]

Much hinges on this. For Jesus agrees with Rousseau that *any* kingdom which is split will be "laid waste" (though the Genevan philosopher, of course, owes his insight to the Galilean prophet). This is the first word of Jesus' politics—and much later, of Rousseau's. And this word is linked, in *Mark*, to Jesus' unflinching formulation of what we might now call power politics.

For having duplicated his 'kingdom'-saying in a 'house'-saying (in *Mark* 3:25), Jesus then says of this 'house' (in *Mark* 3:27):

"No one can enter a strong man's house and plunder his property without first tying up the strong man; then indeed the house can be plundered." The reason this house can be plundered is the same reason a divided kingdom "cannot stand" (*Mark* 3:24). Its power has been neutralized, like a "strong man" who has been bound (*Mark* 3:27). Politics is brutal, says *Mark*'s Jesus, and political reason is a matter of calculation.

This, I believe, is the politics of Jesus. He concedes this basic logic to those who dress in "soft robes" and live "in the houses of kings".[11] As we have seen, this means that he concedes this logic to Hellenistic kings, to Graeco-Roman 'benefactors' and to Judaean judges. *There is no hope for a divided kingdom.* But the question in the gospels, it seems to me, is this. Given the—perhaps depressing—realism of Jesus' politics: *How many kingdoms are there?*

Perhaps this question is imprecise. For not only two, but three 'kingdoms' seem to have a hand in Jesus' death—the Judaean province, the Galilean tetrarchy and the Roman imperium. The question that Jesus introduces is, rather: *How many types of kingdoms are there?* Judaea, Galilee and Rome—and the Zealots— seem to agree that there is only *one* type of kingdom, the archaic temple-state.

Jesus seems to suggest that there are *two* types of kingdoms. One in which 'benefaction' is a screen for domination, and reason is a calculation of force. But there is another type of kingdom—Jesus calls it the "kingdom of God", or in *Matthew*, the "kingdom of heaven". Here, the logic of the political is virtually inverted and ultimately transcended. The law of retaliation is abandoned. Debts are forgiven.[12] Enemies are loved, and so on. The question that Jesus poses in the gospels, and the question his judges weigh, is whether his *transcendent kingdom* is a threat.

They ultimately decide that it is, and Jesus is put to death. The "tragic realism" of the gospels—Erich Auerbach's phrase—is caused by that death.[13]

But Jesus has a politics, and it seems to be as hard-headed as they come. "Beware of men", he warns his cohort; and he urges them to "be intelligent" (*Matthew* 10:16–17). If he had been a Zealot, as Reimarus and his tradition posit, he would have massed his troops and calculated—or, like the Hellenistic king in his parable, he would have begged for a truce (*Luke* 14:31–32).

In the last week of his natural life, when Jesus entered the holy city, he did nothing of the sort.

14

THE ACTION IN THE TEMPLE

One day in the week before he died, we glimpse Jesus sitting quietly in the Temple. In this scene, which is narrated by both *Mark* and *Luke*, the Galilean is placed "opposite the treasury" (*Mark* 12:41).[1] His choice of seating might seem to be a minor point—but in context, it is arresting.

As the scene opens, Jesus is content to watch the faithful freely committing their hard currency—or, as *Mark* puts it, their "bronze" (Greek *chalkos*)—to the Temple fisc. We might recall from chapter 8 that when Pompey entered the Holy of Holies in 63 BCE, he found a massive cache of "sacred currency".[2] Here in the gospels, we see that by freely offering their money to the Jerusalem Temple, the crowds are in their own minds—and apparently, in Jesus' mind—making a sacred offering to God.

The Incident with the Copper Coins

"Many rich people put in much", *Mark* tells us. But Jesus is silent until he sees an impoverished widow drop a couple of "miniscule copper coins" into the treasury. How miniscule?

139

Mark tells us that the value of her coinage (Greek *lepton*) is convertible to the "cent" (Greek *kodrantēs*, from the Latin *quadrans*).[3] Suggestively, this is the infinitesimal value that Jesus cites when he warns that human courts will not release debtors until they have "paid the *very last cent*" (*Luke* has *lepton*; and *Matthew*, *kodrantēs*).[4] This nameless, poverty-stricken woman offers a couple of *those* to the Temple fisc.

On seeing this, we read in *Mark* that Jesus "called his disciples" and said to them:

> Truly (*amēn*), I say to you, this poor widow has put in more than all those who are contributing to the treasury. For they all contributed out of their surplus, but she out of her poverty has put in everything she had, her whole living. (*Mark* 12:41–44; compare *Luke* 21:1–4)

This is, of course, a beautiful act of honour by Jesus.[5] It is a forceful articulation, too, of something that we notice in many of the canonical sayings of Jesus—something that Nietzsche will call, nineteen centuries on, a "transvaluation of values" (*Umwertung der Werte*). For instance, Jesus says that "what is highly valued by humans is detested by God" (*Luke* 16:15); he warns that "the last" in this world-age "will be first" in the world-age to come (*Matthew* 20:16), and so on. He tries to revolutionize human judgements of "the things of humankind".[6]

"Value-Philosophy"

What I find interesting is that, here, with Jesus' saying in the treasury, the monetarist sense of 'value' that haunts any sort of modern "value-philosophy" (*Wertphilosophie*), including Nietzsche's philosophy of "transvaluation" (*Umwertung*), attains a precise and concrete sense. For in this scene, Jesus inverts the first-century Palestinian system of money by assigning the highest value to its lowest unit.

Now, Jesus is unquestionably conscious that the cent *is* the lowest unit. It is the structural value of the cent as *nearest to valueless* that gives meaning to his warnings, that debtors will not be released until "the very last cent" has been paid.[7] Money is a topic on which—as on politics—he seems to be a realist.

There is no 'economic romanticism' in the gospels, any more than political. Thus, Jesus stresses that this poor woman offered "her whole living" to God.[8] The 'transvaluation of values' that he articulates in this scene is thoroughly unromantic and is informed by his prophetic conviction that there is *a system of values which is present in this world-age, but which is constituted by a future world-age.* That system of values is realized in what Jesus calls the kingdom of God.

In economic terms, he argues from *proportionality*. It is the poor woman's poverty which magnifies the value of her offering, and the others' wealth which diminishes the value of theirs. It must nevertheless be said that Jesus, the realist, grounds his 'transvaluation' of this woman's offering on the assertion that *a divine future is present in history.*

But we should return to the setting of this little scene.

"Opposite the Treasury"

What is so arresting about the fact that we catch sight of Jesus as he is sitting "opposite the treasury" in Jerusalem? In the first place, it is interesting that *John* confirms the setting. We read in *John* 8 that Jesus liked to sit and teach "in the treasury of the Temple" (*John* 8:20). This suggests to me a firm association between Jesus and the treasury in the earliest strata of Christian memory. But again: What is so arresting about that?

In a word, *Tempelaktion*. This is the German term of art I will translate as Jesus' Action in the Temple. In an older terminology, it was known as the Cleansing of the Temple.

We will clarify the meaning of Jesus' Action in the Temple in a moment, but its relevance for us, here, is the fact that it is provoked, in all four gospels, by *the presence of currency—of money—in the Temple*. And yet it is placed, in all four gospels, *before* we see Jesus moving calmly about "the treasury of the Temple" (*John* 8:20). The contrast is stark and puzzling. Let me render it more concrete:

  (i) In *Mark* 11 (the oldest synoptic), Jesus goes berserk (if I may say), throwing over "the tables of the money changers" in the Temple. But then, in *Mark* 12, we read that "he sat down opposite the treasury, and watched the crowd putting money into the treasury".[9]

(ii) In *John* 2, Jesus makes "a light whip of cords" (only the fourth gospel tells us this) to drive a sacrificial market out of the Temple. He scatters "the coins of the money changers", too, saying: "Take these things out of here!" But then, in *John* 8, we read that Jesus uttered a highly mystical saying— "I am the light of the world"—"when he was teaching in the treasury of the Temple".[10]

Throughout the canonical gospels, then, two seemingly contradictory things are attested about Jesus. First, there is *something about the presence of currency in the Temple that infuriated Jesus more than anything else he witnessed during his prophetic life*. There is no other scene in which he forcibly moves a beast, a table, or anything else. And second, Jesus had *a definite liking for the part of the Temple where Judaeans put their currency into the Temple fisc*.

We are now able to articulate a precise question: Why is Jesus so disgusted by the moneychangers' coinage that he disrupts their commerce, and so struck by a widow's coins that he calls his disciples over to praise her? To settle this question, we need to step back briefly.

THE ACTION IN THE TEMPLE

"A House of Commerce"

Though their chronologies are sharply divergent, all the gospels narrate a scene in which Jesus creates a disturbance in the Temple. In *John*, it occurs in the early days of his prophetic life (*John* 2:13–22), just after his inaugural 'sign' of transforming water into wine at a wedding in Galilee (*John* 2:1–12). In the synoptics, it occurs just days before his death.[11] And further, the synoptic gospel-writers portray the Action in the Temple as a salient cause of his death.[12] In *John*, there may be a vague echo of this. Just after his Action, Jesus predicts that he will be killed in Jerusalem.[13] Since modern commentators tend to accept that Jesus' disruption of the Temple commerce led to his death, they tend to prefer the synoptic chronology.

There is a tendency in the recent literature, however, to question whether Jesus' *Tempelaktion* is centred on the presence of commerce in the Temple. Some argue that it is meant, rather, to prefigure the Temple's destruction, which he predicts, rather than challenging its 'purity'. Though there is surely some truth in the newer construction—prefiguring the Temple's destruction—it is not finally convincing.

One of the reasons why the historicity of the Action in the Temple is commonly accepted is that the whole collection of gospels attests it. But the whole collection *also* attests to the fact that what Jesus disrupts is Temple *commerce*, and his sayings on the occasion are aimed at that. To establish this, we can glance again at *Mark* and at *John*.

(i) In *Mark* 11, we see first that Jesus "began to drive out those who were *selling* and those who were *buying* in the Temple" and that he concentrated on "the tables of the moneychangers" (*Mark* 11:15). We then hear that Jesus cited the prophets Isaiah and Jeremiah, contrasting their idea of the Temple, "a house of prayer", with its first-century actuality, "a haven for larcenists".[14]

(ii) In *John* 2, we are told that Jesus entered the Temple precincts and "found people selling" doves, sheep, and cattle, and found "moneychangers seated at their tables". He is then shown driving "all of them out of the Temple"—meaning the sheep and cattle—with a "light whip of cords" (*phragellion ek schoiniōn*).[15] We learn in *John*—as in the synoptics—that Jesus "poured out the coins of the money changers". And finally, we read that he says: "Stop making my Father's house a house of commerce!" (*John* 2:14–16).

Personally, I cannot help but hear an echo of the synoptics in this last saying in *John*. What *Mark's* Jesus calls "a house of prayer", *John's* Jesus calls his "Father's house".[16] And what *Mark's* Jesus calls "a haven for larcenists", *John's* calls "a house of commerce".[17] What we could have, then, is this contrastive structure:

Mark	"house of prayer"	"haven for larcenists"
John	"Father's house"	"house of commerce"

If that is correct, then the canonical gospels, as a whole, attest to a structural contrast: "You cannot serve God and Currency."[18] This contrast would be sharpest if we were to select *Mark's* "house of prayer" from the left column and John's "house of commerce" from the right. The logic of Jesus' Action would then become perfectly clear. It is reasonable for one who says, *You cannot serve God and Currency*, to also say, *You cannot have a House of Prayer that is a House of Commerce.*

The Temple, like prayer, belongs to the soul—and what, Jesus asks, "can a human give in exchange for their soul?"[19] You cannot have a space of the unexchangeable that is a space of exchange.

THE ACTION IN THE TEMPLE

"A House of Prayer"

If this structuralist reading of the canonical material is right, then Jesus' Action in the Temple becomes perfectly legible with his choice to sit "opposite the treasury".[20] For Jesus is not only *not* a Zealot, but he is *nothing like* a Zealot. He permits Judaeans to pay Roman taxes, and he himself pays the Judaean Temple tax from a city in Galilee (*Matthew* 17:24–27). In the latter scene, he even suggests that it is *more* rational for Judaeans to pay the Roman tax than their own Temple tax.[21] To a Zealot, this line of reasoning is a form of apostasy.

More to my point, Jesus concedes (only in *Luke*) that the "children of light" can invest "dirty money", or "illicit money" (*mamōna tēs adikias*), in a world-age to come (*Luke* 16:8–9). And perhaps this is what Jesus sees as he sits by the treasury, just a couple of days after his disruption of the Temple commerce: the *sacrifice* of Currency. The form of giving of which he approves is, in the philosopher Georges Bataille's terms, pure expenditure. And, in the case of the impoverished woman who delights Jesus, it is the pure expenditure of one's "whole living".[22]

Jesus is content to sit by the treasury because it is there that Currency is used to *nullify* the logic of exchange. It is there that the Judaean faithful give to God on the terms set by the unexchangeable. Or, said differently, it is there that Currency becomes prayer.

Jesus praises the woman with her two copper coins—but it is worth noting that he does not criticize the rich, here, as he does elsewhere. Whatever else they may get wrong, Jesus seems to approve the rich when they nullify their Currency in the Temple by freely giving it to God.

"The Zeal of Your House"

Looking ahead, Jesus' Action in the Temple holds relevance for his coming trial before Pilate. In the first place, his Action helps to clarify why the Temple elites—the Sadducees—decide to kill him. The priestly aristocracy would perceive Jesus' symbolic 'attack' on the Temple as an attack on the Judaean temple-state. There seems to be a scholarly consensus on this point. Jesus' Action also explains why Pilate remains unconvinced of his zealotry; Jesus holds none of the commitments that a Roman prefect would expect from a Galilean rebel.

In the second place, the *Tempelaktion* is relevant because of the way in which it reveals that Jesus *is* a zealot—or, in post-Enlightenment terms, a fanatic. For there is one place—and *only* one place—in the fourfold gospel where he is depicted as acting out of 'zeal'. We read in *John 2* that he:

> poured out the coins of the money changers and overturned their tables. He told those who were selling ... "Stop making my Father's house a house of commerce!" His disciples remembered that it was written, *"The zeal of your house* will consume me."[23]

This line regarding zeal, which comes to the disciples' minds, is taken from *Psalm* 69. Its significance, however, is deeply changed by Jesus himself. For it is he, in *John 2*, who contrasts the House of God and House of Commerce. And it is he, in the synoptic gospels, who contrasts the Things of God and Things of Caesar.

Jesus *is* a zealot, then, but his zeal is circumscribed. His zeal is for a 'house', a 'house' that he himself has reconceived—in light of the Hebrew prophets—as a 'pure' Temple. A line from the prophet Zechariah reads in the Septuagint's Greek: "On that day there shall no longer be a trader in the house of the Lord."[24] For the Judaean, Roman, and Galilean elites who kill him—and indeed, for the Zealots—divine zeal is necessarily zeal for a *temple-state*.

Within the horizons of the gospels, however, Jesus' Action in the Temple is a scene in which he symbolically drives the archaic *'state'* out of the *'temple'*.

THE ACTION IN THE TEMPLE

Jesus, not Tiberius

Jesus' Action in the Temple is the first act in a world-historical drama that is still unfolding. It is his insistence on a sort of 'temple' which had perhaps never existed—a 'pure' temple. And in this insistence, a sort of 'state' which had never existed begins to become conceivable—a state in which the 'temple' is not a site of imperial power or a house of commerce.

This decoupling of the archaic temple-state is inscribed in Jesus' sayings regarding God and Caesar, God and Currency. When he uttered these sayings, Caesar was a quasi-divine monarch with an empire-wide cult. And Caesar's Currency bore the image and inscription of a "son of a god". Politics and economics are not only both originally religious, but *intensely* and *essentially* religious.

It is not Tiberius Caesar (*divi filius*), but Jesus (*filius dei*) who decouples God and Caesar, God and Currency. And the scenes in which he articulates this most sharply are clustered around his Action in the Temple. The temptation scene in which Jesus makes his God–Caesar contrast, occurs, in all the synoptics, in the tense days that fall between his *Tempelaktion* and the crucifixion.[25]

"By What Authority?"

There is another scene which is tightly linked to the *Tempelaktion*. In it, Jesus invokes a divide which he then *returns to* in his God–Caesar contrast.[26] For on the day *after* his disruption of the Temple commerce, he is stopped by a priestly clique as he is walking in the Temple.[27] They ask him, bluntly: "By what authority (*exousia*) are you doing these things?" Like Pilate's question, "Are you the King of the Judaeans?"[28] this question by the Temple authorities is transmitted by *Matthew*, *Mark* and *Luke* in identical Greek.[29]

But Jesus cancels their right to question him, by saying: "I will ask *you* one question."[30] His question sets a trap into which they are too clever to fall, and the scene ends in stalemate. In a portico of the Temple, Jesus flatly refuses—again, in identical Greek—to tell the Temple's emissaries "by what authority I am doing these things".[31]

The scene's prophetic dialectics cannot detain us. All I will say is that Jesus' trap is set by the figure of John the Baptist—a prophet recently killed and, in Jesus' mind, a martyr.

But Jesus' counter-question to his critics delineates *two sources of authority*. There is an authority which comes "from heaven" (*ex ouranou*), and an authority which comes "from humans" (*ex anthrōpōn*).[32] In one of the next synoptic scenes, Jesus says that there is a sphere that pertains to 'God' and a sphere that pertains to 'Caesar'. And in his *Tempelaktion*, he dramatizes the prophetic idea that there is a 'house' which belongs to God, and a 'house' which belongs to Commerce.

The Action in the Temple is thus not only one of the most crucial scenes in the week of Jesus' death. It is a signal event in the history of empire.

15

THE INCIDENT WITH THE ALABASTER JAR

In the synoptic gospels, it is Jesus' Action in the Temple and bold sayings in Jerusalem that lead to his death. He warns that the Temple will be destroyed,[1] that the Temple elites will be disgraced,[2] and that a brutal epoch will commence which *Luke* calls "the times of the gentiles".[3]

One of his parables seems to have enraged the holy city's aristocracy. It is a transparent allegory of the radical misgovernment by Judaea's ruling class, and not by Romans. "When they realized that he had told this parable against them", we read in *Mark*, "they wanted to arrest him, *but they feared the crowd*".[4] This last phrase must be reckoned with.

"They Feared the Crowd"

The figure of 'the crowd'—a term preferred by *Mark* and *Matthew*—is critical for us.[5] In *Luke*, it is called 'the people'; and in *John*—lamentably—it becomes 'the Judaeans'. For it is not only in the scenes leading up Jesus' arrest, but during his interrogation by Pilate, that 'the crowd' is decisive. We read in *Mark*, for instance, that "Pilate, *resolving to satisfy the crowd* ... handed Jesus over to be crucified".[6] Within a matter of pages, the gospels therefore suggest

(i) that it is 'the crowd' which unnerves the Temple elites, forcing them to arrest Jesus in secret; and
(ii) that it is 'the crowd' which unnerves Pilate, driving him to crucify Jesus.

Said differently, the Temple elites delay the arrest of Jesus, and interrogate him at night, because they fear 'the crowd'—and Pilate condemns Jesus because he fears 'the crowd'.

What is going on?

There is not, I think, a narrative incoherence in the gospels; rather, there are different crowds. The crowd feared by the Jerusalem elites is not the crowd feared by Pilate. On the contrary, Pilate fears a lynch mob controlled by the Temple elites. This is stated in *Mark* and *Matthew*, it is subtly observed in *John*, and somewhat blurred in *Luke*. In *Mark* 15, for instance, we read that "the chief priests stirred up the crowd" to demand that Pilate kill Jesus. And in *Matthew* 27, we notice that "the chief priests and the elders persuaded the crowds to ... have Jesus killed".[7]

There are two 'crowds' in Jerusalem, then, in the days before Jesus' death. One sees him as a prophet, or Christ-figure; and the other—headed by the Temple elites—sees him as a deranged or demon-inspired "impostor" and a threat to what the Sadducees call "our holy place and our nation".[8] The first crowd, feared by the Temple elites, threatens unrest if Jesus were to be seized in the Temple or killed by Judaeans. The second crowd, controlled by the Temple elites, will insist on Jesus' death.

What happens in the hours and days after Jesus' Action in the Temple, then, seems to be this: Jerusalem's scribal (Pharisee) and sacerdotal (Sadducee) elites conspire to have him killed.[9] This is clearly stated in all the gospels. *Mark* tells us that the Jerusalem priests and scribes "were looking for a way to arrest Jesus *by stealth* and kill him" without causing "a riot among the people" (*Mark* 14:1–2). It is Pilate—a Roman—who will kill Jesus without causing 'a riot'.

But who will give the Temple elites a way to arrest Jesus by stealth?

"Day after day", as Jesus says during his arrest, he is "in the Temple teaching".[10] And we will recall that though the scribal and sacerdotal cliques "wanted to arrest him" in the Temple, "they feared the crowd"—meaning, *his* crowd (*Mark* 12:12). In the hours and days after the *Tempelaktion*, the logic of Jesus' Passion calls for someone who knows where Jesus will be at night, and in seclusion, when he is not in the Temple.[11]

"One of the Twelve"

One of the most scandalous aspects of the Passion is that Jesus is betrayed by one of his disciples, by "one of the Twelve".[12] And Jesus himself, in *Matthew*'s arrest scene, calls him "comrade" or "friend" (*hetairos*)—a cold-blooded irony, however gracious the tone. "Do what you are here for", Jesus then says, with incomparable simplicity.[13]

Celsus seems to think that Judas' betrayal proves that Jesus had "deceived his disciples".[14] The rabbi *must* have lost his disciple's trust, so the pagan philosopher claims, because he was dishonest. Origen's rebuttal is apt. "From the lives of the philosophers", he writes, "one might find many cases similar to the desertion of Judas".[15]

Returning to the gospels, the Judaean elites' resolution to kill Jesus seems to be inspired—in *Matthew*, *Mark* and *Luke*—by his Action in the Temple and harsh prophetic sayings. In the absence of Judas, however, that resolution is politically inert. It is therefore a mistake to shift immediately from Jesus' Action in the

Temple to his trials and death. Jesus' Action marks an incident without which the Temple elites might not have conspired to kill him. Nevertheless, the gospel-writers insist that this conspiracy would have *come to nothing* without Judas (*Mark* 14:1–2).

Indeed, it is clear in the gospels that Judas *initiates the betrayal*. "Judas Iscariot", we read in *Mark*, "*went to the chief priests* in order to betray him". And after that conversation, *Mark* tells us, Judas "began to look for an opportunity" to betray him.[16]

In light of this we must ask: Is there an incident in the gospels which might move Judas to betray Jesus? I believe there is, and we can call it the Incident with the Alabaster Jar. Just as three of the gospels (all but *John*) narrate the Action in the Temple within the drama of Jesus' condemnation, three of the gospels (all but *Luke*) narrate the Incident with the Alabaster Jar within the drama of Jesus' betrayal.

I have made much of the confusion of Jesus' judges, and this motif may be linked to the Incident with the Alabaster Jar. If Jesus has the capacity to shock and anger one of the Twelve, there is no reason to doubt that he has the capacity to mystify his critics and his judges.

"Why this Waste?"

The scene is this. Jesus is at the house of Simon the Leper (in *Matthew* and *Mark*), or Lazarus the Dead Man (in *John*).[17] The house is in a settlement called Bethany (in *Matthew*, *Mark* and *John*), which is not far from Jerusalem.[18] Jesus knows he is a marked man, and the Twelve know this, too.[19] Even in *John*, which sharply breaks with the synoptic chronology, his *Tempelaktion* is in the past and the Temple aristocracy's intentions are half-declared (*John* 11:57).[20] There is some reason to believe that Jesus and the Twelve are effectively hiding out in Bethany, in what we could perhaps call a safe house.[21]

THE INCIDENT WITH THE ALABASTER JAR

A woman then enters the scene. In *John*, her name is Mary—one of Lazarus' sisters.[22] In *Matthew* and *Mark*, we read only that "a woman came" to Jesus.[23] In the synoptic gospels (including *Luke*), we are told that she is carrying an immensely costly aromatic substance, likely nard, in "an alabaster jar". But in *John*, we are given a weight: Mary comes to Jesus bearing "a pound ... of pure nard" (*John* 12:3).

This woman—Mary, perhaps?—anoints Jesus in a totally unreasonable manner. In *Matthew* and *Mark*, she anoints his head; in *Luke* and *John*, his feet. In *Matthew* and *Mark*, she pours the fragrant substance out; in *Luke* and *John*—incredibly—she rubs it on Jesus with her hair.[24]

It is a shocking scene, regardless of whether the woman is, as only *Luke* suggests, a 'sinner' who is bathing a 'prophet' in her perfume and tears. "If this man were a prophet", Jesus' host thinks in *Luke*, "he would know ... what kind of woman this is who is touching him!"[25] But it is variously constructed *by* the gospel-writers *as* a shocking scene.

Yet, whenever this scene is integrated into Jesus' Passion, the onlookers are *not* most shocked by the intimacy of the gesture. They are confused and angered by the *economic irrationality of the gesture*. "Why this *waste*?" is a question murmured by the Twelve in *Mark* and *Matthew*.[26] In *John*, it is Judas who criticizes Jesus: "Why was this perfume not sold for three hundred denarii and the money given to the poor?"

In *Mark* and *Matthew*, the Twelve's question is a reasonable one. And Judas' question is intensely reasonable—even if, per *John*'s editorial comment, "he said this not because he cared about the poor, but because he was a thief" (*John* 12:4–6). Three hundred denarii—a figure given in both *Mark* and *John*—is a lot of money to commit to such a gesture,[27] roughly converting into a year's wages for the first-century labouring classes. All there is to show is that a "house was filled with the fragrance of the perfume" (*John* 12:3).[28]

153

In terms of economic rationality, the woman's gesture is a waste.[29] Jesus' reasoning, however, makes this scene into a sort of diptych with the Incident with the Copper Coins. There, a woman without a husband offers a couple of "miniscule copper coins". Here, a woman without a husband lavishes 300 denarii on a wanted man in a humble setting. There, Jesus honours her for having "put in more than all those who are contributing to the treasury".[30] Here, Jesus honours her for sensing that he is about to die. In an objective sense, one gesture is meaningless and the other is exorbitant. "You always have the poor with you", he reasons—again, we glimpse his economic realism—"but you will not always have me".[31]

What is the sumptuary value of Jesus' life? Or indeed, of *any* life, when we recall the question: "What can a human give in exchange for their soul?"[32] In the gospels, the unexchangeable defies the rationality of exchange.

In these two incidents we see Jesus' prophetic logic of sacred expenditure, which seems not only to have enraged the Temple elites, but one of the Twelve. If the narrative logic of the gospels is followed, Judas' betrayal is provoked by Jesus' acquiescence to a wildly exorbitant gesture.

"The Price of Blood"

The next day, or so *Mark* and *Matthew* let us conjecture (their chronology is vague),[33] Judas tells the Temple aristocracy that he can hand Jesus to them discreetly—meaning outside the city, and at night. In sharp contrast to the woman with the alabaster jar, Jesus' death is perfectly legible in economic terms for one of the Twelve. We read in *Mark* that the Temple elites are "greatly pleased" when Judas comes to them, and that they offer "to give him money".[34] A price is put on Jesus' head—literally, on his "blood" (*timē haimatos*, *Matthew* 27:6). In contriving the death of Jesus, Commerce is served.

Reader beware, however. Steiner dwells on the cyclical, ritual "identification of Judas with money" in the Passion narratives. "For Jews, till this day", he warns, "the consequences will be hideous".[35] It is with this history in mind that I stress that Judas' betrayal narrative was penned by Judaeans, (in part) for Judaeans, and has antecedents in the Hebrew scriptures. We could think, for instance, of the ultimately redemptive family epic in *Genesis* in which Joseph is sold into slavery by his brothers (*Genesis* 37:12–35).[36] The Passion, too, is a family epic.

Judeophobia may have been rife in the first century, but—unlike many modern commentators—I do not see it in the canonical memoirs of Jesus' life.[37] "The Gospels", as René Girard puts it, "have no favourites".[38]

A close reading of the Passion narratives reveals that there is no Judeophobic taint, as such, in the blood-money motif.[39] And looking beyond the gospels, when Paul (or pseudo-Paul) writes that "love of money is the root of all evils", he seems to be citing a pagan saying (*I Timothy* 6:10). It is a pagan saying because the 'love of money' is a pagan reality. The phrase "Love of money is the mother-city of all evils" is attributed to a Cynic philosopher, Bion of Borysthenes.[40] And Bion, who was trafficked as a sexual slave in his youth, spoke with some authority.[41]

Only a fool could construe the 'love of money' as a bizarrely Judaean trait or temptation. By the first century BCE, Rome was the city—not Jerusalem—where everything could be bought (*Romae omnia venalia esse*).[42] And in the first century CE, as in the twenty-first, 'love of money' is a darkly human reality. As Mikhail Bulgakov puts it in his clandestine, Soviet-era Jesus-book: "Mankind loves money."[43]

The hard truth is that blood-money is as ancient, and as contemporary, as money. And to be sure, Jesus is in no way the first, or the last, to have been sold—by Judaeans or gentiles—to killers.

PART SIX

THE AUTHORITY OF DARKNESS

16

JESUS THE GALILEAN

Jesus dies on a cross because he is under a Roman judgement (*Luke* 23:40). In the hours before his death, however, he is interrogated by a Judaean high priest (or two in *John*); by a Judaean council at night (or the next morning in *Luke*); and by a Herodian dynast (only in *Luke*). This excess of courts and judges is unique to the canonical Jesus-tradition. It is only in the New Testament that he is captured, tortured and put to death by "both Herod and Pontius Pilate, with the gentiles and the peoples of Israel" (*Acts* 4:27).[1]

The idea seems to be, and the early Christian memory seems to be, that Jesus is not only rejected by "his own" (the peoples of Israel) but by "the world" (the gentiles). This is mystically interesting—"the world", in *John*'s phrase, "did not know him" (*John* 1:10–11)[2]—but it is historically interesting, too. And it is not, as such, incredible.

"The Rulers Gathered"

One of the earliest dramatizations of the Passion is found in *Acts of the Apostles*. Here, after Peter and John are questioned by

159

members of Judaea's "high-priestly line", the author of *Luke–Acts* quotes the Septuagint's version of a soaring stanza from *Psalm* 2.[3]

> Why did the gentiles rage,
>> and the peoples plot in vain?
> The kings of the earth set themselves in array,
>> and the rulers were gathered together,
>>> against the LORD and his Anointed.[4]

Here, the conspiracy against the Anointed (*Christos*) of God is a *gentile conspiracy*. 'The kings of the earth' are gentile monarchs. This is what the phrase means, too, in *Matthew*, when Jesus contrasts 'the kings of the earth' with the priestly nobility of Judaea's temple-state (*Matthew* 17:25). The apostolic recitation of *Psalm* 2 in *Acts* 4, then, seems to lay bare a gentile conspiracy to kill Jesus. And the Passion is a drama which culminates in the most detested gentile punishment—the cross.[5]

And yet, the pages of *Acts* make clear that early Christ-believers thought of Jesus' Passion as *pre-eminently* a Judaean drama. Both can be true, of course, but only if we grasp the complexity of the Jesus-tradition in the gospels. One of the sources of this complexity is the idea, or memory, that 'rulers gathered' in Jerusalem. They gathered in the days before Jesus' death to mark the observance of the Passover.

The tetrarch Herod is likely to have come from one of his fortress palaces or new-built cities in Galilee and Peraea. The prefect Pilate is likely to have come from his palace on the Judaean coast. And the prophet-king Jesus is likely to have come from some obscure settlement "beyond the Jordan".[6] It is only the Judaean high priest, Joseph Caiaphas—on whom there are no real data in first-century texts—who seems to have remained in the holy city in the days before Jesus' death.

There is reason to believe, then, that a week or so before the Romans splayed Jesus between two convicted rebels (Greek *lēstai*,

Latin *latrones*), more than one of 'the kings of the earth'—and a
prophet-king—went up to Jerusalem.[7]

Pilate is a gentile, as he dryly reminds Jesus. "I am not a
Judaean, am I?" (*John* 18:35).[8] In this way we confirm that, for
the Roman, Jesus *is* a Judaean.[9]

Herod Antipas is a sort of gentile, the son of a Samaritan
mother, Malthace, and a part-Idumaean father, Herod I, who
some derided as "half-Judaean" (*hēmiioudaios*).[10] Of course, the
Herodian dynasty spectacularly patronized the Second Jerusalem
Temple. It nevertheless seems likely that both John the Baptist
and Jesus regarded the Herodians as 'kings of the earth'—gentile
or half-gentile rulers of Israel's contested patrimony.

Herod's "Foster-Brother", and the Wife of His Manager

There is only one place in the gospels where Jesus sends a message to Herod Antipas. His tone is intensely disparaging (*Luke*
13:31–33).[11] Jesus' aversion to the Herodian tetrarch heightens
the interest of traditions in *Luke–Acts*, which place one of
Herod's courtiers within Jesus' orbit, and another within the first
church in Syria.

We note first, in *Luke*, that one of Jesus' deaconesses, Joanna,
is described as "the wife of Herod's manager, Chuza"—apparently
a Nabatean or Arab name (*Luke* 8:3).[12] The idea that the wife of
one of Galilee's higher functionaries invested money in the 'kingdom of God' is a remarkable one (*Luke* 16:8–9).

Second, we note in *Acts of the Apostles* that the apostolic church
in Antioch had a circle of prophets and inspired exegetes (*Acts*
13:1). One of those named is Manaen or Menahem, who is said to
have been an "intimate" of the tetrarch of Galilee—literally, his
"foster-brother" (Greek *suntrophos*, Latin *conlactaneus*).[13]

These figures, Joanna and Manaen, remind us that Jesus had
a 'Herodian' in his retinue, and that there was another in the

very first circle of Christ-believers in Syria. So even before they gathered in Jerusalem, 'the kings of the earth' were not unknown to Jesus and his circle.

Jesus had heard of Pilate's harsh measures in Judaea (*Luke* 13:1). Herod had certainly heard of Jesus' prophetic ministry in Galilee (*Matthew* 14:1). And one of Jesus' disciples is said to have been "known to the high priest" in Jerusalem (*John* 18:15).[14]

The drama of Jesus' death had therefore begun in the months or years before its crisis in the holy city. Only traces of that drama remain in the gospels and *Acts*. Crucially, however, this drama did not *begin* in the holy city.

"No Prophet Is to Rise from Galilee"

Jesus is himself a Galilean of obscure parentage (*John* 9:29).[15] By rite, creed and maternal descent, he is Judaean; but he is not Judaean by dialect or jurisdiction.

In Judaea, city-dwellers recognize Jesus and disciples as Galileans (*Matthew* 21:11; *John* 7:52). They speak in a Galilean manner. The diction of one of his disciples is noted on the night before his death (*Mark* 14:70; *Matthew* 26:73). And Jesus' own Galilean-style utterance of a Hebrew line from the *Psalms*, when he is on the cross, confuses some of those who hear him (*Mark* 15:34–35; *Matthew* 27:46–47).[16]

By jurisdiction, Jesus and his cohort belong to the Herodian tetrarchy of Galilee and Peraea, not the Roman province of Judaea. Thus, for instance, one of the slave-girls in the high priest's retinue calls him "Jesus the Galilean" (*Matthew* 26:69). This seems to be one reason why the prefect of Judaea is disinclined to have him crucified (*Luke* 23:6–7). And it is the name of a Galilean settlement, not a Judaean city, which is pinned to the cross, under a Roman *titulus* that reads: "Jesus of Nazareth, King of the Judaeans" (*John* 19:19).[17]

Jesus' non-Judaean provenance is therefore heard, observed and legally noted in Jerusalem. This is part of what makes him a divisive figure (*John* 9:16, 10:19). For while some claim that he is a prophet from Galilee (*Matthew* 21:11), many others hold that "no prophet is to rise from Galilee" (*John* 7:52). The Sadducees, and some of the Pharisees, seem to have rejected *a priori* the notion that a first-century Galilean could be a prophet, or *the* prophet (*Luke* 9:20; *John* 6:69).[18]

For this and other reasons, the Galilean's mood is sombre during his ascent to Jerusalem. Uniquely in *Luke*, Jesus begins to weep when he catches sight of its towers glinting in the distance. This is not because he senses that *he* is marked for destruction, but rather that *the holy city is*. Of course, within days he will be betrayed, sentenced and killed. And within decades—as *Luke* has him say—Jerusalem will be encircled, brutalized and razed (*Luke* 19:41–44). Perceived by many, to this day, as an enemy of Jerusalem and the Temple, Jesus is portrayed in the gospels as a mournful son—and friend—of both.

Søren Kierkegaard's comment on this scene is strong. "Christ goes up to Jerusalem", but he "does not prophesy—there is no more time for that—he weeps".[19]

17

JESUS THE REJECT

Within days of Jesus' lamentation for Jerusalem, the "daughters of Jerusalem" are "beating their breasts and wailing for him" (*Luke* 23:27–28). This is because, as *Mark* is the first to tell us, he is arrested one night in "a place called Gethsemane"—a grove of trees, perhaps—by a cohort of armed men sent by the Temple aristocracy (*Mark* 14:32, 43). Jesus is incredulous. They are treating him like an enemy of the state (Greek *lēstēs*, Latin *latro*), but he is a man of words, a rabbi (*Mark* 14:45). "Day after day", he rebukes them, "I was with you in the Temple" (*Mark* 14:48–49).

There is no mention in *Mark*'s arrest scene of Jesus' hands being tied, but he is seized. The Twelve—or rather, the Eleven—desert him (*Mark* 14:46, 50). One of his disciples, who is "wearing nothing but a linen cloth", is stripped in the confusion—and runs naked from the dark grove (*Mark* 14:51–52).[1] This is how, in the first gospel to be written, Jesus' death begins.

"I Will Destroy This Temple"

The high priest of Judaea is not named in *Mark*; we surmise that it is Caiaphas. Jesus is brought before him. Caiaphas has summoned a council of high-ranking priests, elders and scribes (*Mark* 14:53). Jerusalem's scribes, and perhaps some of the elders, are likely to have been Pharisees. But the priestly core of this council is likely to have been Sadducee—and the high priest himself, without doubt, is a Sadducee.

The status of this council is a matter of conjecture, but in *Mark*, something like a court seems to have been formed by Caiaphas and the Temple elites. *Mark* calls it a Sanhedrin, an Aramaic word for 'council' which comes from the Greek *sunedrion* and later becomes *concilium* in the Latin gospels (*Mark* 14:55).

Hostile witnesses are summoned to testify in chambers, while one of the Twelve, Peter, a man of the "humblest" origins—in Auerbach's words—idles with "servant girls and soldiers" in the courtyard (*Mark* 14:54–72).[2] *Mark* seems more concerned with the drama of Jesus' own circle—namely, Peter—than with the deposition of witnesses. Much of the latter part of *Mark* 14 is given to this inglorious figure, Peter—"a hero of such weakness" that, as Auerbach says, he "derives the highest force *from* his weakness". We see him cursing, terror-struck, after being called "a Galilean", until he finally says of his rabbi—and his Christ: "I do not know the man" (*Mark* 14:66–71).[3]

How are we to interpret this melancholy, coal-fire-lit scene?[4] "The incident [is] entirely realistic both in regard to locale and *dramatis personae*", in Auerbach's judgement. "Peter and the other characters", he concludes, "are caught in a universal movement of the depths". And what could that mean? Auerbach tells us:

> What we see here is a world which on the one hand is entirely real, average, identifiable as to place, time, and circumstances, but which on the other hand is shaken in its very foundations, is transforming and renewing itself before our eyes. For the New Testament authors ... these occurrences on the plane of everyday life assume the importance of world-revolutionary events, as later on they will for everyone.[5]

For the first gospel-writer, Peter's questioning by a slave-girl in a gloomy yard seems to be no less 'world-revolutionary' than Jesus' questioning by the Judaean elites. It is not only the drama of the master, but of the disciple, which gives rise to the church.

The spiralling structure of both dramas—Jesus', and Peter's—should not be missed. *Mark* tells us first that Peter is "sitting with the guards" in Caiaphas' courtyard, "warming himself at the fire" (*Mark* 14:54). In the next sentence, the gospel-writer tells us that the Sanhedrin is hearing a number of witnesses hostile to Jesus, who are "looking ... to put him to death" (*Mark* 14:55). The accusation is that Jesus had said that he would "destroy this Temple *made with hands*"—meaning the Herodian Temple—and "in three days" erect a shrine "*not* made with hands" (*Mark* 14:57). Jesus is *not* found guilty on this charge, yet—after the high priest and Sanhedrin have heard numerous witnesses, and Jesus' own witness—he is finally condemned (*Mark* 14:55–65).

"The Gospel is not gentle with persecutors."[6] But neither is it cruel to them. For Jesus' nocturnal interrogation in *Mark* does not end with a weird demonization of the high priest and his circle, nor a bitter denunciation of Jesus' hostile witnesses. Rather, it ends with an escalating scene in which one of the Twelve, Peter, denies his connection to Jesus (*Mark* 14:66–72). In other words, Jesus' Judaean trial ends with *the transformation of one of his disciples into a hostile witness.*

"The Gospels", to recall Girard's line, "have no favourites".[7]

In *Mark*, it is Jesus' *most* committed disciple who becomes a figure "replete with problem and tragedy", in Auerbach's reading. "Because his faith was deep, but not deep enough", writes Auerbach, the "worst happened" to Peter on the night before his master's death.[8] In Girard's interpretation: "Peter makes Jesus his victim."[9]

A decisive question that the high priest puts to Jesus will concern us later. Here, we can note how *Mark* stresses Jesus' impassiveness throughout the proceedings. He is accused by many, but he refuses to speak. "He was silent", *Mark* writes, "and did not answer" (*Mark* 14:61). The testimony of hostile witnesses seems to confirm, in a garbled way, texts in which Jesus foretells the fall of the Herodian Temple (*Mark* 14:58). Nevertheless, *Mark* stresses that their testimonies "did not agree". And this is credible—since Jesus' sayings, singly and collectively, are hard to interpret. Further, this chimes with something that we have seen, that Jesus *confuses his judges*—as, indeed, he confuses his own disciples.

Mark's statement that the testimonies of Caiaphas' witnesses "did not agree" is not, of course, disinterested (in a mystical or a 'political' sense). But the gospel-writer does not exploit this moment to denigrate Caiaphas or the Temple elites. On the contrary, *Mark* suggests that *because* the "testimony did not agree", Caiaphas and his council *declined* to condemn Jesus on the grounds of that testimony. In this way, the gospel-writer cedes to the high priest and his council a desire—perhaps minimal—to honour judicial norms (*Mark* 14:56–57, 59).[10]

In *Mark*'s Passion, it is precisely the council's refusal to judge Jesus, on the testimony of conflicting witnesses, that leads the high priest to force the Galilean to incriminate himself. It is Caiaphas who finally compels Jesus to reply to his question: "Are you the Christ, the Son of the Blessed One?" (*Mark* 14:61). We will try to elucidate this moment in chapter 18. Here, we only note that, having heard Jesus' reply, Caiaphas turns to his council, saying: "What is your decision?" *Mark* then tells us that they "condemned him as deserving death" (*Mark* 14:64).

What cannot be doubted, here, is that *Mark*'s judicial circle *judges* Jesus (Greek *katekrinan auton*, Latin *condemnaverunt eum*). The legal reality of this judgement is unclear in the gospels and in modern historiography; but whatever its legal reality, it is a judgement. Jesus is judged by the Judaean elites in *Mark*. He is then treated in ways that are consistent with the perception that he is a blasphemer, a false prophet and a messianic impostor (*Mark* 14:65). Although, here, the gospel-writer might have in mind a line from the prophets, in the Septuagint translation: "My cheeks [I gave] to slaps, and my face I did not turn away from the disgrace of being spat upon" (*Isaiah* 50:6).[11]

At dawn the next day, the Jerusalem council seems to reconvene for a consultation. Again, *Mark* calls this council a Sanhedrin. We read that Jesus' hands are tied (again?) and that the Temple elites then hand him over to Pilate (*Mark* 15:1).

"Do Not Pass Judgement"

The scenes of Jesus' capture and high-priestly interrogation in *Matthew* are firmly rooted in *Mark*. There is only one thing for us to note. After "one of those who were with Jesus" cuts off the ear of one of Caiaphas' slaves—the lone act of violence by one of Jesus' circle in the whole canonical collection—he utters, only in *Matthew*, an ultra-realist dictum that is still in circulation today: "All who take the sword will perish by the sword" (*Matthew* 26:52).[12]

For Reimarus and his tradition, this is a scene in which Jesus and the Twelve are revealed to be the most ineffectual zealots in Judaean history.[13] But in the centuries that fell between Gethsemane and Reimarus, the scene was read very differently. Jesus' disciple behaves in a way that is *indispensable to those who hold 'secular power'*, and that becomes—only with Jesus—*impermissible for those who are vested with 'sacred authority'*.

Whatever the origins of Jesus' saying, in terms of the history of western legal thought, "Put your sword back into its place" is not linked to the miscarriage of a new, Zealot-style temple-state. It is linked to the birth of a new idea of the sacred—one in which the logic of coercion has been renounced. The world-historical meaning of this moment could, to my mind, be formulated like this: *Jesus decouples the means of survival of the archaic temple-and-state, at the very moment that he is apprehended by the archaic temple-state.*

And it is certainly not meaningless that Jesus' critique of violence, here, on the night before his judicial murder, shares a structure with his critique of judgement in *Matthew*'s Sermon on the Mount. The one who says

(i) "All who take the sword will perish by the sword" (*Matthew* 26:52),

is the one who says

(ii) "Do not pass judgement, in order that judgement not be passed on you. For with whatever judgement you judge, you will be judged—and with whatever measure you measure, it will be measured to you" (*Matthew* 7:1–2).[14]

The structure of violence, like the structure of judgement, is closed. Only the "blessed", Jesus seems to believe, are not enclosed.[15]

"This Is Your Hour"

Luke adheres to the Marcan template, but less meticulously than *Matthew*. There is no need for more than a brief notetaking of several Lucan elements on the night before the crucifixion—in which Judaea's high priest figures prominently, but Caiaphas is not named.[16]

Only in *Luke* does Jesus give a name to the drama in which he figures. A man of words and teacher of the 'kingdom of God'—Girard's "incomparable victim"—is treated as the enemy of a failed state.[17] "This", he says to those who have come to lay hands on him, "is the authority of darkness (*exousia tou skotous*)" (*Luke* 22:52–53).

JESUS THE REJECT

That *Luke* notes the presence of "commanders of the Temple force" (*stratēgous tou hierou*) is interesting in light of our temple-state theme. And in *Luke*, Jesus' reprimand to the disciple who cuts off a slave's ear is less discursive than in *Matthew*: "No more of this!" It is only in *Luke* that he touches the ear of this mutilated man to heal him (*Luke* 22:50–51).[18] And it is this act of healing—the healing of an enemy—which prepares Jesus' saying about the authority of darkness.

Procedurally, *Luke* differs most sharply from *Mark* and *Matthew* by the fact that he omits the high priest's nocturnal interrogation of Jesus. On the night before his death, according to *Luke*, Jesus is led "into the high priest's house". Peter loiters in the courtyard and utters his all-too-human denials of the one he once called "the Christ of God" (*Luke* 9:20, 22:54–62). Jesus is then mocked, blindfolded and struck—like a Christ-impostor—during the night; but this judicial brutality is not shown to be consequent to a prior condemnation (*Luke* 22:63–65). It is only "when day came" that *Luke's* council, which he calls a Sanhedrin, arraigns the Galilean.[19]

Perhaps most interesting is the fact that uniquely in *Luke*, Jesus seems to give a reason for his near-total silence during his brief dawn-time interrogation before Caiaphas—and, we can conjecture, before Herod and Pilate. This is how I read his reply to a question on his reticence to call himself the Christ. "If I tell you", he says, "you will not believe; and if I question you, you will not answer" (*Luke* 22:66–68). I find this reply to be, within the horizons of the fourfold gospel, intensely credible.

The first half of Jesus' reply can be read, not as a bitter indictment of the Judaean council, but a monotone observation—one that is wholly in keeping with his political realism. Jesus' steely silence on the morning of his death is, he implies—or *Luke* says—politically determined. It belongs both to the authority of darkness, and the drama of truth in which

171

Jesus figures. The law-courts convened to hear him testify, but they *will not believe him when he testifies*. What then, he asks, is the point of his testimony?

In keeping with Jesus' political sayings, he is therefore content to sullenly, or sublimely, let the machine of judgement run on without him. Jesus contributes nothing because the mentality of his judges nullifies whatever he might contribute, *and he knows it*. "This is your hour", he says in Gethsemane, "and the authority of darkness" (*Luke* 22:53).

The influence of Jesus' death on the history of legal culture begins in this rushed proceeding in which, in Christian belief and many centuries of western consciousness, it is *totally useless for history's supreme witness to truth to open his mouth*. Because it is useless, this man Jesus—whose life is, he says in *John*, "to testify to the truth" (*John* 18:37)—very nearly testifies to nothing.

The second half of Jesus' reply is even more striking. "If I question you", he says to the Judaean nobility, "you will not answer" (*Luke* 22:66–68). This, too, is credible within the horizons of the gospels. We may recall the scene after Jesus' Action in the Temple, when he is urged to declare the authority by which he is speaking and acting in Jerusalem. He subtly denies the right of his questioners to question him, saying to them (here in *Luke* 20): "I will also ask *you* a question, and you tell *me*."[20] Jesus is a master of the counter-question. When they refuse to answer him, he ends the conversation—asserting a right to interrogate his interrogators.[21]

In Gethsemane, *Luke* shows Jesus questioning the "commanders of the Temple force" (*Luke* 22:53). But once he is in captivity, he only replies to his judges in the most sullen and prosaic—yet world-altering—affirmatives. "You say that I am", to the Judaean council; and "You say so", to the Roman prefect (*Luke* 22:70, 23:3).

Following his arrest, Jesus seems to perceive that he has been stripped of this prophetic right. Trapped in a process which makes it impossible for him—so he determines—to dialectically trap his judges, he withdraws from what Foucault might call the "game of truth".[22] Jesus refuses to speak, during his Passion, because *he senses that he is no longer in the game*. And this coheres with what he says to the Twelve, uniquely in *Luke*, hours before his arrest: "I tell you, this scripture must be fulfilled in me, 'And he was counted among the lawless (*anomōn*)'."[23]

For a man who *must* be 'counted among' the guilty, there is no reason—political or theological—to waste his breath in protestations of innocence. There is both a prophetic hauteur and a political cynicism to Jesus' silence—and to this uniquely Lucan defence of his silence. These appear, to me, to cohere beautifully with the figure we observe in many other scenes in *Luke* and the other gospels.

"Why Do You Persecute Me?"

The next time in *Luke–Acts* that we hear Jesus questioning a functionary of the courts is when his blinding apparition asks Saul—later Paul—on a road in Roman Syria: "*Saoul, Saoul*, why do you persecute me?" (*Acts of the Apostles* 9:4).

It is affecting that Jesus calls his persecutor *Saoul*, in Aramaic—and not *Saulos*, in Greek. The resurrected Christ is still using his mother-tongue.[24] And it is remarkable, too, that *Luke's* Jesus only begins to question agents of the court once his questions will have some effect:[25] Why do you persecute me?

Whether one takes this to be a sign of mystical, historical or novelistic perfection, it is a piece of consummate artistry and immense psychological depth. I have long felt that Jesus' question to Paul is the most compelling witness to the resurrection-event. Jesus is a questioner throughout his natural life, and after his death it is exquisitely true to form that he would introduce himself to a judicial adversary in Syria—one who will ultimately die for him in Italy—by means of a question.[26]

But during his trials in *Luke*, Jesus is obdurately silent. The authority of darkness has—if *Acts* can be trusted, temporarily—cancelled his right to question his persecutors.

"Why Do You Ask Me?"

Not so in *John*, where the synoptic gospels' Gethsemane is a nameless garden, the Pharisees are among those who seize Jesus, and the chaotic desertion of the disciples is a provision made by the wanted man himself. "If you are looking for me", Jesus tells the high priest's cohort, "let these men go" (*John* 18:1–8).

Caiaphas is named in *John*, and it seems to be implied that he questions Jesus on the night before his death. It is from his house in *John*, as in the synoptics, that Jesus is led to Pilate on the day of the crucifixion (*John* 18:24, 28). However, on the night before the crucifixion, *John*—and only *John*—sketches a scene in which Jesus is questioned by Annas, a former high priest and Caiaphas' father-in-law. For, though the high priests were installed and deposed by Romans, the office had a quasi-hereditary character.

In *John*, Jesus is bound before he is taken to the high priest—meaning, in the first instance, to Annas (*John* 18:12). Peter is not alone in this high priest's courtyard but is pictured with another of Jesus' disciples. They are both drawn to "a charcoal fire", says *John*, "because it was cold" (*John* 18:15–18). It is here, warming himself at the fire, that Peter denies his love for Jesus (*John* 18:25–27). But there is no sign in *John* that the other disciple, who is not named, is ever troubled about his ties to Jesus. This may be because, as we are told, this other disciple is somehow "known to the high priest" (*John* 18:16); Peter is a stranger.

Annas tries to draw Jesus out in a preliminary investigation—and he fails. *John* only says that the high priest (as *John* calls him, out of deference for the office) asks Jesus "about his disciples and about his teaching". The Galilean seems to think that the pontiff is disingenuous. "I have spoken openly to the world", he says, "I have said nothing in secret". Then he poses a counter-question: "Why do you ask me?" (*John* 18:19–21). *John*'s Jesus—unlike *Luke*'s—interrogates his interrogators.

The audacity of this prophetic tactic is not unfelt by those present. "When he had said this", we read, "one of the attendants standing nearby struck him on the face, saying, 'Is that how you answer a high priest?'" (*John* 18:22). Jesus is unimpressed by the question and by the judicial torture. His next question to Annas will concern us later.

Here, we can say that Annas' interrogation of Jesus is brief and heated. *John* tells us that, during the night, "Annas sent Jesus bound to Caiaphas the high priest" (*John* 18:24). But this is the last we hear of the prisoner, or the high priest, till "early in the morning" when Jesus is being led "from Caiaphas to Pilate's praetorium" (*John* 18:28).

"The Hour Is Coming"

Caiaphas is a tremendously important character in *John*, not because of anything he says on the night before Jesus' death—in fact, he says nothing—but because of something *John* (or an editor) says about him, seemingly in passing. "Caiaphas", says *John* shortly after Jesus' arrest, "was the one who advised the Judaeans that it was better to have one person die for the people" (*John* 18:14).

This is a formal citation in *John* 18 of a scene in *John* 11 which comes immediately before the Incident with the Alabaster Jar. It is here, in *John*'s chronology—and not, as in *Mark* and *Matthew*, on the night before his death—that a Judaean council decides to neutralize Jesus (*John* 11:45–53). The scene is heavy with prophecy, politico-theological reasoning and ecclesiological imagery.

In *John*'s Passion narrative, however, we are only reminded that Caiaphas is a figure who reasons that it is "better to have one person die for the people" (*John* 18:14). In the case of Jesus, reasons *John*, Caiaphas' piece of *Realpolitik* reasoning is a divinely inspired prophecy (*John* 11:51). This is fascinating. But we can only ask, here, *why* is Caiaphas so certain that *Jesus* must be the one to die?

The high priest tells us with stunning clarity in *John* 11. "If we let him go on like this", he says, "the Romans will come and destroy both *our holy place* and *our nation*" (*John* 11:48).[27] We could not hope for a sharper delineation of the archaic temple-state which, *by putting Jesus to death*, Caiaphas inadvertently helped to destroy.

For Caiaphas is nervous that one archaic temple-state, Rome, will destroy another. And this is, of course, what occurs some forty years after Jesus' death. But *John* modulates Caiaphas' idea about Jesus dying "for the nation"—that is, for the Judaean nation—by commenting that Jesus would, *unknown* to Caiaphas, be dying for all "the dispersed children of God" (*John* 11:51–52).

Nothing could matter less, in this context, than the historicity of Caiaphas' saying or the truth of *John*'s gloss. What is crucial is just that we glimpse, here, a Christian divergence. *John* imagines a Christian divergence from the idea of a temple-state which, however much their 'religions' may have differed, Rome and Judaea had in common.[28]

The mystery of Jesus' life and death in *John* is that it begins to "gather into one (*sunagagei eis hen*) the dispersed children of God"—Judaeans and gentiles—*without* gathering them into a territorial 'holy place' or an ancestral 'nation' (*John* 11:51–52). What this history of mystical, non-national 'gathering' intimates is precisely a birth of *religion*.[29] The sense of this term is something that much recent scholarship has correctly seen as a Christian form and derivation. And there is nothing modern or late modern about this idea.

We see this in Jesus' conversation with a woman of Samaria in *John* 4. "Our ancestors worshipped on this mountain", she tells Jesus (gesturing to Mount Gerizim), "but you say that the place where people must worship is in Jerusalem" (gesturing to Mount Zion). Note the symmetry. It is not the topographical difference, but the *structural symmetry* that is crucial. It is this symmetry that I have called the *temple-state*.

In Jesus' reply, it is precisely this symmetry that he perceives—and transcends. "Woman, believe me", he says, "the hour is coming when you will worship the Father *neither* on this mountain *nor* in Jerusalem". To the Samaritan woman's 'ancestors' and 'mountain', and to Caiaphas' 'holy place' and 'nation', Jesus in *John* 4, in a coolly prophetic tone, brings what he calls "worship in spirit and truth" (*John* 4:19–24).

The meaning of this is, perhaps, not clear in *John* 4. It may not ever be clear. (Or, conceivably, the hour is still coming.) All that is certain is that *John*'s Jesus, with 'spirit' and 'truth', transcends the Samaritan logic of 'ancestors' and 'mountain'. And *John* (or his redactor), with 'the dispersed children of God', transcends the Judaean logic of 'holy place' and 'nation'. Something new is being formulated in these pages, and it is surely related to what later Christians—and many post-Christians—think of as religion.

It could thus, perhaps, be said that Jesus' rejection by the temple-state of Judaea, and his crucifixion by the temple-state of Rome, not only give rise to a religion, but, further, these give rise to *religion*.

officeholder in Jerusalem, circa 30, is a pontiff—and the highest officeholder in Rome, circa 30, is a pontiff. The Roman emperor, at the time of Jesus' death, is the "supreme pontiff" (*pontifex maximus*) of the Roman cultus.[7]

Pilate is therefore not a secular prefect who receives Jesus from a religious court in Jerusalem. Pilate resides in Caesarea—a city named for the divine and semi-divine Caesars—as a legate of the Roman temple-state in the Judaean temple-state. As Tiberius' officer, Pilate speaks and acts on behalf of the supreme pontiff of the Roman imperium. And from the tumults chronicled by Philo and Josephus, we may conclude that Pilate was zealous in asserting the sacred rights of the Roman temple-state.[8]

Jesus' transfer to a Roman tribunal must be seen as a shift from the jurisdiction of Caiaphas' temple-state to Tiberius'. Early on the morning of his death, Jesus is led by officers of the Judaean high priest, Caiaphas, to the praetorium of an officer of the Roman high priest, Tiberius. The reformulation of charges is not a question of recasting a Judaean *religious* crime as a Roman *secular* crime. Rather, what we can detect is that the charge of sedition is transposed from the Judaean temple-state (Greek *blasphēmia*) to the Roman temple-state (Latin *maiestas*).

I am by no means *identifying* the charge of blasphemy in Judaea with the charge of majesty in Rome. It is apparent that there is not an exact equivalency between the Judaean and Roman charges; this is a part of the drama. Pilate is *unconvinced* that Jesus' sedition within the Judaean temple-state constitutes sedition within the Roman temple-state. And if *Luke*'s Herod-trial is accepted, Herod is unconvinced, too. There are vast and intricate differences *between* the legal apparatuses of first-century Judaea and Rome—and *within* them.

The only symmetry I am proposing, between *blasphēmia* and *maiestas*, is at the highest level—at the level of the 'temple-state'. Judaean blasphemy differs from Roman majesty, just as the office of high priest in Jerusalem differs from that in Rome. But both signify *the crime of perceived hostility—hostility to a political order and a sacrificial cult, converging upon a single figure—a supreme pontiff.*

In Rome, the supreme pontiff is Tiberius, whom Pilate represents; in Jerusalem, the supreme pontiff is Caiaphas. The crime of blasphemy, decided by Caiaphas, stigmatizes Jesus as an enemy of the Judaean temple-state; the crime of majesty, decided by Pilate, dooms him as an enemy of the Roman temple-state.

"Betrayed into Human Hands"

Jesus' conveyance to Pilate marks a legal and dramatic shift. He is transferred from the jurisdiction of his *ancestral* temple-state to that of a *gentile* temple-state. Yet it is worth noting that, when he predicts his death, he does *not* say that he will be abandoned by the courts of 'God' to the powers of 'Caesar'. Rather, Jesus predicts that he will be handed over by the Judaean elites to the Romans.

To be more concrete: what he warns his disciples, in all the synoptic gospels, is that

(i)   he will be "rejected" by the Temple elites and killed;[9]
(ii) he will be "betrayed into human hands" and killed;[10] and
(iii) although the Temple elites will "condemn him to death", they will "then hand him over to the gentiles" to be humiliated and killed.[11]

As in prediction (i), the synoptic gospels and *Acts of the Apostles* conceive Jesus' Passion as a rejection-drama by the rulers of his ancestral cult in Jerusalem. He is portrayed as the Christ throughout the gospels, and yet is condemned by Judaea's rulers as an impostor.

In prediction (iii), this rejection-drama is intensified by his humiliation at the hands of gentile rulers—that is, by the 'kings of the earth' of *Psalm 2* and *Acts of the Apostles* 4.[12] Since it is the task and grace of Israel's Anointed to vanquish the 'kings of the earth' (as in *Psalm* 2), Jesus' punishment by gentiles represents the total degradation for a Christ-figure. Note, though, that neither his prophecy of rejection by Judaeans, nor humiliation by gentiles, runs along the God–Caesar divide he has articulated.

Rather, in prediction (ii), Jesus says that he will be betrayed "into human hands" (Greek *eis cheiras anthrōpōn*, Latin *in manus hominum*). This is interesting. The humanity of the hands that will brutalize Christ links together the Judaeans in prediction (i) and his gentile executioners in prediction (iii). The conceptual bond that Jesus draws in *Mark*, the bond that he draws between the Judaean and Roman phases of his Passion, is precisely that of "human hands".[13] The rejection of Jesus by Judaeans is a *human* thing, and the execution of Jesus by Romans is a *human* thing.

In the gospels, there is no consciousness that the Judaean indictment of Jesus is religious, but that his Roman punishment is secular. In his predictions of his Passion, Jesus describes both phases—if my reading is correct—as *human*. And yet the prophetic context seems, to me, to intimate that both powers which punish him are human in precisely such a way that they, *like* Peter (in *Mark* 8), have not discerned the *rupture* which Jesus introduces between "the things that are God's" and "the things of humankind".[14]

It is precisely *because* both Judaea and Rome are temple-states that Jesus stresses their *humanity*. Far from enhaloing the religious character of Caiaphas' tribunal, Jesus refers indifferently to the "human hands" of the Judaean and Roman temple-states. That is to say, in light of his God–Caesar contrast, neither Caiaphas nor Pilate seems to represent 'God'. By stressing their humanity, Jesus seems to have placed the Judaean elites who reject him under the rubric of 'Caesar'. This, ironically, is where they place themselves in the last phase of *John*'s Pilate trial.

Both tribunals *regard themselves* as vested with a divine (or semi-divine) authority. It is Jesus who implies that their authority is *merely human*. The hands with which they seize, strike and punish him are what he derisively—or, de-mystifyingly—calls "human hands".[15] The high priest of Judaea and the prefect of Rome *only* symbolize, and *only* realize, "the things of human-kind" in Jesus' Passion. In his sufferings, and in his bizarre insistence on the things of God and things of Caesar, it is Jesus himself who represents, in the tribunals of *both* Caiaphas and Pilate, "the things that are God's".[16]

It is Jesus who says—condescendingly, or prophetically—that the judgements uttered, and the punishments inflicted, are not sanctified by the divinized Caesars or by Moses' divine law code. They are merely the work of human hands.

This is certainly not a total picture of Jesus' prophetic conception of the powers—pagan or Judaean—which end his natural life in Roman Judaea, circa 30. But this politically realist, de-mystifying Jesus can help to correct a modern historiography which sees Christianity as a supreme force of *political mystification*.[17]

In the first centuries of our era, it is precisely for *political reasons* that pagans perceived Christians as *atheists*. One of the most radically de-mystifying sayings of Jesus is found in *John* 16, where he warns the Eleven (Judas has exited the scene) that "the hour is coming when those who kill you will think that by doing so, they are offering worship to God" (*John* 16:2). Jesus' sayings concerning punishment by "human hands" in the synoptics and "the world" in *John*, seem to diminish, somehow, the divine-law sanction of Caiaphas, and the divinized-ruler sanction of Pilate.[18]

One of the aspects of Jesus' drama of truth, and of what he calls "the authority of darkness" (*Luke* 22:52–53), is that the political elimination of an innocent man is misconceived as an act of "worship to God" (*John* 16:2). Jesus strips the theological patina on violence from the temple-state of Judaea, no less than of Rome. As for Galilee and Peraea, Jesus refuses to even speak to Herod Antipas, a man whose father refurbished the Temple (*Luke* 23:8–9). The divine self-conception of these temple-states is part of what Jesus consigns to "the things of humankind".

In the gospels, the divinization of human power is depicted as a *human affair*. And, according to Jesus, it is *intensely human* to condemn the innocent *in the name of God or the gods*.

"If You Had Known What This Means"

This is most trenchantly stated in a saying unique to *Matthew*, in which he tells the Pharisees: "If you had known what this means, 'I desire mercy and not sacrifice'"—a line from the prophet Hosea—"'you would not have condemned the guilt-less'".[19] Perhaps Jesus' contrast of 'mercy' and 'sacrifice' in this saying could be inscribed within the contrastive logic that we have seen:

God	Caesar
God	Currency
House of God	House of Commerce
Things of God	Things of Humankind
Authority from Heaven	Authority from Humans
Mercy	Sacrifice

That Jesus seems to assign 'mercy' to a new form of life, and 'sacrifice' to the unconscious persecution of "the guiltless", is interesting (*Matthew* 12:6–7). For sacrifice—a highly formalized cult of animal immolation—is something that Rome and Judaea have in common. Early Christians incrementally abandoned sacrifice, and late antique Christians legally abolished it.[20]

However that may be, the final condemnation of 'the guiltless'—putting an end to Jesus' life—is not made by the Temple courts, but by Pilate. And it is time to see how Pilate is depicted in the gospels' trial narratives.

PART SEVEN

DARKNESS AND LIGHT

19

JESUS THE CONVICT

Pilate's decisive question to Jesus, on the morning of his death, is this: "Are you the King of the Judaeans?" In *Mark*, *Matthew* and *Luke*, the Galilean prophet only speaks once to the gentile prefect. He says: "You say so" (*Mark* 15:2).[1]

After uttering this enigmatic reply, *Mark's* Jesus is mystifyingly silent—during his trial, judicial torture, and suspension from a stake and crossbeam—until he cries out in his death-throes: "My God, my God, why have you deserted me?" (*Mark* 15:34). This desolate cry is an echo of *Psalm 22*, but no less crucially, it is a *question*.

The Gospel According to Silence

Though Jesus questions God with one of his last breaths, he never questions Caesar's deputy in *Mark*. It is precisely Jesus' silence, his manifest uninterest in swaying his judge or deflecting his accusers, that seems to shock and intrigue Pilate. For *Mark* stresses the number of charges that are levelled against him. The legal brief is so heavy that Pilate urges the Galilean to defend himself. "See how many charges they bring against you", the prefect says. Jesus is unmoved; and Pilate is amazed (*Mark* 15:3–5).

This tradition of Jesus' silence, and Pilate's amazement, is not unrealistic. I read it as a luminous moment in what Sigizmund Krzhizhanovsky calls, in a Soviet-suppressed novel of the 1920s, *The Gospel According to Silence*. What is this lost 'gospel'? Though it is purely fictional, the novelist's insight is not. For what Krzhizhanovsky imagines is a medieval 'text' composed by a nameless monk, consisting entirely of biblical scenes in which Jesus remains silent.[2] And it is true that the Galilean's uncanny silence is one of his defining traits—as in the Incident of the Adulteress, where he bends, unrushed, to write something inconclusive in the dirt before he speaks. In literary terms, it is perfectly natural for Pilate to be struck by such silence.[3]

And in *Mark*, Jesus' silence alone seems to convince Pilate that he is not a Zealot-style rebel (Greek *lēstēs*). That the Roman senses the incorrectness of the charge—sedition (or *maiestas*)—recurs clearly in all the canonical Passion narratives. In *Mark*, it is signalled by Pilate's question, "What evil has he done?"[4] It would be a mistake to diminish the force of this question.[5] For in Pascal's words: "Jesus Christ did nothing but teach humans that they loved themselves, that they were slaves, blind, sick, unhappy, and sinners."[6] Where is the evil in that?

We must recall, too, that a reluctance to convict Jesus solely on the strength of hostile testimony is something that Judaean and Roman judges have in common. In *Matthew*, *Mark* and *Luke*, we see that Caiaphas and his council *refrain* from condemning him until he has 'implicated' himself by speaking unequivocally—and this is what he refuses to do in Pilate's hearing.[7]

"No Respect for Humans"

A number of narrative elements seem to structure the Pilate trial in the canonical gospels. To enumerate these in *Mark* is not to 'harmonize' his trial narrative with *Matthew*, *Luke*, and *John*.

Rather, it is to uncover a narrative structure which seems, to me, to inspire the shifting traditions.

If premodern 'harmonies' of the gospels often muted real dissonances, modern critical readings tend to dissolve any 'harmonizable' logic among the four Passions. It is this deep structure—and not a 'harmonized' chronology—which concerns us in the coming pages.

The logic of Jesus' Pilate trial in *Mark* is determined by the following elements:

(i) Pilate senses that he is being used by the Temple aristocracy.[8]

In *Mark*, we read he "realized that it was out of jealousy"—which is to say, *not* out of concern for Roman legality—"that the chief priests had handed Jesus over" (*Mark* 15:10).

(ii) A crowd is massed before Pilate's tribunal, and it is under the influence of the Temple elites.[9]

Mark notes how "the chief priests stirred up the crowd" during Jesus' Roman trial (*Mark* 15:11).

(iii) Pilate knows that there is a convict in prison, Barabbas (a name that may mean no more than "son of a father"), whose guilt is not in doubt.[10]

Mark writes that Barabbas "was in prison with the rebels who had committed murder during the insurrection" (*Mark* 15:7). The only other mention of this 'insurrection' is in *Luke*, who copies it from *Mark* (*Luke* 23:19).

(iv) Pilate has a custom of liberating one prisoner at Passover (the historicity of this custom, the so-called *privilegium Paschale*, is doubted), and he makes a bid to liberate Jesus.[11]

In *Mark*, Pilate asks the crowd that has formed before his tribunal: "Do you want me to release for you the King of the Judaeans?" (*Mark* 15:9).

Notice how tight the construction is, thus far, in *Mark*. Pilate's sense (i) that he is being used by the Temple aristocracy justifies (iii) his preference of Jesus, whom he has not sentenced, over Barabbas, whom he (or some other Roman judge) has sentenced. And (ii) the presence of a crowd justifies (iv) Pilate's invocation of his habit of giving one prisoner *to* the crowd at Passover (*Mark* 15:6). The basic logic of the scene is conserved by *Matthew* and *Luke* and is, I think, discernible in *John*. With it, the gruesome dénouement of the Pilate trial could already be predicted.

Some other basic elements are introduced by *Mark* and reflected in all the canonical Passions:

(v) "Stirred up" by the Temple elites, the crowd insists that Jesus (convicted by a *Judaean* court) must be crucified, and Barabbas (convicted by a *Roman* court) must be liberated.[12]

It is not hard to believe that a Judaean crowd would prefer a man convicted by the Romans (Barabbas) to one convicted by Judaeans (Jesus).

(vi) Pilate's reluctance to condemn Jesus is rooted in his sense that the Galilean is not a hardened fighter seeking the *passé*.

Herodian title of "King of the Judaeans". This reluctance has an institutional logic, too. The imperial prefect resists being used by the provincial nobility.[13]

(vii) Pilate makes a concession to the crowd by liberating Barabbas, a Roman convict, and sentencing Jesus, a Judaean convict.[14]

Pilate's willingness to yield to a Judaean crowd—"overwhelmed by the purity of their superstition"—is attested by both Philo and Josephus.[15]

(viii) Before the Galilean is crucified *by the Romans*, he is humiliated *by the Romans*.[16]

The first gospel, *Mark*, places it out of doubt that it is Pilate's troops who "led Jesus out to crucify him", and that they only did this after they had brutalized him in "the courtyard of the palace" (*Mark* 15:16–20).

(ix) The juridical inscription on Jesus' cross is Roman, not Judaean.[17]

In the narrative logic of *Mark* and the other gospels, this is a conclusive sign that Jesus is sentenced by a Roman judge who is *not* convinced of his guilt ('majesty')—and not by a Judaean judge who *is* ('blasphemy').

If this reconstruction of the gospels' logic is correct, then it is a well-constructed narrative. Because a 'crowd' in Jerusalem holds Jesus to be a prophet or the Christ, the Temple elites can only arrest Jesus at night—with Judas' help. For the same reason, the Temple court can only kill him with Pilate's help. The prefect senses that he is being used, and dislikes it. However, he can only pacify the 'crowd', who holds Jesus to be an impostor, by crucifying him.

The secrecy of Jesus' capture and nocturnal interrogation is determined by one faction in Jerusalem which hopes that he is "the one to redeem Israel" (*Luke* 24:21). The political necessity of his crucifixion is determined by another faction which believes that he is "perverting [the] nation" (*Luke* 23:2).

But Jesus is not flogged or crucified by a mob in Jerusalem, nor by the Judaean nobility. He is condemned by a Roman judge who declares himself *unconvinced* of Jesus' guilt, and he is nailed up by gentile conscripts. It is hard not to be reminded of the judge in Jesus' parable who has "no fear of God or respect for humans" (*Luke* 18:2). Jesus seems not to have held lawyers and judges in high regard, and there certainly is nothing high-minded in the legal ordeal that *Mark* narrates. Pilate tortures, ritualistically degrades and kills a man he sees to be no normal enemy of Rome.

But it is precisely this which leads us to *Matthew*, the only gospel in which Jesus' gentile judge tries to rinse the bloodguilt off his hands.

Three Traditions, Two Myths

Matthew enhances *Mark*'s Pilate trial with three vivid traditions. First, he offers a humanizing account of Judas' suicide.[18] Second, he relates a dream in which Jesus' innocence is revealed. It is Pilate's wife, Procula—her name in Christian tradition—who sends word of this dream once her husband has taken his place "on the judgement seat" (*Matthew* 27:19). But she is "more awake than Pilate", says Kierkegaard, "who did not dream".[19] And in the end, her husband's reality-principle prevails.

It is *Matthew*'s third tradition that concerns us here. He writes that before Pilate "handed Jesus over to be crucified", he "took some water and washed his hands before the crowd, saying, 'I am innocent of this man's blood'" (*Matthew* 27:24–26). In this brief, histrionic gesture—unique to *Matthew*—is born the myth of Pilate's innocence, and, with it, centuries of Christian bitterness. For coupled with Pilate's protestation of innocence, there is a moment—unique to *Matthew*—in which "the people as a whole" cry out: "His blood be on us and on our children!" (*Matthew* 27:25).

In the text of *Matthew*, Pilate's gesture and the Judaeans' cry are counterpoised. But in the dismal reception history of *Matthew*'s Passion, a myth of Pilate's innocence is tied to a myth of undying Judaean bloodguilt. We cannot concern ourselves here with the sad history of both myths.[20] Rather, we can only glance at the meaning of (i) Pilate's gesture, and (ii) the Judaeans' cry within the literary horizons of *Matthew*. It is clear that the trope of Pilate's innocence, and the sick notion of undying Judaean bloodguilt, are both myths in the lowest sense—catastrophic failures of interpretation.

To my mind, it is *not* necessary to suspect anti-Judaean biases in *Matthew*, but it *is* necessary to recognize anti-Judaean biases in many Christian churches. Put differently, though these myths are *derived* from the gospels, I have become convinced that they represent a failure of many in the churches to read their most revered texts.

"See to It Yourselves"

Pilate concludes his hand-rinsing act by saying to 'the crowd' of Judaeans, "See to it yourselves"—meaning, see to the crucifixion of Jesus (*Matthew* 27:24). But *Matthew*'s prose is pellucid. It is Pilate who releases Barabbas. And it is Pilate who, after having Jesus scourged, hands him over to be crucified.

Further, *Matthew* tells us in words which defy mis-construal who it is that tortures Jesus, and then crucifies him. It is "the soldiers of the governor (*tou hēgemonos*)", meaning Pilate. They then lead Jesus into the courtyard of the Jerusalem palace, in which Pilate is in residence. It is these Roman conscripts who then brutalize the Galilean convict before leading him off to crucify him (*Matthew* 27:26–31).

The text of *Matthew* is perfectly clear. It is Pilate's troops who degrade, torture, and crucify Jesus. What, then, is the meaning of this line: "See to it yourselves"? Is it meaningless? Or is it a fore-echo of the second-century Christian myth—that Judaeans, and not Romans, nail Jesus to the cross?[21]

It is neither.

It is an echo of the Temple elites' words to Judas. Earlier in *Matthew* 27, after Judas says that he has "sinned by betraying innocent blood", the conspirators' reply is pitiless. "What is that to us?" they say, "See to it yourself" (*Matthew* 27:4).[22] The only thing that Judas sees to is his own demise. But having said to Jesus' betrayer, 'See to it yourself', the Temple elites then 'see to'

Jesus' blood-money by purchasing "a burial-place for foreigners" (*Matthew* 27:5–10).

The historicity of this sequence is of no interest for us. What matters here is just that, in *Matthew* 27, the Temple elite's line, 'See to it yourself', is calloused when first uttered. It is then revealed, following Judas' death, to be hypocritical. No one holds that this blood-money pericope shows Judas to be innocent.[23] And it is impossible to construe the Sadducees' reply, 'See to it yourself', as exculpatory.

The structure of Pilate's hand-washing scene, twenty lines later, is identical. Just as the Judaean rulers say to one who has 'handed over' an innocent man to them, "See to it yourself" (*Matthew* 27:4); a gentile ruler says to those who have 'handed over' an innocent man to him, "See to it yourselves" (*Matthew* 27:24). In Judas' blood-money scene, and in Pilate's hand-washing scene, the line is cold—and hypocritical.

Though it has roots in Hebrew prophecy and Cynic philosophy, the prominence of 'hypocrisy' in western consciousness owes much—perhaps most—to the sayings of Jesus. In a stanza from the book of *Isaiah*, which Jesus quotes, a hypocrite is anyone who does not honour in their heart what they honour with their lips.[24] Jesus is a scourge of 'hypocrites'—the Greek word for 'stage actors' (*hupokrites*)—and it is in large part thanks to his sayings that we have such a sharp notion of what one is.

A hypocrite is someone who, as Jesus says in *Matthew* 23, looks "righteous to others" on what he calls "the outside", but is full of "lawlessness" and "filth" on what he calls "the inside".[25] The genealogy of 'interiority' is a recurring question in intellectual history. Jesus is manifestly inspired by *Isaiah*'s contrast between 'lips' (outer) and 'heart' (inner), but he accentuates this contrast—and with it, a concern with 'hypocrisy'—in radical ways.[26] To my mind, western interiority begins here.

And it is shocking that Christians have convinced themselves that Pilate's hand-washing is somehow a mark of his 'innocence' in *Matthew* 27. Jesus denounces just such hypocritical ablutions four chapters earlier, in *Matthew* 23. This is Jesus, speaking to "the crowds and to his disciples"—in the Temple, it seems[27]—days before his death:

> Woe to you ... hypocrites! For you clean the outside of the cup and of the plate, but inside you are full of greed and self-indulgence ...
>
> Woe to you ... hypocrites! For you are like whitewashed tombs, which on the outside look beautiful, but inside they are full of the bones of the dead. (*Matthew* 23:25–28)

The relevance of this prophetic denunciation is glaring. In *Matthew* 27, Pilate actualizes the image of the 'whitewashed tomb', dipping his hands in a basin while he fills himself with 'the bones of the dead'. That Christians could have *failed* to read this in the light of *Matthew* 23 is terrible. Sadly, however, they did.

The responsibility for the misreading of Pilate's gesture lies with Christian interpreters, however, not with the gospel-writer. For it is only in *Matthew* that Jesus compares pagan and Judaean prayer cultures, criticizing both (*Matthew* 6:5–8).[28] There is no reason whatever, strictly within the confines of this gospel, why his bold critique of Judaean purity culture cannot be brought to bear on Pilate's ad hoc ablution.

And it is *Matthew*—only *Matthew*—who has Jesus say, unflinchingly: "If your right hand causes you to sin, cut it off and throw it away" (*Matthew* 5:30). Now, it is crucial to note that Jesus gives no prophetic sanction to the practice of mutilation. On the contrary, in all the gospels, he is a *healer* of paralysed or disfigured—which is to say, powerless—hands. But this bloody saying about self-mutilation—the bloodiness marks its serious, oracular nature—shows that it certainly takes more than dipping one's hands in a fingerbowl to clear oneself, in *Matthew*, of judicial murder.

I JUDGE NO ONE

"Weep for Yourselves and Your Children"

The Jesus of *Matthew* links his own wrongful death—and "the blood of the prophets"—to the doom of Jerusalem and the desecration of the Temple. He censures his contemporaries for being "descendants of those who murdered the prophets"—by which he means, descendants who will themselves murder prophets.[29]

This is insulting now—and, undeniably, it was insulting then. In *Luke* 11 (which has parallels in *Matthew* 23), a lawyer cautions Jesus: "Teacher, when you say these things, you *insult* us (*hēmas hubrizeis*)!" But Jesus is undeterred, saying: "Woe to you lawyers! For you have taken away the key of knowledge" (*Luke* 11:45, 52). This is not a conciliatory move—but it is not the task of a prophet to flatter or conciliate.

Jesus is an heir of the prophets who said, in God's name, to a certain Judaea: "I hate, I despise your festivals" (*Amos* 5:21); and to a certain Judaean elite: "Many houses will become desolate, great mansions left unoccupied" (*Isaiah* 5:9). Ezekiel is a prophet who is, in Spinoza's commentary, "seething with fury"—and Jeremiah is a prophet obsessed with "the calamities of the Jews".[30]

Prophets denounce.

The question is, then, *to whom* is the guilt of Jesus' death linked in the gospels, particularly in *Matthew*? And Jesus tells us himself: "All this will come upon this generation" (*Matthew* 23:36).

This is, of course, precisely what we hear in the Judaeans' horrifically misinterpreted cry: "His blood be on us and on our children!" (*Matthew* 27:25). This self-imprecation is a gospel-writer's gloss on Jesus' saying. For within the literary horizons of the gospels, Jesus clearly foretells that destruction would come on *his contemporaries in Jerusalem, and on their children.*

There is a more compassionate gloss on the same motif in *Luke*, where Jesus says to the "daughters of Jerusalem", just moments before he is crucified: "Do not weep for me, but weep for yourselves and your children" (*Luke* 23:28). He is clearly warning his contemporaries that they *and their children* will suffer greatly. In this and numerous other sayings, the fall of Jerusalem in 70 CE is 'foretold'. (Note that Socrates, too, "prophesies" or "utters an oracle" against the Athenian citizen-judges who condemn him.)[31] Jerusalem's doom is prophetically tied to Jesus' death, but it is severely circumscribed. The gospel-writers believed that it *fell* on the generation of Jesus' contemporaries, and their children.

And the original sense of Judaean 'bloodguilt' is not only circumscribed by a generation. It is circumscribed by *a city*, or more accurately, by *the province of Judaea*. The 'people' who claim Jesus' death in *Matthew* 27 are nothing like Eve, "the mother of all the living", or Abraham, "the father of a multitude of nations" (*Genesis* 3:20, 17:5). They are, in the strictest sense, Judaeans circa 30 CE. Not Hebrews of first-century Antioch nor Judaeans of fourth-century Rome, much less *Jüden* of sixteenth-century Saxony or Jews of twenty-first-century London.[32] Jesus' dicta in *Matthew* regarding the coming judgement are centred on Jerusalem and Judaea. "Those in Judaea", he warns, "must flee to the mountains" (*Matthew* 24:16).[33]

Josephus informs us that many Judaeans saw a stinging defeat of Herod Antipas as the divine retribution for his murder of John the Baptist. A pagan philosopher, Mara bar Sarapion, infers that Judaeans were punished for Jesus' death, *just as* Hellenes were for Socrates' death. And *Matthew* believes that Jesus' death is one cause of the fall of Jerusalem and desecration of the Herodian Temple in 70 CE—but only that. This notion is not *racialized* and is not, per se, *anti-Judaic*. The gross idea that some miasma of bloodguilt outlasts Jesus' generation is not only odious, but utterly foreign to *Matthew*.

Whatever one makes of the veracity of Pilate's hand-rinsing and the Judaeans' self-inculpating cry, the reception history of

Matthew's Passion is marked by base passions. The irony is, of course, that *Matthew* is the most 'Judaic' of the gospel-writers. There is no reason to doubt the heartbreak of his Jesus when he mourns Jerusalem: "Your house is left to you desolate!" (*Matthew* 23:38).

It cannot be denied, however, that imposing Christian commentators have gloated, century after century, where Jesus wept.

20

"WHAT IS TRUTH?"

In *John* 11, Jesus and the Twelve are living in the wilds beyond the Jordan, near the place where John the Baptist initiated those who came to hear him preach. They are living in seclusion because of a scene narrated in *John* 10. Namely, this.

Jesus is in Jerusalem in the wintertime to celebrate the Feast of Dedication (Hanukkah), and one of his discourses is nearly fatal for him. For one day, as he is "walking in the Temple, in the portico of Solomon", he says this of God: "The Father and I are one." On hearing this, we read, "the Judaeans took up stones ... to stone him".

Jesus is incredulous. "I have shown you many good works", he says, "for which of these are you going to stone me?" They reply: "It is not for a good work ... but for blasphemy, because you, though only a human being, are making yourself God." He deflects the charge. "Is it not written in your law", he asks—and it is striking that he calls the scriptures, "*your* law"—"'You are gods'?" (*John* 10:22–34).

I JUDGE NO ONE

"You Are Gods"

Jesus is citing a line, or a couplet, from *Psalm* 82. The poet imagines the God of Israel seated on a dais "in the divine council", encircled by beings he calls "the gods" (*Psalm* 82:1). The Lord then says to the luminous beings who govern the earth:

"You are gods,
    children of the Most High, all of you;
nevertheless, you shall die like mortals,
    and fall like any prince." (*Psalm* 82:6–7)

For historians of religion, *Psalm* 82 is a fascinating text since it seems to echo non-Israelite notions of divine kingship. The historical intrigue of this psalm is massively intensified by Jesus' (or *John's*) decision to cite it in his own defence.

Is Jesus only interested in this rare ascription of divinity to humans ('You are gods')? Or is he evoking the whole couplet, and in that way subtly predicting his own death ('You shall die like mortals')? These are questions we cannot pursue.

What matters for us in this scene is that it reveals Judaea to be a dangerous place for him. It is because of this that when he says to the Twelve, "Let us go to Judaea again", his disciples protest. "Rabbi", they say, "the Judaeans were just now trying to stone you, and are you going there again?" (*John* 11:7–8).

Jesus insists that they must re-enter Judaea. And the pericope ends with Thomas, the great doubter, saying: "Let us also go, that we may die with him" (*John* 11:16). What Thomas means is clear. Judaea is a place of death for Jesus, and of peril for the Twelve.

"We Have a Law"

The figure of 'the crowd' in the Roman trial of *Mark* and *Matthew*, which becomes 'the people' in *Luke*, becomes 'the Judaeans' in *John*. It is therefore common in premodern texts—

and in modern critical texts—for the Pilate trial in *John*, in which Jesus is lazily 'defended' by Pilate and feverishly charged by 'the Judaeans', to be interpreted in race-heavy terms.

It is 'the Judaeans' who inform a Roman prefect: "We have a law, and according to that law Jesus ought to die" (*John* 19:7). Exegetes must ask, then: Who are 'the Judaeans'? It is impossible to deny that *John* (and the Johannine circle) knew that this scene reflected badly on 'the Judaeans'. But who are they?

It is a terrible fact that the reception history of *John*'s Passion, like *Matthew*'s, is linked to racialized notions of 'Judaeans'. But it is also a fact that the gospel-writer states, in the first lines of his text, that a divine Word "illuminates every human" (*phōtizei panta anthrōpon*), and that "children of God" are not born "of blood, nor of the will of the flesh, nor of a husband's will" (*John* 1:9, 13). This powerfully contradicts any racialized idea of divine belonging. And this is a vision shared by a second-century Christian philosopher, Clement—to name only one—who recognizes "a certain divine effluence instilled into all humans without exception".[1]

Who, then, for the hand that wrote *John* 1, are 'the Judaeans' of *John* 19? The answer lies in the wilderness scene of *John* 11.

What does Jesus say to the Twelve? "Let us go to Judaea again." And what do the Twelve reply? "Rabbi, the Judaeans were just now trying to stone you" (*John* 11:7–8). This exchange settles the question of who 'the Judaeans' are in *John*—or rather, who they are *not*. They are certainly not a 'race' or a 'proto-race'. For Jesus and the Twelve are all Judaean by descent. Nor are they devotees of the Judaean cultus, since Jesus and the Twelve are devotees of that cultus, too. (Thus, Jesus' desire to 'go to Judaea' for the high holy days.) Nor are they are marked by their use of Israel's mother-tongue, for we notice what Jesus' nervous disciples call him, in *John*'s Greek, in this scene. They use the Hebrew honorific, *Rhabbi*.

But if 'the Judaeans' in *John*'s Passion are not defined by 'race', or cult, or mother-tongue, then how are they defined?

The answer—which is hid in this exchange in *John* 11 and can be read off the Pilate trial in *John* 19—is simple. 'Judaea' is a territorial entity defined *by law*, and 'the Judaeans' are a people defined *by law*. For what is the gospel-writer's anticipatory line in *John* 1? "The law was given through Moses." And what is Jesus' defence in *John* 10? There is a line written in "your law" (*nomōi humōn*). What is it that 'the Judaeans' say to Pilate in *John* 19? "We have a law" (*hēmeis nomon*).[2] Judaea, in *John*, is a polity—more precisely, a temple-state. And Judaeans, in *John*, are the members of that temple-state.

Judaea is a place of death for Jesus, and 'the Judaeans' are a threat to him, because—as *John* has them say—they 'have a law'.

All this is by way of introduction, but the clarification is an important one. It is time for anti-Semitic interpretations of *John*—by critical exegetes and, most urgently, by anti-Semites—to be rejected, finally. As the uniquely Johannine character of Nicodemus, "a Pharisee" and "ruler of the Judaeans" who comes to Jesus by night, shows: *John* is conclusively *not* one who thinks of divine belonging in terms of birth, but of rebirth (*John* 3:1–10). This idea of rebirth in *John* is akin, I think, to that of "repentance" (*metanoia*)—a change of mind and change of life—in the synoptic gospels. In any case, a proto-racist conception of Judaeans is demonstrably, *metaphysically* alien to the fourth gospel.

"I Find No Cause"

The Pilate trial in *John* cannot be decoded until we realize that Jesus is caught, not between symbols of 'race' or 'mentality'—Pilate and 'the Judaeans'—but between law-codes, neither of which recognizes him as a king.

The Judaean law is salient for *John* because Jesus and his accusers hold it in common. The gospel's rejection-drama is announced in *John* 1, where we read that Jesus "came to what was *his own*, and *his own* did not accept him" (*John* 1:11). But it is *Roman* legal reasoning—or, more precisely, a Roman political *threat*—which is conclusive of *John*'s Passion.

It is much clearer in *John* that the task of Jesus' accusers—the Temple elites and 'Judaeans'—is to express his crime within *their* legal culture as a crime within *Pilate's* legal culture. Their efforts, which are sequentially narrated by *John*, might seem to take them from the terrain of 'religious' Judaean law, on which Jesus claims to be the "Son of God" (*John* 19:7), to the terrain of 'secular' Roman law, on which he claims to be the "King of the Judaeans" (*John* 19:12). On a close reading, this is not what occurs.

From the very beginning, Pilate makes it clear that the Judaean charges have no place in a Roman court. After he converses with Jesus, he remains convinced. The Galilean has not committed, or incited, acts which are punishable by a Roman tribunal in the provinces. But Pilate is totally unconcerned with Jesus' fate. Much as *Matthew*'s Pilate says to the crowd, "See to it yourselves" (*Matthew* 27:24), *John*'s says to the Judaeans, not once but twice:

(i) "Take him yourselves and judge him according to your law." (*John* 18:31)
(ii) "Take him yourselves and crucify him." (*John* 19:6)

It is in light of this that we must read Pilate's judicial finding. He is not objecting to the proceedings for moral reasons, but for legal ones. And his language, in *John*, is legal:

(i) "I find no cause against him." (*John* 18:38)
(ii) "I find no cause against him." (*John* 19:4)
(iii) "I find no cause against him." (*John* 19:6)

The meaning of the word 'cause' (Greek *aitia*, Latin *causa*), here, is crucial. In a rare reflection on the obscure ties between the legal and philosophical concepts of 'cause' and 'guilt'—Latin *causa* and *culpa*—Giorgio Agamben observes that 'cause' is an archaic word which lacks a Latin etymology, and which marks "the threshold of the edifice of the law". He elaborates. "*Causa* is a certain situation, an 'affair'—in itself non-juridical—at the moment in which it is included in the sphere of the law."[3] Pilate's *judicial finding* is thus that the affair of the strange Galilean, Jesus, has no place within the sphere of Roman law.

This is not a declaration of Jesus' innocence.

That Pilate is categorically uninterested in 'innocence' is part of his glamorously nihilistic question: "What is truth?" (*John* 18:38). *John*'s prefect is bored by nebulous concepts like 'truth' and 'innocence', but he is—far more than the synoptics' prefect—a man of the law. He is a Roman judge, and his first question to Caiaphas and his clique is brusque and precise: "What accusation (*katēgorian*) do you bring against this man?" (*John* 18:29). When Pilate later states, three times, that he can find no cause, he is not speaking in Jesus' defence—he is speaking as a Roman functionary.

Pilate has not established, in Roman legal terms, the accusation levelled by the Judaeans. The prefect knows that the Temple court wants Jesus to be punished—that is, to be killed. And he of course knows that Judaeans have their own law. "Judge him", he says coolly, "according to your law" (*John* 18:31). But Romans, too, have *their* law—which is *his* law. And he has no desire to crucify 'this man' unless he is convinced that *the Judaeans' outrage can be rendered into Roman legal terms.*

The procedural logic of the Johannine trial is, I believe, as it should be:

(i) Pilate asks the Judaeans for the charge against Jesus (*John* 18:29).

(ii) After a brief skirmish (*John* 18:30–31), they allege that he claims to be King of the Judaeans—a Herodian title that Rome had annulled in 4 BCE (*John* 18:33–35).

(iii) Pilate then interrogates Jesus, asking him, "What have you done?" (*John* 18:35).

(iv) Jesus replies (*John* 18:36–37).

It is only after Pilate has (i) heard a charge which is construable in Roman legal terms, and (iv) has heard Jesus' reply, that

(v) He says for the first time, "I find no cause against him" (*John* 18:38).

Jesus' mystical 'kingship' is, for Pilate, legally null—and, for that matter, philosophically null ('What is truth?'). And this is not unrealistic.[4] The trial only ends when Pilate becomes convinced that his *notoriety* as 'King of the Judaeans' is legible in Roman legal (and political) terms. This occurs when

(vi) The Judaeans argue: "Everyone who claims to be a king sets himself up against Caesar" (*John* 19:12).

Now Pilate has his 'cause'. For "when Pilate heard these words",

(vii) "He brought Jesus outside and sat on the judge's chair" (John 19:13).

This moment in which Tiberius' legate seats himself on the *sella curulis*, or portable Roman tribunal, symbolizes Pilate's judgement of Jesus.[5]

Now, *John*'s Greek here can legitimately be taken to mean that Pilate "brought Jesus outside and made him"—Jesus—"sit on the judge's chair" (*John* 19:13).[6] This would mark a heightening of the theatre of cruelty which begins, in *John*, when Jesus is displayed "wearing the crown of thorns and the purple robe" (*John* 19:5).

This *Ecce homo*, or "Here is the man" sequence in *John* is a real grotesquery. Less than a century after *John* was written, Celsus comments that he cannot believe that any god or demi-god would permit his captors to "put a purple robe round him and the crown of thorns".[7] But it is, in a hermeneutical sense, harder to believe that Pilate would parody *himself* by placing Jesus on Rome's sacred tribunal.

I conclude that where *Luke* writes that "Pilate gave sentence" (*Luke* 23:24), *John* writes that he "sat on his judge's chair" (*John* 19:13). The dramatic meaning of these lines is the same. Pilate sentences Jesus to death in *John*, as in *Luke*. This is one of the "juridical facts" which modern commentators must decipher, as Elias Bickerman stressed in the 1930s.[8]

For Jesus is crucified, in *John*, as a Galilean convicted by Rome in the province of Judaea. All this is revealed in the death-script (Greek *titlos*, from the Latin *titulus*) that Pilate composes in the languages "of the Hebrews, the Romans, and the Greeks"—namely,

JESUS OF NAZARETH, KING OF THE JUDAEANS.

(*John* 19:19–20)[9]

Or, rather, Jesus' Galilean provenance and Judaean 'crime' are both revealed in this *titulus*. It is the form of Jesus' death—his cross, death-script, and sentence written in the Romans' tongue (*Rhōmaisti* in *John*'s Greek)—which marks him as a non-citizen, and Galilean, put to death for a Roman political crime.

"The Noble Scorn of a Roman"

Jesus is not a judge, a punisher or a rebel. He is not a political Christ (à la Reimarus), and his prophetic life is not essentially political. Yet he is not silent on Roman politics.

He criticizes "the great ones" who tyrannize pagan nations (*Mark* 10:42–43), and he refuses to imitate "the kings of the gentiles" who are called "benefactors" but are, in truth, exploiters (*Luke* 22:25–26). He is not uninformed about the Romans' brutalization of non-Romans—though he never criticizes the Caesars, or the prefect of Judaea, by name (*Luke* 13:1–5).

And he is not silent on Graeco-Roman religion. He criticizes pagan forms of prayer (*Matthew* 6:7–8), though no more severely than he criticizes Judaean forms (*Matthew* 6:5–6). In his Sermon on the Mount, he seems to suggest that "the gentiles" (*hoi ethnikoi*) are "the same" as Judaeans, in that gentiles only greet other gentiles in first-century cities (*Matthew* 5:47). His main critique of pagan gods seems to be that their devotees live in anxiety about what they will eat, drink and wear (*Matthew* 6:32; *Luke* 12:30). In this he differs from many of the Hebrew prophets, who denounced pagan cults and mores—and the Judaeans who blurred into them.

Jesus is a critic, but not a *resister* of the pagan regime in Judaea. The word he brings is not what Kant calls a "political faith", and the logic of coercion is one that he renounces—*as* the Christ, *as* the "King of Israel" (*John* 12:13).[10] We never see him "laying down ordinances as a legislator", in Spinoza's phrase; rather, we see him "offering doctrine" like a philosopher, because his task is to "correct ... people's minds".[11]

In the synoptic gospels, Jesus' renunciation of the logic of coercion occurs in the first days of his prophetic life, in three dreamlike scenes of his temptation. In *John*, it occurs in the last hours of his prophetic life, during his interrogation and torture by a pagan magistrate.

In *John*'s Passion, we hear more than once the unconscious premise of Hierocles' fragment (in chapter 3), which is now being formulated by Jesus' critics and his judge. Because he is *charged*, in the last Passion narrative to be written, he is held to be *guilty*. This is even more philosophically inert than Hierocles' inference that because Jesus is a Roman *convict*, he must be guilty of insurrection. Consider:

(i) When Pilate asks the Temple elites for the accusation against Jesus, they reply: "If this man were not a criminal, we would not have handed him over" (*John* 18:29–30).

(ii) When Pilate asks Jesus "What have you done?" he echoes the elites' reasoning: "Your own nation and priesthood"—in a word, temple-state—"have handed you over to me" (*John* 18:35).

In reply, Jesus tells Pilate what he has done in the highly mystical and seemingly philosophical memoir we call *John*.[12] His prophetic calling, he says, is not to strive or fight with the temple-states of this world, but to testify to the truth. In his life, then, he has testified to the truth (*John* 18:36–38).

Pilate says, grinningly: What is truth?[13]

For Nietzsche, this question radiates the "noble scorn of a Roman, before whom a disgraceful misuse of the word 'truth' was perpetrated". For him, this judicial insult is "the only phrase *that has value*" in the gospels (his stress).[14]

The commentary of an old African prelate, Augustine, is more detached. His reading? Pilate's mind is on other, more mundane things. He is facing a hard question of legal procedure, and he thinks that he could, perhaps, crucify Barabbas—a political criminal—and rid himself of the mystifying rabbi. So, says Augustine, Pilate "did not wait for Jesus to reply to him concerning what the truth is".[15] He did not want a delay in the proceedings.

"I Did Not Come to Judge"

What *is* the truth to which Jesus testifies in *John*? "I did not come to judge the world", he says, "but to save" (*John* 12:47).

One aspect of Jesus' truth, in *John* and in the synoptic gospels, is that there can be no salvation—no *true* human liberation (*John* 8:32)—without a critique of human judgement. He calls us to

the hard practice of judging ourselves, and not others, by revealing that we judge ourselves *by* judging others. "With the judgement you make you will be judged" is not only a prophetic truth,
but a formal one (*Matthew* 7:2). That *judges are judged by their
judgements* is one of Jesus' formal insights.

This insight does not only consist in the thought that one
cannot judge others without placing oneself under the law, but
in the further thought that "no one keeps the law" (*John* 7:19).
The *guilt of human judges* is an *a priori* truth of human judgement, in the gospels.

But Jesus' formal insight is deeper and more complex. For he
notices that most human judgements only *appear* to refer to law
in its essence, and to others in their true being. Most human
judgements are not *even* a matter of the guilty judging the guilty
as they are, and according to the law *in its essence*. Rather, most
human judgement is a form of misjudgement (*John* 7:24). It is
because of this that Jesus urges us not to judge (*Matthew* 7:1).

What Jesus' sayings reveal is that most of the judgements of
Rome and Judaea are judgements "by appearances" (*John* 7:24).
John's Passion dramatizes this. By handing Jesus over to the gentile prefect, the Temple court insists that he is guilty *by appearances*. By hearing the Judaeans' charges against him, the gentile
prefect notes that he is guilty *by appearances*. When the prophetic critic of this judgement has the audacity, or higher
naivety, to refer to truth, he is met with sarcasm.

The Politics of Pilate's Judgement

This brings us to the question of whether Pilate's judgement of
Jesus is essentially legal, or is, rather, political. In other words, in
John, is Jesus' punishment by Pilate is determined by the forms of
Roman law or by Pilate's *Realpolitik* calculations? By Pilate's legal
reasoning or his perception of the vying forces in Roman Judaea?

It could seem that the painful conclusion of Jesus' political life is determined by Judaean law:

(i) "We have a law, and according to that law Jesus ought to die, because he has made himself the Son of God" (*John* 19:7);

and by Roman law:

(ii) "Everyone who claims to be a king sets himself up against Caesar" (*John* 19:12).

On this reading of *John*'s Passion, the Temple court delivers Jesus to Pilate because he is held to be guilty of blasphemy (Greek *blasphēmia*), and Pilate condemns him because he is seen to be guilty of sedition (Latin *maiestas*). It is because of a Judaean legal judgement that Jesus is brought to Pilate, and it is because of a Roman legal judgement that Pilate "sat on the judge's chair" to condemn him (*John* 19:13). On this reading, the end of Jesus' political life is *legally* determined. And though they may have misjudged him, *both the Temple court and Pilate were trying to uphold their laws.*

But I believe that Jesus' critique of judgement is reflected in *John*'s Passion. The motif of hypocrisy in the whole canonical collection implies that *the law—even the divine law—can be a cover for darker impulses and brutal calculations.* And this seems to be the drama-within-the-drama of Jesus' legal ordeal in *John*. He is condemned as a blasphemer by the Temple court and as an insurgent by Pilate. The *form* of his condemnations, and the *surface* of the narrative logic, is legal—but its *essence*, and *inner meaning*, is political.

For, before Jesus is charged by the Judaean temple-state, various political concerns are voiced:

(i) "If we let Jesus go on like this ... the Romans will come and destroy both our holy place and our nation." (*John* 11:48)

1. *Benedict de Spinoza*, by an unknown artist.

8. *Blaise Pascal*, stipple engraving, 1844, after a chalk drawing by Jean Domat, 1637.

9. *Charles Sanders Peirce*, 1891.

10. *Entombment of Christ with Mary Grieving* (unfinished), by Johannes de Mare (after Titian), circa 1848.

11. *The Woman Taken in Adultery*, by William Blake, circa 1805.

... et dans le disque même du soleil, rayonne la face de Jésus-Christ.

12. ... *And in the Very Disk of the Sun, Shines the Face of Jesus Christ*, by Odilon Redon, 1888.

(ii) "Look, the whole world has gone after him." (*John* 12:19)

And before Pilate seats himself on his curule chair (*sella curulis*), he hears not a legal, but a political threat from Jesus' critics:

(iii) "If you"—Pilate—"release this man, you are no friend of Caesar." (*John* 19:12)

This material indicates that it is not the law of Rome, but the politics of Caesar, which induces *John*'s Pilate to crucify Jesus. And that it is not the law of Moses, but the politics of Judaea, which induces *John*'s Temple elites to call for his crucifixion.

Though Jesus is convicted in *John*, the deeper logic of his Passion seems to be that the laws of Judaea and Rome are just a cover for *Realpolitik* calculations. Though the Galilean's life is not essentially political, the dramatic logic of his death is.

21

DEATH AND PARADISE

Jesus' prophetic life and political death are minor occurrences which become "world-revolutionary", in Erich Auerbach's words, because they inspire a "universal movement of the depths". Though Jesus is a provincial labourer and his first hearers are provincials, nevertheless "time and again", in the gospels, "the impact of Jesus' teachings, personality, and fate upon this and that individual is described".

What we witness in the gospels is "the birth of a spiritual movement in the depths of the common people". Auerbach elaborates:

> The random fisherman or publican or rich youth, the random Samaritan or adulteress, come from their random everyday circumstances to be immediately confronted with the personality of Jesus; and the reaction of an individual in such a moment is necessarily a matter of profound seriousness.[1]

The last encounters in Jesus' political life are with the two 'random' criminals between whom he is crucified.[2] In Luke, one of them recognizes his own guilt and the logic of his punishment. He says that although they are dying "under the same sentence", he has been "condemned justly"; while Jesus has "done nothing wrong". He then says to Jesus, calling him by name—"Jesus, remember me when you come into your kingdom" (*Luke* 23:40–42).[3]

The gospels never deny the hard realities of political life. Jesus does not question this half-dead man's certainty that he has been "condemned justly". Though Jesus clearly believes that murderers must be punished,[4] he says to his supplicant, "Today you will be with me in Paradise" (*Luke* 23:43). (See fig. 12.)

Nietzsche reasons that the "today" in this saying is still, for us, a "today".[5] Jesus' Paradise "has no yesterday and no tomorrow", he writes, "it will not come in 'a thousand years'—it is an experience of the heart".[6] And of what is it an experience? Love. For Nietzsche, the true legacy of Jesus' death is what he calls—by no means uncritically—"a religion of love".[7] Is he right?

This talk of 'love' might seem modern. But it is not.

An eleventh-century Syrian Christian, Abdallah ibn al-Fadl al-Antaki, calls Jesus' injunction to love others as we love ourselves "the philosophical commandment" (*al-waṣiyya al-falsafiyya* in Arabic). "Search out for me an expression", he hazards, "among the philosophers". He then asks: "Does it reach the nobility that [Jesus'] philosophical commandment has truly reached?"[8]

Kant's rhetoric is cooler, but the *Aufklärer* says much the same. "The person who can be revered"—he means Jesus—crystallized all human duties in one "*universal* rule" and one "*particular* rule". The universal is, "Love God", and the particular is, "Love every one as yourself". In other words, the law of God (or reason) can only be fulfilled in human love.[9]

And Spinoza's idea of "the supreme philosopher"—Jesus—is no different. He concludes, in light of Jesus' sayings and *John's* letter (where we read: "God is love"), that one "who has love, truly has God".[10]

This is a Christian intuition that is still altering history, and Paul formulated it before the gospels were even written. "Love does no wrong", he says, "therefore, love is the fulfilling of the law" (*Romans* 13:10).[11] In the dark churn of history, this idealization—and realization—of law-fulfilling love may be the essence of what Kristeva calls Christian difference.[12]

The 'religion of love' is not a negation of political reason, but it is a challenging reminder that our highest desires lie beyond the political. And our sense of that beyond owes incalculably much to the one who, misjudged to the end, never judged—but tried to save.

AUTHOR'S NOTE

It is a pleasure to thank my colleagues at the Danube Institute and the Batthyány Lajos Foundation in Budapest. I could not have finished this book without their generosity and camaraderie.

I warmly thank my former colleagues at Eötvös Loránd University in Budapest for the chance to give a seminar course on philosophy and the gospels. And I am grateful to my students for many flashes of insight which would not have occurred without our conversations.

I wish to thank my new colleagues at Vita-Salute San Raffaele University for the invitation to continue my research in Milan. And I am indebted to many colleagues in other cities for illuminating conversations, and for help in obtaining documents.

A thousand thanks go to the book's editor, Lara Weisweiller-Wu—to its publisher, Michael Dwyer—and to the rest of Hurst Publishers. I owe signal debts, too, to the very learned and open-handed readers that Hurst consulted.

Part of chapter 4 is drawn from my *TLS* essay, "'A World like a Russian Novel': The Trials of Socrates and Jesus" (10 April 2020). I wish to thank *The Times Literary Supplement* for permission to use that material here.

Having finished a book on Jesus it feels necessary to say, "I know that I am human and may have erred" (Spinoza, claiming a Roman maxim); and "Let those I love try to forgive what I have made" (Pound, ending the *Cantos*).

The book is dedicated to my brother, Timothy Dusenbury—a poet and *kapellmeister* in the classical sense. He read it closely in manuscript, sharpening the prose.

Finally, I want to remember a young *haredi* boy who called me *tzadik* on my last, dusk-blue night in Jerusalem. It is thanks to him that I left that holy city, last year, with a quiet heart.

Budapest, 2022
D.L.D.

LIST OF FIGURES

1. *Benedict de Spinoza*, by an unknown artist. (Engraving on paper. Held since 1816 and digitized by the Rijksmuseum, Amsterdam. Public domain.)
2. *Hermann Samuel Reimarus*, by Johann C. G. Fritzsch (after Theodor Friedrich Stein), 1775. (Engraving on paper. Held since 1905 and digitized by the Rijksmuseum, Amsterdam. Public domain.)
3. *Immanuel Kant*, by Johann Theodor Puttrich, 1793. (Aquatint with etching. Held and digitized by the Wellcome Collection. Public domain.)
4. *Self-portrait*, by William Blake, 1802. (Pencil drawing with washes. Archived by Wikimedia Commons, accessed in September 2022. Public domain.)
5. *Friedrich Nietzsche*, by Hans Olde, before 1917. (Drypoint etching on paper. Held since 1952 and digitized by the Rijksmuseum, Amsterdam. Public domain.)
6. *Carl Friedrich Bahrdt*, by an unknown artist, 1792. (Frontispiece of *Dr. Carl Friedrich Bahrdt's Troubled Life, Death, and Burial, Described for the Curious and Inquisitive* (Halle, 1792). Archived by Wikimedia Commons, accessed in September 2022. Public domain.)
7. *Maurice Merleau-Ponty*, before 1961. (Photograph. Archived by Wikimedia Commons, accessed in September 2022.

NOTES

1. JESUS THE STRANGER

1. L. Wittgenstein, *Vermischte Bemerkungen—Culture and Value*, ed. G. H. von Wright with H. Nyman, trans. P. Winch (Oxford, 1980), 33–33e. (Translation lightly modified.)
2. F. Nietzsche, *Human, All Too Human*, trans. R. J. Hollingdale (Cambridge, 1996), 175; idem, *Menschliches, Allzumenschliches I und II*, ed. G. Colli and M. Montinari (Berlin—New York, 1988), 310. For more on which: P. Lepers, "Noblest of Men, Great Egoist or Idiot? Nietzsche on Jesus", *Nietzsche und die Reformation*, ed. H. Heit and A. Urs Sommer (Berlin, 2020).
3. F. Nietzsche, "The Antichrist. Curse upon Christianity", in *The Case of Wagner. Twilight of the Idols. The Antichrist. Ecce Homo. Dionysus Dithyrambs. Nietzsche Contra Wagner*, ed. G. Colli and M. Montinari, trans. A. Del Caro, C. Diethe, et al. (Stanford, 2021), 164; idem, *Der Fall Wagner. Götzen-Dämmerung. Der Antichrist. Ecce homo. Dionysos-Dithyramben. Nietzsche contra Wagner*, ed. G. Colli and M. Montinari (Berlin—New York, 1988), 204.
4. I. Kant, *Religion within the Boundaries of Mere Reason, and Other Writings. Revised Edition*, ed. and trans. A. Wood and G. di Giovanni, rev. with intro. R. M. Adams (Cambridge, 2018), 111; idem, *Die Religion innerhalb der Grenzen der blossen Vernunft. Die Metaphysik der Sitten* (Berlin, 1914), 80.
5. B. de Spinoza, *Theological-Political Treatise*, ed. J. Israel, trans. M. Silverthorne and J. Israel (Cambridge, 2007), 19 (translation modified); idem, *Tractatus Theologico-Politicus. Traité Théologico-Politique*, Latin ed. F. Akkerman, French trans. J. Lagrée and P.-F. Moreau (Paris, 1999), 92. Spinoza's comparison of Moses and Jesus makes use of *Exodus* 33:11, where we read that in a proto-Tabernacle called the "tent of meeting", the Lord would "speak to Moses face to face, as one speaks to a friend".
6. How many of us know, for instance, that there is a *Life of Jesus* written by the young G. F. W. Hegel? Or that Jeremy Bentham—the Panopticon inventor and

felicific calculator—wrote a pseudonymous three-volume work titled *Not Paul, but Jesus*, which contains a philosophical commentary on the life of Jesus? Consult the third and final volume, which was recently published for the first time by The Bentham Project at University College London: J. Bentham, *Not Paul, but Jesus. Volume III: Doctrine* (London, 2013).

7. Nietzsche's early subtitle for *The Antichrist* was "Attempt at a Critique of Christianity": F. Nietzsche, *The Case of Wagner. Twilight of the Idols. The Antichrist. Ecce Homo. Dionysus Dithyrambs. Nietzsche Contra Wagner*, ed. G. Colli and M. Montinari, trans. A. Del Caro, C. Diethe, et al. (Stanford, 2021), 509.

8. J. Kristeva, *This Incredible Need to Believe*, trans. B. B. Brahic (New York, 2011), 84–90.

9. For instance: P. Schäfer, *The History of the Jews in the Greco-Roman World* (London—New York, 2003), 106.

10. A. D. Subin, *Accidental Gods: On Men Unwittingly Turned Divine* (London, 2021), 5.

11. E. J. Bickerman, "The Name of Christians", *Studies in Jewish and Christian History: A New Edition in English including The God of the Maccabees*, ed. A. Tropper (Leiden, 2007), 803. Remarkably, there are only two occurrences of the Greek transliteration, *Messias*, in the New Testament, at *John* 1:41 and *John* 4:25. John Lierman notes "the irony of the fact" that, in *John* 4, this luminous title is not uttered by a Judaean, but by a Samaritan woman: J. Lierman, "The Mosaic Pattern of John's Christology", *Challenging Perspectives on the Gospel of John*, ed. J. Lierman (Tübingen, 2006), 216–17.

12. "Heading a nationalist war against the Romans and their mercenary thugs was totally against [his] nature ... Jesus was not a resistance fighter": H. Bloom, *Jesus and Yahweh: The Names Divine* (New York, 2005), 18.

13. H. S. Reimarus, *Reimarus: Fragments*, ed. C. H. Talbert, trans. R. S. Fraser (London, 1971), 135. (Translation modified.) For more on Reimarus: D. Klein, *Hermann Samuel Reimarus (1694–1768)* (Tübingen, 2009), esp. 133–48; U. Groetsch, *Hermann Samuel Reimarus (1694–1768): Classicist, Hebraist, Enlightenment Radical in Disguise* (Leiden, 2015).

14. G. Steiner, *Lessons of the Masters: The Charles Eliot Norton Lectures* (Cambridge, Mass., 2003), 34.

15. Ironically, this text came to bear Spinoza's name in the eighteenth century, when it circulated as *The Three Impostors, or The Spirit of Spinoza* (*Les Trois Imposteurs, ou l'Esprit de M. Spinosa*). Consult: R. H. Popkin, "Spinoza and the *Three Imposters*", *The Third Force in Seventeenth-Century Thought* (Leiden, 1992); F. Charles-Daubert, "*L'Esprit de Spinosa* et les *Traités des trois imposteurs*: rappel des différentes familles et de leurs principales caractéristiques",

Heterodoxy, Spinozism, and Free Thought in Early-Eighteenth-Century Europe: Studies on the Traité des Trois Imposteurs, ed. S. Berti, F. Charles-Daubert, and R. H. Popkin (Dordrecht, 1996).

16. Spinoza, *Theological-Political Treatise*, 70; idem, *Tractatus Theologico-Politicus*, 212–14. The comparison of Isaiah and Jesus is made by Spinoza, who cites *Isaiah* 58:1–9; but it is likely inspired by the citation of *Isaiah* 29:13–14 in *Matthew* 15:7–9 and *Mark* 7:6–7.

17. Ibid., 160 (Christ's teaching), 173 (love of God and humankind); idem, *Tractatus Theologico-Politicus*, 422, 450–52.

18. *Numbers* 21:10–14; Spinoza, *Theological-Political Treatise*, 122; idem, *Tractatus Theologico-Politicus*, 336: quidam liber, qui *bellorum Dei* vocabatur.

19. Kant, *Religion within the Boundaries of Mere Reason*, 185; idem, *Die Religion innerhalb der Grenzen der blossen Vernunft*, 158.

20. Ibid., 154 (political faith), 156 (moral faith); idem, *Die Religion innerhalb der Grenzen der blossen Vernunft*, 125, 128.

21. Ibid., 164 note; idem, *Die Religion innerhalb der Grenzen der blossen Vernunft*, 137.

22. Nietzsche, *The Case of Wagner. Twilight of the Idols. The Antichrist. Ecce Homo. Dionysus Dithyrambs. Nietzsche Contra Wagner*, 18 (Kant), 148 (Spinoza); idem, *Der Fall Wagner. Götzen-Dämmerung. Der Antichrist. Ecce homo. Dionysos-Dithyramben. Nietzsche contra Wagner*, 28, 184. I am grateful to one of Oxford Univeristy Press's readers for noting that, in some of his late correspondence, Nietzsche seems to temper his harsh portrayal of Spinoza in *The Antichrist*.

23. His italics. Nietzsche, *The Antichrist*, 142; idem, *Der Antichrist*, 178.

24. Nietzsche, *The Antichrist*, 159–61; idem, *Der Antichrist*, 197–200.

25. *Matthew* 2:20–21 (land of Israel), 4:17 (kingdom of heaven).

26. Kant, *Religion within the Boundaries of Mere Reason*, 154; idem, *Die Religion innerhalb der Grenzen der blossen Vernunft*, 125.

27. Jesus' country is "Galilee of the gentiles" in *Isaiah* 9:1; *I Maccabees* 5:15; and *Matthew* 4:15. For more on which: S. Freyne, *Jesus, a Jewish Galilean: A New Reading of the Jesus-Story* (New York—London, 2004), 64, 80–84.

28. This lone act of violence is noted in all four gospels: *Matthew* 26:51; *Mark* 14:47; *Luke* 22:50; *John* 18:10. Columnized in K. Aland, *Synopsis of the Four Gospels: Greek-English Edition of the Synopsis Quattuor Evangeliorum* (Stuttgart, 2003), 300 (no. 331).

29. Kant, *Religion within the Boundaries of Mere Reason*, 126–27 (typography lightly modified); idem, *Die Religion innerhalb der Grenzen der blossen Vernunft*, 94–95.

30. Ibid., 127; idem, *Die Religion innerhalb der Grenzen der blossen Vernunft*, 95–96.

31. Ibid., 179–81; idem, *Die Religion innerhalb der Grenzen der blossen Vernunft*, 151–53.

32. Ibid., 156; idem, *Die Religion innerhalb der Grenzen der blossen Vernunft*, 128.
33. Ibid., 97; idem, *Die Religion innerhalb der Grenzen der blossen Vernunft*, 63.
34. Ibid., 126; idem, *Die Religion innerhalb der Grenzen der blossen Vernunft*, 95.
35. Ibid., 127; idem, *Die Religion innerhalb der Grenzen der blossen Vernunft*, 95–96.
36. This is not to deny that Reimarus' theory inspired a notable tradition of Marxist thought on the life of Jesus. For instance: E. Bloch, *Atheism in Christianity: The Religion of the Exodus and the Kingdom*, trans. J. T. Swann (London, 2009).
37. Nietzsche, *The Antichrist*, 162; idem, *Der Antichrist*, 201.

2. "WHAT IS THIS WISDOM?"

1. *Gospel of Thomas* 13. This non-canonical sayings-gospel is dated to the first or second century. I am grateful to Samuel Noble for consulting the fourth-century Coptic translation in which this originally Greek *logion* comes to us. The critical word is simply transcribed from the Greek with a Coptic particle pre-fixed. It is significant that Matthew is himself a gospel-writer, according to tradition, and also worth noting that Matthew's description is less advanced than Thomas'—who says to Jesus, "My mouth is completely unable to say what you are like".
2. Depending (i) on whether there is a first- or second-century allusion to Jesus in Epictetus, *Discourses* 2.2.20, as suggested by N. Huttunen, "Epictetus' Views on Christians: A Closed Case Revisited", *Religio-Philosophical Discourses in the Mediterranean World: From Plato, through Jesus, to Late Antiquity*, ed. A. Klostergaard Petersen and G. van Kooten (Leiden, 2017), 321 (more on which, in the coming pages); and (ii) on whether the intriguing *Letter of Mara bar Sarapion*, which takes note of Jesus' death, is dated to the first or second century (more on which, in chapter 7). The cache of charming yet spurious fourth-century letters between 'Paul' and 'Seneca'—first put in doubt by Erasmus—attests to a thousand-year Christian *desire* for the New Testament's most forceful letter-writer, Paul, to be in conversation with the urbane epistolary philosopher, Seneca, whose brother Gallio it seems Paul *did* meet in the provinces (*Acts* 18:12–17). Consult Jerome, *On Illustrious Men* 12 (the earliest mention of the letters); and H. M. Hine, "Seneca and Paul: The First Two Thousand Years", *Paul and Seneca in Dialogue*, ed. J. R. Dodson and D. E. Briones (Leiden, 2017).
3. Jesus is called "wise" by Flavius Josephus (a first-century Judaean historian), and by Mara bar Sarapion (a first- or second-century Syrian philosopher). Both testimonies, which are not without difficulties, will be quoted in chapter 7. As to the stern lines on "philosophy" in *Colossians*, Eduard Lohse notes, behind them, a double-structure of early Christian critique. Just as certain rabbinic decisions are demystified as "human tradition" in the gospels (*Mark* 7:1–13), so certain

pagan (or syncretic) speculations are demystified as "human tradition" in this letter (*Colossians* 2:1–23). I would add that this double-structure is dramatized in *Acts* 17:17–18. Though *Colossians* is considered by most modern commentators to postdate Paul, it is still very early. The letter "presupposes a Pauline school tradition", Lohse concludes, "[likely] based in Ephesus as the center of the Pauline mission in Asia Minor". E. Lohse, *Colossians and Philemon: A Commentary on the Epistles to the Colossians and to Philemon*, ed. H. Koester, trans. W. R. Poehlmann and R. J. Karris (Philadelphia, 1971), 96 (human tradition), 181 (Pauline school). For the presence of philosophical concepts, tropes, and concerns in the Pauline corpus: A. J. Malherbe, *Light from the Gentiles: Hellenistic Philosophy and Early Christianity; Collected Essays, 1959–2012. Volume 1*, ed. C. R. Holladay, J. T. Fitzgerald, G. E. Sterling, and J. W. Thompson (Leiden, 2014).

4. Tatian of Adiabene, *Oration to the Greeks* 31. For more on Tatian, including the uncertainty of his ties to Adiabene: W. L. Petersen, "Tatian the Assyrian", *A Companion to Second-Century Christian "Heretics"*, ed. A. Marjanen and P. Luomanen (Leiden, 2005), here 133. For more of this theme in early Christian rhetoric: G. Karamanolis, *The Philosophy of Early Christianity* (London—New York, 2021), 27–54. It is unfortunate that Tatian's novel synthesis of the gospels—the *Diatesseron*, or "Out-of-Four"—is lost. A comprehensive new study of this gospel's remains is J. W. Barker, *Tatian's Diatessaron: Composition, Redaction, Recension, and Reception* (Oxford, 2022).

5. Though Clement's birthplace is unknown, his memory is tied to Egypt. His homily, "Who Is the Rich Man That Is Being Saved?", is on *Mark* 10:17–31. Curiously, his Greek text "substantially differs from the text known to us in the New Testament manuscripts", particularly at *Mark* 10:29–30. For more on the discrepancy: J. Plátová, "The Text of Mark 10:29–30 in Quis dives salvetur? by Clement of Alexandria", *The Process of Authority: The Dynamics in Transmission and Reception of Canonical Texts*, ed. J. Dušek and J. Roskovec (Berlin, 2016). More could be said about the incredibly rich genre of philosophical commentary on the gospels, but (i) European modernity owes much to the logic of toleration laid out in 1687 in the *Commentaire philosophique* by a radical Protestant *érudit*, Pierre Bayle. It was first done into English in 1708: P. Bayle, *A Philosophical Commentary on These Words of the Gospel, Luke 14.23, "Compel Them to Come In, That My House May Be Full"*, ed. J. Kilcullen and C. Kukathas (Indianapolis, 2005). And (ii) in this century, Giorgio Agamben has written a stimulating commentary on Paul's incomparable *Römerbrief*, hopefully proving that the genre has a future: G. Agamben, *The Time That Remains: A Commentary on the Letter to the Romans*, trans. P. Dailey (Stanford, 2005).

6. *Mark* 6:2; compare *Matthew* 13:54; *Luke* 4:22; and *John* 7:15. Columnized in K. Aland, *Synopsis of the Four Gospels: Greek-English Edition of the Synopsis Quattuor Evangeliorum* (Stuttgart, 2003), 128 (no. 139).

7. *Luke* 7:35; compare *Matthew* 11:19.

8. Note, though, that there are "philosophers" in *Acts of the Apostles*—which is a sequel to *Luke*. The unforgettable scene is *Acts* 17:16–33, here verse 18: "Some Epicurean and Stoic philosophers debated with [Paul]."

9. Compare *Matthew* 13:57; *Mark* 6:4; *Luke* 4:24; *John* 4:44; and *Gospel of Thomas* 31. For the question of what the prophet's "own country" means in this saying—Nazareth? Galilee? Israel?—consult this intriguing note: R. L. Sturch, "The Πατρίς of Jesus", *The Journal of Theological Studies* (N.S.) 28, 1 (1977), 94–96.

10. R. M. Thorsteinsson, *Jesus as Philosopher: The Moral Sage in the Synoptic Gospels* (Oxford, 2018), 38–45, here 39.

11. Dio of Prusa, *Orations* 47.6. For more on Dio and the philosopher's country: P. Desideri, "City and Country in Dio", *Dio Chrysostom: Politics, Letters, and Philosophy*, ed. S. Swain (Oxford, 2000). For more on Dio and the gospels: G. Mussies, *Dio Chrysostom and the New Testament: Collected Parallels* (Leiden, 1972).

12. Epictetus, *Discourses* 3.16.11. For Epictetus' relevance to early Christianity: R. M. Thorsteinsson, *Roman Christianity and Roman Stoicism: A Comparative Study of Ancient Morality* (Oxford, 2010), 55–70.

13. Of course, it is noted in the gospels (and in Josephus) that John was thronged by listeners. But John, too, was accused of being demon-possessed, according to *Matthew* 11:18 and *Luke* 7:33.

14. Epictetus, *Discourses* 3.16.11.

15. Compare *Mark* 6:1; *Matthew* 13:54; *Luke* 4:16; Aland, *Synopsis of the Four Gospels*, 127–29 (no. 139).

16. Compare *Matthew* 13:55–56; *Luke* 4:22; *John* 6:42. It is eye-catching that he is called "the son of Mary": A. Yarbro Collins, *Mark: A Commentary*, ed. H. W. Attridge (Minneapolis, 2007), 290–91.

17. Compare *Mark* 6:5 and the muted form it is given in *Matthew* 13:58. Significantly, there is no parallel in *Luke*.

18. Note the identical Greek at the phrase, "They laughed at him", in *Mark* 5:40; *Matthew* 9:25; *Luke* 8:53; Aland, *Synopsis of the Four Gospels*, 127 (no. 138).

19. The Greek is identical in *Mark* 6:3 and *Matthew* 13:57.

20. Dio of Prusa, *Orations* 47.5. Adela Yarbro Collins notes that *Mark*'s Jesus is a prophetic healer-legislator who, in some ways, resembles the philosophical healer-legislator in Porphyry's *Life of Pythagoras*—a text which, of course, post-dates *Mark* by roughly 200 years: A. Yarbro Collins, *Mark: A Commentary*, ed. H. W. Attridge (Minneapolis, 2007), 212.

21. Dio of Prusa, *Orations* 47.6.

22. It is worth noting that although the iconic Cynic philosopher, Diogenes, was

exiled (for obscure reasons) by the citizens of his native Sinope, he was "loved (*ēgapato*) by the Athenians": Diogenes Laertius, *Lives of the Philosophers* 6.2.43.

23. The reference is, of course, to Moses in *Exodus* 2:22: "I have been a stranger in a strange land" (Authorized Version).

24. Steiner, too, holds that a "recurrent pattern of conflict between the life of the mind and that of the [Hellenic] city" is tied to a "Hebraic intuition [which] will insist that prophets and teachers of wisdom are slain by their fellow citizens": Steiner, *Lessons of the Masters*, 10.

25. For a vague, but not unrelated conjecture that "Jesus' healing ministry, attested in all the gospels", might have drawn him from the Galilean hill-country (Nazareth) to the Sea of Galilee (Capernaum), where the air is "mild" and the water is "sweet to the taste" (as we read in Josephus): Freyne, *Jesus, a Jewish Galilean*, 56–57.

26. Philosophical antecedents of the symposium-motif in *John* have recently been argued for in G. van Kooten, "John's Counter-Symposium: 'The Continuation of Dialogue' in Christianity—A Contrapuntal Reading of John's Gospel and Plato's *Symposium*", *Intolerance, Polemics, and Debate in Antiquity: Politico-Cultural, Philosophical, and Religious Forms of Critical Conversation*, ed. G. van Kooten and J. van Ruiten (Leiden, 2019), esp. 286–93.

27. "As the [Hellenistic] poet Herodas had stated it: 'every door shudders before the tax-collectors'. In the New Testament, 'publicans and sinners' appear almost as synonyms, and similar opinions are expressed in non-Jewish literature. Rabbinical writings, too, display a marked aversion for customs officials." E. Schürer, *The History of the Jewish People in the Age of Jesus Christ (175 B.C.– A.D. 135)*, rev. and ed. G. Vermes and F. Millar, with P. Vermes and M. Black (Edinburgh, 1973), 1.376.

28. Compare *Matthew* 9:10–13; *Luke* 5:29–32; Aland, *Synopsis of the Four Gospels*, 42 (no. 44). Further, compare *Luke* 4:23—"Physician, cure yourself!"—which has no parallel in the other gospels.

29. A study of this motif in early Christian funerary art in Provence and northern Italy is D. Knipp, *'Christus Medicus' in der frühchristlichen Sarkophagskulptur. Ikonographische Studien zur Sepulkralkunst des späten vierten Jahrhunderts* (Leiden, 1998). See, too, a new contribution on *Christus medicus* in medical literatures of the early modern Low Countries: B. A. Kaminska, "*Christus Medicus* and Beyond: The Thaumaturgic Power of Christ and Medical Metaphors in the Premodern Netherlands", *Images of Miraculous Healing in the Early Modern Netherlands* (Leiden, 2021).

30. Thorsteinsson, *Jesus as Philosopher*, 54–55.

31. For other *comparanda* in *The Letters of Diogenes* (first century BCE?), Plutarch's

Sayings of Spartans (first century CE?), and Lucian's *Life of Demonax* (second century CE): Yarbro Collins, *Mark*, 195 and notes.

32. K. Lampe, *The Birth of Hedonism: The Cyrenaic Philosophers and Pleasure as a Way of Life* (Princeton, 2015), 16–18.

33. In the synoptic gospels, Simon of Cyrene is "compelled to carry Jesus' cross" (in *Matthew*'s phrase). Compare *Matthew* 27:32; *Mark* 15:21; *Luke* 23:26.

34. Diogenes Laertius, *Lives of the Philosophers* 2.8.70.

35. Antisthenes may have had a foreign-born, and not a free-born, mother: Diogenes Laertius, *Lives of the Philosophers* 6.1.1 (Thracian), 6.1.4 (not free-born).

36. For Antisthenes: Diogenes Laertius, *Lives of the Philosophers* 6.1.3. For Jesus: *Matthew* 5:11; compare *Luke* 6:22.

37. Diogenes Laertius, *Lives of the Philosophers* 6.1.6.

38. And *nouveaux riches*? The Greeks already had the concept, as we see in Aristotle, *Rhetoric* 2.9.9: "The new-rich (*hoi neoploutoi*) who attain office due to their wealth cause more irritation than the old-rich (*hoi archaioploutoi*)."

39. For Euripides: Clement of Alexandria, *Miscellanies* 1.14.59. For Menander: Jerome, *Commentary on Titus*, gloss on *Titus* 1:12–14.

40. There is a colossal literature on the 'Son of Man' (Greek *huios tou anthrōpou*, Latin *filius hominis*). For a concise reception history: M. Müller, *The Expression 'Son of Man' and the Development of Christology: A History of Interpretation* (New York—London, 2014).

3. JESUS THE PHILOSOPHER

1. W. Blake, "The Everlasting Gospel", *Blake's Poetry and Designs*, ed. M. L. Johnson and J. E. Grant (New York—London, 1979), 364–65. (Typography lightly modified.)

2. Irenaeus of Lyon, *Against Heresies* 3.11.8.

3. In fact, 'modern' (*modernus*) comes to us from early Christian Latin: J. Moorhead, "The Word *modernus*", *Latomus* 65, 2 (2006), 425–33.

4. I have in mind *Mark* 7:26 and *John* 12:20; but this is not the gospel-writers' only term for 'pagans'. There is a "Canaanite" woman in *Matthew* 15:22, and so on.

5. I. Tanaseanu-Döbler, "The Logos in Amelius' Fragment on the Gospel of John and Plutarch's *De Iside*", *Plutarch and the New Testament in Their Religio-Philosophical Contexts: Bridging Discourses in the World of the Early Roman Empire*, ed. R. Hirsch-Luipold (Leiden, 2022), 177.

6. Eusebius of Caesarea, *Preparation for the Gospel* 11.19. Here using the translation of, and relying on the new analysis of, Tanaseanu-Döbler, "Logos in Amelius'

Fragment on the Gospel of John", 180–81. Note, however, that I have made typographic and verbal changes to her translation and have replaced a pronoun with "the Barbarian" for clarity.

7. G. G. Stroumsa, *Barbarian Philosophy: The Religious Revolution of Early Christianity* (Tübingen, 1999).

8. Eusebius of Caesarea, *Preparation for the Gospel* 11.18.

9. Augustine of Hippo, *On Christian Doctrine* 2.28.43.

10. This could be hyperbolic. Augustine could have in mind something like Celsus' critique of *Matthew* 5:39 and *Luke* 6:29 in Origen, *Against Celsus* 7.58. Note, too, that we read in Origen, *Contra Celsum* 5.65, that Celsus "contrasts certain phrases which are continually being used by believers in Christian doctrine with quotations from the philosophers, wanting to make out that the opinions which Celsus thinks to be right in the doctrines held by the Christians have been expressed both better and more clearly by the philosophers, so that he may draw away to philosophy those who are impressed by doctrines that in themselves are manifestly good and religious".

11. Diogenes Laertius, *Lives of the Philosophers* 2.5.41; G. van Kooten, "John's Counter-Symposium: 'The Continuation of Dialogue' in Christianity—A Contrapuntal Reading of John's Gospel and Plato's *Symposium*", *Intolerance, Polemics, and Debate in Antiquity: Politico-Cultural, Philosophical, and Religious Forms of Critical Conversation*, ed. G. van Kooten and J. van Ruiten (Leiden, 2019), 284.

12. *Matthew* 8:28. The toponym is problematic, but "country of the Gadarenes" (rather than "Gerasenes" or "Gergesenes") seems to be the best reading.

13. Note, however, Hans Dieter Betz's warning: "The evidence for Cynicism is limited to Gadara and Tyre, Hellenistic cities outside of Galilee." H. D. Betz, "Jesus and the Cynics: Survey and Analysis of a Hypothesis", *The Journal of Religion* 74, 4 (1994), 453–75, here 471.

14. For this catalogue of territories—and though many other texts could be cited—see the tight clustering of Galilee, Judaea, Decapolis, and Syria in *Matthew* 4:24–25.

15. Socrates Scholasticus, *Ecclesiastical History* 3.16.

16. I am both citing and contesting the point of departure in M. Foucault, *Confessions of the Flesh. The History of Sexuality, Volume 4*, ed. F. Gros, trans. R. Hurley (New York, 2021), 3. For my review of which: D. L. Dusenbury, "A Choice, and Not a Law: The Role of Virginity in Foucault's Thinking", *TLS. The Times Literary Supplement* (16 July 2021); archived online at https://www.the-tls.co.uk/articles/history-of-sexuality-volume-four-michel-foucault-book-review-d-l-dusenbury/; accessed on 7 August 2022.

17. For philosophical contrast-imitation in of *Luke's* and *John's* Passion narratives:

G. Sterling, "*Mors philosophi*: The Death of Jesus in Luke", *The Harvard Theological Review* 94, 4 (2001), 383–402; G. van Kooten, "The Last Days of Socrates and Christ: *Euthyphro, Apology, Crito*, and *Phaedo* Read in Counterpoint with John's Gospel", *Religio-Philosophical Discourses in the Mediterranean World: From Plato, through Jesus, to Late Antiquity*, ed. A. Klostergaard Petersen and G. van Kooten (Leiden, 2017).

18. E. Auerbach, *Mimesis: The Representation of Reality in Western Literature*, trans. W. R. Trask (Princeton, 2003), 40.

19. To confine myself to a single contribution on Polybius' relevance to *1 Maccabees*, and Ben Sira's to the gospels: P. Wajdenbaum, "The Books of the Maccabees and Polybius", *The Bible and Hellenism: Greek Influence on Jewish and Early Christian Literature*, ed. T. L. Thompson and P. Wajdenbaum (London—New York, 2014); D. A. deSilva, *The Jewish Teachers of Jesus, James, and Jude: What Earliest Christianity Learned from the Apocrypha and Pseudepigrapha* (Oxford, 2012), 58–85.

20. Josephus, *Against Apion* 1.22.176–82. For Josephus' use of this scene: A. Kasher, "Polemic and Apologetic Methods of Writing in *Contra Apionem*", *Josephus' Contra Apionem: Studies in its Character and Context with a Latin Concordance to the Portion Missing in Greek*, ed. L. H. Feldman and J. R. Levison (Leiden—Cologne, 1996), 179–80.

21. Porphyry of Tyre, *On Abstinence from Killing Animals* 2.26.3.

22. D. Ridings, *The Attic Moses: The Dependency Theme in Some Early Christian Writers* (Gothenburg, 1995).

23. Both texts are quoted, here, as by Celsus in Origen, *Against Celsus* 7.58. For Socrates: Plato, *Crito* 49b–e. For Jesus: *Matthew* 5:39; *Luke* 6:29.

24. E. Haenchen, *The Acts of the Apostles: A Commentary*, trans. H. Anderson and R. M. Wilson (Philadelphia, 1971), 594 note 5.

25. Seneca, *Moral Epistles* 81.17: Errat enim, si quis beneficium accipit libentius quam reddit.

26. R. M. Thorsteinsson, *Jesus as Philosopher: The Moral Sage in the Synoptic Gospels* (Oxford, 2018); T. Engberg-Pedersen, *John and Philosophy: A New Reading of the Fourth Gospel* (Oxford, 2017); G. H. van Kooten, "The 'True Light which Enlightens Everyone' (*John* 1:9): John, *Genesis*, The Platonic Notion of the 'True, Noetic Light', and the Allegory of the Cave in Plato's *Republic*", *The Creation of Heaven and Earth: Re-interpretations of Genesis i in the Context of Judaism, Ancient Philosophy, Christianity, and Modern Physics*, ed. G. H. van Kooten (Leiden, 2005); idem, "John's Counter-Symposium: 'The Continuation of Dialogue' in Christianity—A Contrapuntal Reading of John's Gospel and Plato's *Symposium*", *Intolerance, Polemics, and Debate in Antiquity: Politico-*

Cultural, Philosophical, and Religious Forms of Critical Conversation, ed. G. van Kooten and J. van Ruiten (Leiden, 2019); M. D. Litwa, *Iesus Deus: The Early Christian Depiction of Jesus as a Mediterranean God* (Minneapolis, 2014); idem, *How the Gospels Became History: Jesus and Mediterranean Myths* (New Haven—London, 2019).

27. *Gospel of Thomas* 13.

28. Josephus, *Judaean Antiquities* 18.63–64; E. Schürer, *The History of the Jewish People in the Age of Jesus Christ (175 B.C.–A.D. 135)*, rev. and ed. G. Vermes and F. Millar, with P. Vermes and M. Black (Edinburgh, 1973), 1.437; S. Pines, *An Arabic Version of the Testimonium Flavianum and Its Implications* (Jerusalem, 1971), 9–10. This is, of course, the infamous *Testimonium Flavianum*—more on which in chapter 7.

29. Josephus, *Against Apion* 1.22.182.

30. I take "knife men" from B. D. Shaw, "The Myth of the Neronian Persecution", *The Journal of Roman Studies* 105 (2015), 73–100, here 76.

31. Auerbach, *Mimesis*, 72.

32. For more on Christ-as-fighter in ancient *antichristiana*: W. Horbury, "Christ as Brigand in Ancient Anti-Christian Polemic", *Jesus and the Politics of His Day*, ed. E. Bammel and C. F. D. Moule (Cambridge, 1984), 188–95.

33. For more on the context of this fragment: D. L. Dusenbury, *The Innocence of Pontius Pilate: How the Roman Trial of Jesus Shaped History* (London, 2021), 39–48.

34. Lactantius, *Divine Institutes* 5.3.4. Consult, too, the text and commentary in M. Stern, *Greek and Latin Authors on Jews and Judaism. Volume Three: Appendixes and Indexes* (Jerusalem, 1984), 43–44: "Jesus emerges as a leader of a robber gang, after running away from Jews".

35. W. H. C. Frend, "Prelude to the Great Persecution: The Propaganda War", *Journal of Ecclesiastical History* 38 (1987), 1–18; E. DePalma Digeser, *A Threat to Public Piety: Christians, Platonists, and the Great Persecution* (Ithaca, New York, 2012).

36. T. D. Barnes, "Sossianus Hierocles and the Antecedents of the 'Great Persecution'", *Harvard Studies in Classical Philology* 80 (1976), 239–52, here 243–46.

37. Lactantius, *Divine Institutes* 5.2.12–17.

38. R. Girard, *The Scapegoat*, trans. Y. Freccero (Baltimore, 1989), 27.

39. Minucius Felix, *Octavius* 29.2.

40. Lactantius, *Divine Institutes* 5.12.5–6 = Cicero, *Republic* 3.17.27.

41. Lactantius, *Divine Institutes* 5.12.8.

42. Cassius Dio, *Roman History* 47.8.3–4; G. Samuelsson, *Crucifixion in Antiquity:*

An Inquiry into the Background and Significance of the New Testament Terminology of Crucifixion (Tübingen, 2013), 128.

43. Plato, *Republic* II (361e–362a); Samuelsson, *Crucifixion in Antiquity*, 65–66; S. R. Slings, *Critical Notes on Plato's Politeia*, ed. G. Boter and J. van Ophuijsen (Leiden, 2005), 24–28.

44. D. L. Dusenbury, *Platonic Legislations: An Essay on Legal Critique in Ancient Greece* (Cham, 2017), 47–53.

45. For more on the meaning of Plato's rare verb, here: Samuelsson, *Crucifixion in Antiquity*, 66.

46. For Paul's rhetorical, first-person formulation of this dramatic structure, see *Galatians* 4:16.

47. Epictetus, *Discourses* 2.2.20; N. Huttunen, "Epictetus' Views on Christians: A Closed Case Revisited", *Religio-Philosophical Discourses in the Mediterranean World: From Plato, through Jesus, to Late Antiquity*, ed. A. Klostergaard Petersen and G. van Kooten (Leiden, 2017), 321. Though Huttunen's reading is contested, a subtle evocation of Jesus' death by crucifixion cannot be ruled out.

48. Jesus is called "the just one" in *Acts* 3:14 (by Peter), 7:52 (by Stephen), and 22:14 (by Paul).

49. Kant, *Religion within the Boundaries of Mere Reason*, 113; idem, *Die Religion innerhalb der Grenzen der blossen Vernunft*, 82.

4. JESUS AND THE DESIRE TO DIE

1. Compare *John* 8:20, 59.

2. Christopher Matthews concludes that the name *Philip* filtered into "aristocratic Palestinian Jewish circles" as a result of its "use by the Hellenistic kings". What is more: "The Fourth Gospel's identification of Bethsaida as the home town of the disciple Philip (John 1:44) would make him a namesake of Philip the Tetrarch (Luke 3:1) who ruled this territory": C. R. Matthews, *Philip, Apostle and Evangelist: Configurations of a Tradition* (Leiden, 2002), 16–17.

3. For more on the gentile identity of the Greeks and the Greek names of Jesus' disciples: Matthews, *Philip, Apostle and Evangelist*, 114–17; G. H. van Kooten, "The 'True Light which Enlightens Everyone' (*John* 1:9): John, *Genesis*, The Platonic Notion of the 'True, Noetic Light', and the Allegory of the Cave in Plato's *Republic*", *The Creation of Heaven and Earth: Re-interpretations of Genesis i in the Context of Judaism, Ancient Philosophy, Christianity, and Modern Physics*, ed. G. H. van Kooten (Leiden, 2005), 189–90.

4. "[A] straight narratological line runs from the Diaspora of the Greeks, which Jesus' opponents deemed potentially receptive of Jesus' teaching in John 7, through the dismantling of the Judaism-Hellenism divide in John 10, [to] the

arrival of the Greek visitors at the Jewish Pascha festival and Jesus' Eleusinian statement to them in John 12": G. van Kooten, "Christ and Hermes: A Religio-Historical Comparison of the Johannine Christ-Logos with the God Hermes in Greek Mythology and Philosophy", *Im Gespräch mit C. F. Georg Heinrici. Beiträge zwischen Theologie und Religionswissenschaft*, ed. M. Frenschkowski and L. Seehausen (Tübingen, 2021), 277.

5. *John* 21:20, 24. There is an inconclusive literature on the identity of this disciple-whom-Jesus-loved, and his connection to the writer (or editors) of *John* in its canonical form. It is impossible, here, to engage with this literature.

6. Letter of 4 January 1889 to Cardinal Mariano Rampollo (whom Nietzsche calls "*Kardinal Mariani*"), and letter of 4 January 1889 to King Umberto I, in F. Nietzsche, *Friedrich Nietzsche Briefe. Januar 1887–Januar 1889*, ed. G. Colli and M. Montinari with H. Anania-Hess (Berlin—New York, 1984), 577.

7. F. Nietzsche, *Human, All Too Human*, trans. R. J. Hollingdale (Cambridge, 1996), 233; idem, *Menschliches, Allzumenschliches I und II*, ed. G. Colli and M. Montinari (Berlin—New York, 1988), 414.

8. Nietzsche, *Human, All Too Human*, 233; idem, *Menschliches, Allzumenschliches*, 414.

9. There are Judaic and Islamic traditions, too, concerning this sequence of trials and deaths. For Socrates: Y. Halper, *Jewish Socratic Questions in an Age without Plato: Permitting and Forbidding Open Inquiry in 12–15th Century Europe and North Africa* (Leiden, 2021), 15–45 (Judaic tradition); I. Alon, *Socrates in Medieval Arabic Literature* (Leiden—Jerusalem, 1991), 41–100 (Islamic tradition). And for Jesus: Dusenbury, *Innocence of Pontius Pilate*, 79–91 (Judaic tradition), 93–107 (Islamic tradition).

10. Nietzsche, *Human, All Too Human*, 233; idem, *Menschliches, Allzumenschliches*, 414.

11. The most commanding reflections on this still seem to be G. Steiner, "The Scandal of Revelation", *Salgamundi* 98–99 (1993), 42–70; idem, "Two Suppers", *Salgamundi* 108 (1995), 33–61.

12. Nietzsche, *The Antichrist*, 147; idem, *Der Antichrist*, 183.

13. F. Nietzsche, *Twilight of the Idols, or How to Philosophize with a Hammer*, in *The Case of Wagner. Twilight of the Idols. The Antichrist. Ecce Homo. Dionysus Dithyrambs. Nietzsche Contra Wagner*, ed. G. Colli and M. Montinari, trans. A. Del Caro, C. Diethe, et al. (Stanford, 2021), 51; idem, *Der Fall Wagner. Götzen-Dämmerung. Der Antichrist. Ecce homo. Dionysos-Dithyramben. Nietzsche contra Wagner*, ed. G. Colli and M. Montinari (Berlin—New York, 1988), 68.

14. Nietzsche, *Twilight of the Idols*, 56; idem, *Götzen-Dämmerung*, 73.

15. Nietzsche, *The Antichrist*, 162–63; idem, *Der Antichrist*, 201–203. (Typography lightly modified.)

16. F. Nietzsche, *The Case of Wagner. Twilight of the Idols. The Antichrist. Ecce Homo. Dionysus Dithyrambs. Nietzsche Contra Wagner*, ed. G. Colli and M. Montinari, trans. A. Del Caro, C. Diethe, et al. (Stanford, 2021), 525 note 163.

17. Nietzsche, *The Antichrist*, 161–62; idem, *Der Antichrist*, 200–201.

18. Ibid., 167–68; idem, *Der Antichrist*, 207–208.

19. Ibid., *The Antichrist*, 161–62; idem, *Der Antichrist*, 200–201.

20. Nietzsche, *Twilight of the Idols*, 51; idem, *Götzen-Dämmerung*, 67.

21. Nietzsche, *The Antichrist*, 167–68; idem, *Der Antichrist*, 207–208.

22. Nietzsche, *Twilight of the Idols*, 56; idem, *Götzen-Dämmerung*, 73. Nietzsche's own death—unlike his collapse—is forgotten. His mind famously cracked in December 1888 when he was living in the Italian city of Turin (renowned for a Christ-stained burial cloth). By the end of January 1889, he had sunk into a catatonic state from which he never emerged. He died placidly on 25 August 1900, after suffering a wave of strokes. For the causes of his collapse and death: J. Young, *Friedrich Nietzsche: A Philosophical Biography* (Cambridge, 2010), 522–27, 550–62. And for more on Turin's fantastic relic: A. Nicolotti, *From the Mandylion of Edessa to the Shroud of Turin: The Metamorphosis and Manipulation of a Legend* (Leiden, 2014).

23. Nietzsche, *Twilight of the Idols*, 61; idem, *Götzen-Dämmerung*, 79.

24. For Barhdt as a "pre-Jacobin": T. Hoeren, "Präjakobiner in Deutschland. Carl Friedrich Bahrdt (1740–1792)", *Zeitschrift für Religions- und Geistesgeschichte* 47 (1995), 55–72.

25. I. Kant, *Religion within the Boundaries of Mere Reason, and Other Writings. Revised Edition*, ed. and trans. A. Wood and G. di Giovanni, rev. with intro. R. M. Adams (Cambridge, 2018), 112, and 121 note; idem, *Die Religion innerhalb der Grenzen der blossen Vernunft. Die Metaphysik der Sitten* (Berlin, 1914), 82.For the relevant pages in Bahrdt's corpus: C. F. Bahrdt, *System der moralischen Religion zur endlichen Beruhigung für Zweifler und Denker. Allen Christen und Nichtchristen lesbar* (Berlin, 1790), chapters 9 ("On the Authority of Jesus, Judged Philosophically") and 10 ("Continuation"). Kant's critique of Bahrdt is our only interest in this chapter, however.

26. Kant, *Religion within the Boundaries of Mere Reason*, 48; idem, *Die Religion innerhalb der Grenzen der blossen Vernunft*, 13.

27. Ibid., 156; idem, *Die Religion innerhalb der Grenzen der blossen Vernunft*, 128.

28. Ibid., 112; idem, *Die Religion innerhalb der Grenzen der blossen Vernunft*, 82.

29. Ibid., 111; idem, *Die Religion innerhalb der Grenzen der blossen Vernunft*, 80.

30. Ibid., 95; idem, *Die Religion innerhalb der Grenzen der blossen Vernunft*, 61.

31. Ibid., 112; idem, *Die Religion innerhalb der Grenzen der blossen Vernunft*, 82.

32. M. Kuehn, "Kant's Jesus", *Kant's Religion within the Boundaries of Mere Reason*, ed. G. Michalson (Cambridge, 2014), 168 and notes.

33. H. S. Reimarus, *Reimarus: Fragments*, ed. C. H. Talbert, trans. R. S. Fraser (London, 1971), 135. (Translation modified.)

34. Reimarus, *Fragments*, 146–47. (Typography lightly modified.)

35. Kant, *Religion within the Boundaries of Mere Reason*, 112; idem, *Die Religion innerhalb der Grenzen der blossen Vernunft*, 82.

36. Ibid., 112, 156.

37. Ibid., 112. (Translation and typography lightly modified.)

38. Ibid., 112. (Typography lightly modified.)

39. Ibid., 112–13; idem, *Die Religion innerhalb der Grenzen der blossen Vernunft*, 82.

40. Vladimir Nabokov's nacreous line about "that wonderful Jewish sect whose dream of the gentle young rabbi dying on the Roman *crux* had spread over all Northern lands" comes to mind: V. Nabokov, *Bend Sinister* (New York, 1990), 193. Nabokov writes, too, about "intimations of bliss" when reading the gospels and coming across "unexpected, sunlit" phrases like "green grass": idem, *Glory*, trans. D. Nabokov (London, 2012). He is thinking of *Mark* 6:39, where we see—surprisingly—that Jesus "instructed them all to recline in parties (*sumposia*) on the green grass (*chlōrō chortō*)". To my mind, a few other bliss-intimating literary touches—just in *Mark*—are that John the Baptist eats "*wild honey*" (*meli agrion*, *Mark* 1:6); that Jesus is asleep, during a storm, with his head "*on a cushion*" (*epi to proskephalaion*, *Mark* 4:38); and that a transfigured Christ wears garments that are "intensely white, *as no fuller on earth could bleach them*" (*Mark* 9:3).

5. JESUS AND THE HORROR OF DEATH

1. M. Merleau-Ponty, *Nature: Course Notes from the Collège de France*, ed. D. Séglard, trans. R. Vallier (Evanston, Illinois, 2003), 137–38.

2. For the Matthaean changes here: B. M. Metzger, *A Textual Commentary on the Greek New Testament* (London—New York, 1975), 70 (*Matthew*), 119–20 (*Mark*). For the contrast with *Luke* and *John*: K. Aland, *Synopsis of the Four Gospels: Greek-English Edition of the Synopsis Quattuor Evangeliorum* (Stuttgart, 2003), 320–21 (no. 347).

3. For the time-markers: *Mark* 15:1 (daybreak), 15:24 (crucifixion), 15:33 ("when the sixth hour had come"), 15:34 ("at the ninth hour").

4. Metzger, *Textual Commentary on the Greek New Testament*, 122–26, here 125.

5. Apropos of which, Harold Bloom says that "Mark is both a bad writer and a

great one". He concludes, "I would grant Mark his curious literary power": H. Bloom, *Jesus and Yahweh: The Names Divine* (New York, 2005), 60, 71.

6. For Jesus as "Son of God": *Mark* 1:11, *et pass*. The ascription in *Mark* 1:1 is omitted in some ancient manuscripts: Metzger, *Textual Commentary on the Greek New Testament*, 73.

7. B. Pascal, *Pensées*, trans. A. J. Krailsheimer (London—New York, 1966), 126 (no. 316) (translation modified); idem, *Pensées*, ed. L. Brunschvicg (Paris, 1972), 379: *Pourquoi le font-ils faible dans son agonie?* (I have inserted 'the gospel-writers' and 'Jesus' for clarity.) A fine reflection on Pascal's Jesus is L. Goldmann, *The Hidden God: A Study of Tragic Vision in the Pensées of Pascal and the Tragedies of Racine*, trans. P. Thody (London—New York, 2016), 62–86.

8. *John* 11:35; *Luke* 22:44 (absent in many ancient manuscripts). I am grateful to Timothy Dusenbury for reminding me, here, of this powerful image in the *textus receptus* of *Luke*. Modern text-critics have determined that *Luke* 22:44 is "no part of the original text", but its antiquity is not denied: Metzger, *Textual Commentary on the Greek New Testament*, 177.

9. *Mark* 3:5; *Matthew* 12:13; *Luke* 6:10; Aland, *Synopsis of the Four Gospels*, 45 (no. 47).

10. Origen, *Against Celsus* 2.27.

11. *Mark* 14:33–36; *Matthew* 26:37–39; *Luke* 22:41–42; *John* 12:27; Aland, *Synopsis of the Four Gospels*, 297 (no. 330).

12. Aland, *Synopsis of the Four Gospels*, 271–73 (no. 302).

13. George van Kooten calls this an "Eleusinian-type answer". It is in keeping with "the spring festival of the Pascha", that Jesus refers to his "death and resurrection in the veiled language of the dying and growing of a grain of wheat": G. van Kooten, "Christ and Hermes: A Religio-Historical Comparison of the Johannine Christ-Logos with the God Hermes in Greek Mythology and Philosophy", *Im Gespräch mit C. F. Georg Heinrici. Beiträge zwischen Theologie und Religionswissenschaft*, ed. M. Frenschkowski and L. Seehausen (Tübingen, 2021), 277.

14. Origen, *Against Celsus* 2.55; compare 2.58. For "impaling-stake" (and other aspects of this passage): M. M. Mitchell, "Origen, Celsus and Lucian on the 'Dénouement of the Drama' of the Gospels", *Reading Religions in the Ancient World*, ed. D. E. Aune and R. D. Young (Leiden, 2007), 221 note 31: "... perhaps disparagingly, Celsus uses the term σκόλοψ for the cross, rather than σταυρός (Mt 27:32), a predilection he shares with Lucian's depiction of Jesus' form of death."

15. For an unnatural darkness: *Mark* 15:33; *Matthew* 27:45; *Luke* 23:44–45. For an earthquake: *Matthew* 27:51–53. I owe this determination of Celsus' refer-

ence to Mitchell, "Origen, Celsus and Lucian on the 'Dénouement of the Drama' of the Gospels", 221.

16. *Matthew* 27:46; *Mark* 15:34.

17. Origen, *Against Celsus* 2.33.

18. Ibid. 2.36.

19. The line is Homeric: Homer, *Iliad* 5.340, 218–19. In the context that gives it meaning for Celsus' critique of the gospels, it is attributed to Alexander: Plutarch, *Vita Alexandri* 28.2. Later in the tradition, however, the same line is attributed to the philosopher Anaxarchus of Abdera—a denier of Alexander's divinity. The sceptic is said to have said this while pointing at Alexander's wounds: Diogenes Laertius, *Lives of the Philosophers* 9.10.60.

20. Origen, *Against Celsus* 7.53.

21. Plato, *Phaedo* 118.

22. Pascal, *Pensées*, 313 (no. 919) (translation modified); idem, *Pensées*, 244 (no. 553).

23. Origen, *Against Celsus* 2.24.

24. Note, however, Pascal's conclusion that "Jesus prays, uncertain of the will of the Father, and fears death (*et craint la mort*)": Pascal, *Pensées*, 313 (no. 919) (translation modified); idem, *Pensées*, 245 (no. 553).

25. R. M. Thorsteinsson, *Jesus as Philosopher: The Moral Sage in the Synoptic Gospels* (Oxford, 2018), 63.

26. Origen, *Against Celsus* 6.10.

27. Ibid., 2.24.

28. Ibid., 2.24.

29. "Father, into your hands I commit my spirit!" (*Luke* 23:46); "It is finished" (*John* 19:30).

30. We should not forget that Celsus' *True Word* is lost. Origen might be treating Celsus' text in the high-handed way that he accuses his pagan opponent of treating the gospels. But here can we confine ourselves to the text of Origen and fragments of Celsus which, through him, we possess.

31. Origen, *Against Celsus* 2.24.

32. Thus, Ezra Pound in his 1909 poem on the crucifixion: "He cried no cry when they drave the nails and the blood gushed hot and free." E. Pound, *Collected Early Poems of Ezra Pound*, ed. M. J. King, intro. L. L. Martz (New York, 1976), 113 (typography lightly modified).

33. Compare Origen, *Against Celsus* 5.59 (*megalēs ekklēsias*), 5.61 (*tou plēthous*); and an illuminating comment in R. van den Broek, *Gnostic Religion in Antiquity* (Cambridge, 2013), 6.

34. Note, though, that 'Gnosticism' is a modern term—"first coined in 1669 by

the Cambridge Platonist Henry More, in a commentary on the seven letters to the seven churches [in *Revelation*]": van den Broek, *Gnostic Religion in Antiquity*, 5–6.

35. Origen, *Against Celsus* 5.61.

36. *Gospel of Peter* 4.10.

37. It is unnecessary for us to reflect on the nuances of Gnostic and Docetic traditions (or the rich literatures on them), and this line from *The Gospel of Peter* is cited only for its simplicity. Numerous relevant texts are gathered—and brilliantly analysed—in G. G. Stroumsa, "Christ's Laughter: Docetic Origins Reconsidered", *The Crucible of Religion in Late Antiquity* (Tübingen, 2021; reprint of a 2004 article), here 91–97.

38. Origen, *Against Celsus* 2.24.

39. Ibid., 2.24.

40. Epictetus, *Discourses* 1.29.18. As Thorsteinsson notes, Epictetus is echoing Plato's *Crito*—where, however, it is the will of the gods (*theoi*), and not God (*theos*), that must be done: Plato, *Crito* 43d; Thorsteinsson, *Jesus as Philosopher*, 123.

6. JESUS AND THE PRESENTIMENT OF DEATH

1. Josephus, *Against Apion* 1.200–204. Some attribute the scene to a pseudo-Josephus or a pseudo-Hecataeus, but for us, this is immaterial. Our interest in it is philosophical, not historical.

2. The cult of Alexander is relevant in this context, and decisively influenced the Hellenistic practice of elevating kings to the status of divinity: A. S. Bosworth, *Conquest and Empire: The Reign of Alexander the Great* (Cambridge, 1988), 278–90.

3. Some editors change the manuscripts' plural (*Ioudaiōn*), which points to a detachment of Judaean cavalrymen, to the singular (*Ioudaios*), which suggests one Judaean cavalryman within a detachment: Josephus, *Against Apion*, trans. with comm. J. M. G. Barclay (Leiden, 2007), 116 note 680. I prefer the traditional reading. Note, too, that there has been some controversy over how we should render the ancient Greek term *Ioudaioi*. Should it be translated as 'Jews' or 'Judaeans'? I have non-dogmatically, and non-polemically, preferred the latter—for reasons which are suggested by Josephus' extract from the (vaguely hostile) Hellenistic historian Agatharchides of Cnidus (second century BCE), in which Jewish descent, ritual, and law are clearly tied to the land of Judaea—and are, thus, 'Judaean'. This is Agatharchides (apud Josephus): "Those called Judaeans (*hoi kaloumenoi Ioudaioi*) inhabit the best fortified city of all, which, it happens, the natives call Hierosolyma, and it is their custom to do no work every seventh day ... but to pray in the temples until evening, with hands outstretched."

Josephus, *Against Apion* 1.205–212, here 209. Note that, in Agatharchides' description—and throughout this book—the term 'Judaean' is not reductive, but comprehensive. It of course refers to a territory ('Judaea'), and to a people rooted in that territory ('Judaeans'), but it is emphatically meant to refer, too, to their distinctive laws, cultus, and so on.

4. Josephus, *Against Apion* 1.201.

5. The term 'gentile' postdates this incident by many centuries and seems to derive from the Vulgate Bible: S. Penwell, *Jesus the Samaritan: Ethnic Labeling in the Gospel of John* (Leiden, 2019), 23.

6. Josephus, *Against Apion* 1.203.

7. Ibid., 1.204.

8. An important study is K. Johansson, *The Birds in the Iliad: Identities, Interactions and Functions* (Gothenburg, 2012).

9. For the persistence of this idea in late antiquity: Origen, *Against Celsus* 4.89.

10. Josephus, *Against Apion* 1.204.

11. Josephus, *Judaean Antiquities* 18.63–64; E. Schürer, *The History of the Jewish People in the Age of Jesus Christ (175 B.C.–A.D. 135)*, rev. and ed. G. Vermes and F. Millar, with P. Vermes and M. Black (Edinburgh, 1973), 1.437; S. Pines, *An Arabic Version of the Testimonium Flavianum and Its Implications* (Jerusalem, 1971), 9–10. There will be more in chapter 7 on the long-doubted *Testimonium Flavianum*.

12. Josephus, *Against Apion* 1.204.

13. *Matthew* 27:33; *Mark* 15:22; *Luke* 23:33; *John* 19:17. Columnized in K. Aland, *Synopsis of the Four Gospels: Greek-English Edition of the Synopsis Quattuor Evangeliorum* (Stuttgart, 2003), 316 (no. 344).

14. Origen, *Against Celsus* 2.17.

15. Ibid., 5.59.

16. Josephus, *Against Apion* 1.204.

17. Origen, *Against Celsus* 2.17.

18. L. Glück, *Poems 1962–2012* (New York, 2012), 413.

19. For Hebrew and Graeco-Roman parallels: M. D. Litwa, *How the Gospels Became History: Jesus and Mediterranean Myths* (New Haven—London, 2019), 152–54.

20. Josephus, *Judaean Antiquities* 18.63; Schürer, *History of the Jewish People*, 1:437 (translation modified). Compare *Luke* 5:26, the only place in the New Testament where *paradoxos* is used to described Jesus' doings.

21. B. de Spinoza, *Theological-Political Treatise*, ed. J. Israel, trans. M. Silverthorne and J. Israel (Cambridge, 2007), 32; idem, *Tractatus Theologico-Politicus. Traité Théologico-Politique*, Latin ed. F. Akkerman, French trans. J. Lagrée and

P.-F. Moreau (Paris, 1999), 124–25: de rebus enim humanis tantum agebatur, quae quidem limites humanae capacitatis non excedunt, nisi quia futurae sunt.

22. See René Girard's naturalistic defence of Jesus' predictions of Peter's denials: R. Girard, *The Scapegoat*, trans. Y. Freccero (Baltimore, 1989), 157–58.

23. Seneca, *Moral Epistles* 76.35. This and other philosophical parallels to Jesus' prescience are noted at R. M. Thorsteinsson, *Jesus as Philosopher: The Moral Sage in the Synoptic Gospels* (Oxford, 2018), 153–54.

24. *Matthew* 16:3; compare *Luke* 12:56.

25. Philostratus, *Life of Apollonius* 5.24.

26. I stress that Peirce's belongings were recovered. The case nevertheless makes for unpleasant reading. It is reported in T. Sebeok and J. Umiker-Sebeok, "'You Know My Method'", *The Sign of Three: Dupin, Holmes, Peirce*, ed. U. Eco and T. Sebeok (Bloomington, 1983), 11–17.

27. D. Potter, *Prophets and Emperors: Human and Divine Authority from Augustus to Theodosius* (Cambridge, Mass., 1994), 31–35.

28. Clement of Alexandria, *Exhortation* 2.

29. "Those whom you worship were once men ... Legend and the lapse of time have given them their honours": Clement of Alexandria, *Exhortation* 4. But on Clement's reckoning, many gods are *less* than this. Poseidon, for him, is nothing but "water itself". The god takes his name—or, rather, is given his name— "from *posis*, drink": idem, *Exhortation* 5.

30. Eusebius of Caesarea, *Demonstratio Evangelica* 3.5.124.

31. Nemesius of Emesa, *On Human Nature* 3.

32. A. Schiavone, *Pontius Pilate: Deciphering a Memory* (New York—London, 2017).

33. Schiavone, *Pontius Pilate*, 161–65.

34. F. Nietzsche, *Human, All Too Human*, trans. R. J. Hollingdale (Cambridge, 1996), 233; idem, *Menschliches, Allzumenschliches I und II*, ed. G. Colli and M. Montinari (Berlin—New York, 1988), 414.

35. Schiavone, *Pontius Pilate*, 34.

36. E. Auerbach, *Mimesis: The Representation of Reality in Western Literature*, trans. W. R. Trask (Princeton, 2003), 562 note 6.

37. Auerbach, *Mimesis*, 151, 154.

38. Schiavone, *Pontius Pilate*, 140–43.

39. Ibid., 15.

40. Ibid., 156.

41. Josephus, *Against Apion* 1.204.

42. Origen, *Against Celsus* 2.17.

43. A. Watson, *The Trial of Jesus* (Athens, Georgia, 1995), 173–75.

44. Schiavone, *Pontius Pilate*, 126–27.

45. J. W. van Henten, "Jewish Martyrdom and Jesus' Death", *Deutungen des Todes Jesu im Neuen Testament*, ed. J. Frey and J. Schröter (Tübingen, 2012), 145–46.

46. M. Foucault, *Fearless Speech*, ed. J. Pearson (Los Angeles, 2001). *Caveat lector.* This is not what *parrhēsia* means in *John* 18:20, but "fearless speech" is a structuring motif in the gospels and *Acts of the Apostles*. I make use of *John* 18:20, here, to indicate a real, but immensely complex, motif in the gospels.

47. Note the pagan analogues to Jesus' death mentioned by Christian writers in *I Clement* 55:1, "many kings and rulers have surrendered themselves to death, at the instruction of an oracle, in order to rescue their subjects through their own blood"; and Origen, *Against Celsus* 1.31, "Jesus voluntarily accepted death for the sake of the race of men, just like those who died for their fatherland to save it from prevailing epidemics", here as cited by H. S. Versnel, "Making Sense of Jesus' Death: The Pagan Contribution", *Deutungen des Todes Jesu im Neuen Testament*, ed. J. Frey and J. Schröter (Tübingen, 2012), 218–19.

48. Philostratus, *Life of Apollonius* 7.14.

49. See the mention of Socrates' accusers at Philostratus, *Life of Apollonius* 7.13.

50. Origen, *Against Celsus* 2.17.

51. Versnel, "Jesus' Death: The Pagan Contribution", 227–30. A reception history of Socrates as the exemplary martyr-philosopher is K. Döring, *Exemplum Socratis: Studien zur Sokratesnachwirkung in der kynisch-stoischen Popularphilosophie der frühen Kaiserzeit und im frühen Christentum* (Wiesbaden, 1979).

52. P. Wintour, "Persecution of Christians 'Coming Close to Genocide' in Middle East", *The Guardian* (2 May 2019). Archived online at https://www.theguard-ian.com/world/2019/may/02/persecution-driving-christians-out-of-middle-east-report; accessed on 5 June 2019.

53. Origen, *Against Celsus* 2.17.

7. "A GOD WHO WAS CONDEMNED"

1. Eusebius of Caesarea, *Ecclesiastical History* 1.10.6, 2.4.1, etc. For some of the later vagaries of 'passion' in Europe: E. Auerbach, "*Passio* as Passion (1941)", *Time, History, and Literature: Selected Essays of Erich Auerbach*, ed. J. I. Porter, trans. J. O. Newman (Princeton, 2014), here 169–82.

2. *Luke* 22:44, here in the 'Wycliffe' version (which is not from the hand of John Wycliffe): J. Wycliffe, *The Wycliffe New Testament (1388)*, ed. W. R. Cooper (London, 2002). For the conclusion that this verse, though very ancient, is not original to *Luke*'s Passion narrative: B. M. Metzger, *A Textual Commentary on the Greek New Testament* (London—New York, 1975), 177.

3. In *Matthew* 26:50, Jesus greets Judas as a "friend" or "comrade" (*hetaire*), and then asks: "Why are you here?" Compare *Luke* 22:48.

4. *Luke* 22:61 (the text is preterite; "The Lord *turning looked* on Peter", in the Douay-Rheims Translation); *Luke* 23:34 (Authorized Version); *Luke* 23:43 (New Revised Standard Version).

5. For "Skull": *Luke* 23:33; comparing *Matthew* 27:33; *Mark* 15:22; and *John* 19:17. Columnized in K. Aland, *Synopsis of the Four Gospels: Greek-English Edition of the Synopsis Quattuor Evangeliorum* (Stuttgart, 2003), 316 (no. 344). For the *coup de lance* (as it is called): *John* 19:33–34. A strong textual variant of *Matthew* 27:49 places the piercing of Jesus' side *before* his death, and not, like the Johannine *coup de lance*, after he expires: D. M. Gurtner, "Water and Blood and Matthew 27:49: A Johannine Reading in the Matthean Passion Narrative?", *Studies on the Text of the New Testament and Early Christianity*, ed. D. M. Gurtner, J. Hernández, and P. Foster (Leiden, 2015), 134–50.

6. We find two Greek renderings of her name, *Maria* and *Mariam*, in the gospels. *Maria* is preferred in *Mark* and *Matthew* (see *Mark* 6:3; *Matthew* 1:16); *Mariam* is preferred in *Luke–Acts* (see *Luke* 1:27; *Acts of the Apostles* 1:14). Though Jesus' mother figures prominently in *John*, she is never named (see *John* 2:3, "the mother of Jesus"; and *John* 19:25–27, "Jesus saw his mother").

7. T. Eagleton, "Lunging, Flailing, Mispunching", *London Review of Books* 28, 20 (2006), 32–34; idem, *Radical Sacrifice* (New Haven—London, 2018), 30–58.

8. *Romans* 6:4. For an early Christian gloss on this verse: Clement of Alexandria, *Exhortation* 4.

9. B. Pascal, *Pensées*, trans. A. J. Krailsheimer (London—New York, 1966), 123 (no. 300) (translation modified); idem, *Pensées*, ed. L. Brunschvicg (Paris, 1972) 373 (no. 786).

10. E. Auerbach, *Mimesis: The Representation of Reality in Western Literature*, trans. W. R. Trask (Princeton, 2003), 42–43.

11. For the immensely complex history of the premodern quest to obtain dates for Jesus' birth and death: T. C. Schmidt, "Calculating December 25 as the Birth of Jesus in Hippolytus' *Canon* and *Chronicon*", *Vigiliae Christianae* 69, 5 (2015), 542–63; C. P. E. Nothaft, *Dating the Passion: The Life of Jesus and the Emergence of Scientific Chronology (200–1600)* (Leiden, 2012).

12. P. Pokorný, "Jesus as the Ever-Living Lawgiver in the *Letter* of Mara bar Sarapion", *The Letter of Mara bar Sarapion in Context*, ed. A. Merz and T. Tieleman (Leiden, 2012), 129–39, here 135 note 13: "Soon after [William] Cureton's publication of the *Letter* in 1855, Mara's opinion about Jesus was almost forgotten." The *Letter* is still almost forgotten.

13. R. E. Van Voorst, "Jesus Tradition in Classical and Jewish Writings", *Handbook*

for the Study of the Historical Jesus, ed. T. Holmén and S. E. Porter (Leiden, 2011), 2159.

14. F. Millar, *The Roman Near East, 31 BC–AD 33* (Cambridge, Mass., 1993), 461: "If there is an appropriate context [for the *Letter*], it is the early 70s."

15. George van Kooten argues, boldly, not only that Mara's *Letter* is a late-first-century text, but that "there is even reason to assume that Mara is here dependent on John's gospel": G. van Kooten, "The Last Days of Socrates and Christ: *Euthyphro, Apology, Crito*, and *Phaedo* Read in Counterpoint with John's Gospel", *Religio-Philosophical Discourses in the Mediterranean World: From Plato, through Jesus, to Late Antiquity*, ed. A. Klostergaard Petersen and G. van Kooten (Leiden, 2017), 219–21.

16. Theories that make Mara's *Letter* a rhetorical set-piece in epistolary form written in the second or third century (or later), are not convincing: Pokorný, "Jesus as the Ever-Living Lawgiver", 132–33.

17. Van Voorst, "Jesus Tradition in Classical and Jewish Writings", 2160–61.

18. Pokorný, "Jesus as the Ever-Living Lawgiver", 129 (Syriac text), 131 (Stoic text), 134 (Jesus' death).

19. *Letter of Mara bar Sarapion* 18; "The Epistle of Mara, Son of Serapion", *Spicilegium Syriacum: Containing Remains of Bardesan, Meliton, Ambrose and Mara bar Serapion*, ed. with English trans. and notes W. Cureton (London, 1855), 73–74; Pokorný, "Jesus as the Ever-Living Lawgiver", 133.

20. Even before Jesus' death, we read in one of the gospels, "his fame spread throughout all Syria" (*Matthew* 4:24). For the decimation of ancient Christian peoples in the region: E. Griswold, "Is This the End of Christianity in the Middle East?", *The New York Times Magazine* (22 July 2015). Archived online at https://www.nytimes.com/2015/07/26/magazine/is-this-the-end-of-christianity-in-the-middle-east.html; accessed on 1 August 2022.

21. F. F. Bruce, *New Testament History* (New York, 1980), 30.

22. Dio of Prusa, *Orations* 47.6; Josephus, *Judaean Antiquities* 18.116.

23. *Matthew* 23:37–39; *Luke* 13:34–35; Aland, *Synopsis of the Four Gospels*, 253 (no. 285).

24. Though the "desolation" that Jesus warns of is centred upon the temple-city of Jerusalem, it threatens the whole territory of Judaea: *Matthew* 24:15–16; *Mark* 13:14; *Luke* 21:20–22; Aland, *Synopsis of the Four Gospels*, 258 (no. 290). Related to this is a tradition that before Jerusalem fell in 70 CE many Christ-believers fled to "one of the cities of Peraea"—namely, Pella: Eusebius of Caesarea, *Ecclesiastical History* 3.5.3.

25. For the date of Lucian's text: J. N. Bremmer, "Lucian on Peregrinus and Alexander of Abonuteichnos: A Sceptical View of Two Religious Entrepreneurs", *Beyond Priesthood: Religious Entrepreneurs and Innovators in*

the Roman Empire, ed. R. L. Gordon, G. Petridou, and J. Rüpke (Berlin, 2017), 49–78, here 49. For "the man who was crucified": Lucian of Samosata, The Death of Peregrinus 11.

26. For Socrates: Plato Apology 24c; Diogenes Laertius, Lives of the Philosophers 2.5.40. For Jesus: Mark 1:27.

27. It is not Jesus but an imprisoned Cynic-philosopher-turned-Christian, Peregrinus, who is called "the new Socrates" (kainos Sōkratēs). The connection to Jesus' legal ordeal is oblique, but definite: Lucian of Samosata, The Death of Peregrinus 12.

28. Lucian of Samosata, The Death of Peregrinus, 12.

29. Ibid., 11, 13.

30. G. Samuelsson, Crucifixion in Antiquity: An Inquiry into the Background and Significance of the New Testament Terminology of Crucifixion (Tübingen, 2013), 273–74.

31. Tacitus, Annals 15.44. For more on crucifixion in Tacitus' corpus: G. Samuelsson, Crucifixion in Antiquity: An Inquiry into the Background and Significance of the New Testament Terminology of Crucifixion (Tübingen, 2013), 161–67.

32. For Tertullian: Tertullian of Carthage, On the Veiling of Virgins 1. For Marcellus: H. Denzinger, ed., Enchiridion Symbolorum definitionem et declarationem de rebus fidei et morum, rev. A. Schönmetzer (Barcelona, 1963), 21.

33. See Menaham Stern's commentary: M. Stern, Greek and Latin Authors on Jews and Judaism. Volume Two: From Tacitus to Simplicius (Jerusalem, 1980), 88–93 (Tacitus).

34. Pliny the Younger, Letters 10.96.7.

35. Suetonius, Lives of the Twelve Caesars, Claudius 4.

36. E. Haenchen, The Acts of the Apostles: A Commentary, trans. H. Anderson and R. M. Wilson (Philadelphia, 1971), 65, 532, 538–39.

37. Tertullian of Carthage, Apology 3.5. Tacitus may make a pun on this confusion. See the ingenious reading of Tacitus, Annals 15.44 in Haenchen, The Acts of the Apostles, 65.

38. Tacitus, Annals 15.44.

39. Suetonius, Lives of the Twelve Caesars, Nero 16.

40. Menaham Stern is more forceful. "There exists hardly any serious doubt", he writes, "that here Chrestus = Christus, i.e. Jesus". Stern concludes that Suetonius' syntax "need not imply [the] physical presence [of Chrestus–Christus in Rome] but only an act of instigation". Thus, in his judgement: "The disturbances referred to here by Suetonius reflect the earliest stage of the diffusion of Christianity within the city of Rome. They occurred only a few years after the death of Jesus, when the Christians were still considered by the Roman

41. Ibid., Suetonius, *Lives of Twelve Caesars*, Nero 16.

42. Lucian of Samosata, *The Death of Peregrinus* 11.

43. For Justin's Trypho: W. Varner, "On the Trail of Trypho: Two Fragmentary Jewish-Christian Dialogues from the Ancient Church", *Christian Origins and Hellenistic Judaism: Social and Literary Contexts for the New Testament*, ed. S. E. Porter and A. Pitts (Leiden, 2013); J. M. Hubbard, "Does Justin Argue with Jews? Reconsidering the Relevance of Philo", *Vigiliae Christianae* (forthcoming). For Celsus' Judaean: M. R. Niehoff, "A Jewish Critique of Christianity from Second-Century Alexandria: Revisiting the Jew Mentioned in *Contra Celsum*", *Journal of Early Christian Studies* 21, 2 (2013), 151–75; J. N. Carleton Paget, "The Jew of Celsus and *Adversus Judaeos* Literature", *Zeitschrift für Antikes Christentum* 21, 2 (2017), 201–42.

44. Justin the Philosopher, *Dialogue with Trypho the Judaean* 108.2; Carleton Paget, "Jew of Celsus and *Adversus Judaeos* Literature", 236.

45. Justin the Philosopher, *First Apology* 13.

46. Carleton Paget, "Jew of Celsus and *Adversus Judaeos* Literature", 222 note 122.

47. I have in mind, here, the terrible blood libel. For its anti-Christian versions in the first centuries CE: J. Rives, "Human Sacrifice among Pagans and Christians", *Journal of Roman Studies* 85 (1995), 65–85.

48. Origen, *Against Celsus* 2.1.

49. Carleton Paget, "Jew of Celsus and *Adversus Judaeos* Literature", 241–42.

50. Origen, *Against Celsus* 2.4.

51. Ibid., 2.5.

52. Ibid., 2.10.

53. Ibid., 2.34.

54. Origen doubts the Euripidean ornamentation in *Against Celsus* 2.34: "Judaeans are not at all well read in Greek literature. But supposing that some Judaean *had* become so well read as this ..."

55. Origen, *Against Celsus* 2.5, 2.34.

56. H. J. De Jonge, "Joseph Scaliger's Historical Criticism of the New Testament", *Novum Testamentum* 38, 2 (1996), 176–93, here 189–91.

57. E. Schürer, *The History of the Jewish People in the Age of Jesus Christ (175 B.C.–A.D. 135)*, rev. and ed. G. Vermes and F. Millar, with P. Vermes and M. Black (Edinburgh, 1973), 1.428–41.

58. I follow the text in Geza Vermes' and Fergus Millar's "new Schürer", but the translation is a composite. I have consulted Josephus, *Judaean Antiquities* 18.63–64; Schürer, *History of the Jewish People*, 1.437; and J. P. Meier, *A Marginal Jew:*

Rethinking the Historical Jesus, Volume One: The Roots of the Problem and the Person (New Haven, 1991), 61.

59. S. Pines, *An Arabic Version of the Testimonium Flavianum and Its Implications* (Jerusalem, 1971), 7. (Typography lightly modified.)

60. Pines, *Arabic Version of the Testimonium Flavianum*, 7–8 (and notes). (Typography lightly modified.)

61. For more on this difficult name: Pines, *Arabic Version of the Testimonium Flavianum*, 52 note 184, 53 note 188.

62. Pines, *Arabic Version of the Testimonium Flavianum*, 8. (Typography lightly modified.) Note that this text is connected to certain apocrypha on Pilate.

63. Ibid., 8.

64. Ibid., 9–10. (Typography lightly modified and translation lightly modified: 'Judaeans' as in this book; 'Christ' in keeping with Pines's notes.)

65. For more on this: Pines, *Arabic Version of the Testimonium Flavianum*, 19–20.

66. Lactantius, *Divine Institutes* 5.12.8.

67. The divergence is least clear in our Roman sources. It nevertheless seems legitimate to note a certain difference in tone between Pliny (who puts Christians to death) and Tacitus (who only recounts how Nero put them to death). For whatever reason, in Pliny's much-cited letter to Trajan, he makes no negative comment about the Christians' eponymous Christ.

68. Eusebius of Caesarea, *Demonstration of the Gospel* 3.6–7, here 3.7.1. Compare Augustine of Hippo, *The City of God against the Pagans* 19.23; A. Busine, *Paroles d'Apollon. Pratiques et traditions oraculaires dans l'Antiquité tardive (IIe–VIe siècles)* (Leiden, 2005), 280–81.

69. Augustine of Hippo, *The City of God against the Pagans* 19.23.

8. JURISDICTIONS AND *DRAMATIS PERSONAE*

1. F. Nietzsche, *The Case of Wagner. Twilight of the Idols. The Antichrist. Ecce Homo. Dionysus Dithyrambs. Nietzsche Contra Wagner*, ed. G. Colli and M. Montinari, trans. A. Del Caro, C. Diethe, et al. (Stanford, 2021), 162.

2. E. Schürer, *The History of the Jewish People in the Age of Jesus Christ (175 B.C.–A.D. 135)*, rev. and ed. G. Vermes and F. Millar, with P. Vermes and M. Black (Edinburgh, 1973), 239.

3. Josephus, *Judaean War* 1.148–49; Schürer, *History of the Jewish People*, 1.238–39.

4. Josephus, *Judaean War* 1.152–54. The Essenes so "hate[d] their Hasmonean rivals that they actually rejoiced when ... Pompey conquered Jerusalem and defiled the temple: after all, the temple had already been defiled, as they saw it,

by their priestly opponents." P. Fredriksen, *When Christians Were Jews: The First Generation* (New Haven, 2018), 31.

5. Josephus, *Judaean War* 1.152–54. For a precis of the many conflicts and convolutions marking Hyrcanus' high priesthood: Schürer, *History of the Jewish People*, 1.233–41.

6. Schürer, *History of the Jewish People*, 1.267–80; M. Goodman, *The Ruling Class of Judaea: The Origins of the Jewish Revolt against Rome A.D. 66–70* (Cambridge, 1987), 31–33.

7. Frederick Bruce notes that the "very existence of some eastern cities [in our period] was so closely bound up with their sacred associations … that they had special constitutions as temple-cities". Jerusalem is one; other 'temple-cities', in this stricter sense, are Ephesus in Asia (temple-city of Artemis) and Hierapolis in Syria (temple-city of Artagatis): F. F. Bruce, *New Testament History* (New York, 1980), 18–19.

8. For *pontifex*, see *John* 18:13; for *princeps sacerdotum*, see *Matthew* 26:57 and *Luke* 22:54; and for *summus sacerdos*, see *Mark* 14:53.

9. The provincial status of Roman Judaea is not entirely clear. I rely on Schürer, *History of the Jewish People*, 1:357, where he writes that the prefect of Judaea remained, in our period, "to some extent subordinate to the imperial legate, *legatus Augusti pro praetore*, in Syria". Judaea thus belongs to what Schürer calls a "third class of imperial provinces".

10. For the Roman origins of this cultus: I. Gradel, *Emperor Worship and Roman Religion* (Oxford, 2002).

11. *Mark* 8:27 (Caesarea Philippi); *John* 6:1 (Sea of Tiberias). It is worth noting, too, that a settlement the gospels call *Bethsaida* bears the name *Julias*—for Augustus' unfortunate daughter, Julia, or for Tiberius' later-deified mother, Livia Julia—in other first-century texts. For Augustus' daughter: Josephus, *Judaean War* 3.10.7. For Tiberius' mother: C. R. Matthews, *Philip, Apostle and Evangelist: Configurations of a Tradition* (Leiden, 2002), 109 note 52.

12. Schürer, *History of the Jewish People*, 1:357–62.

13. J. Scheid, *The Gods, the State, and the Individual: Reflections on Civic Religion in Rome*, trans. C. Ando (Philadelphia, 2015).

14. Schürer, *History of the Jewish People*, 1.379–81.

15. Josephus, *Judaean War* 2.408–21; Schürer, *History of the Jewish People*, 1.381–82.

16. Schürer, *History of the Jewish People*, 1.340–42.

17. Schürer, *History of the Jewish People*, 1.341–42; H. W. Hoehner, *Herod Antipas: A Contemporary of Jesus Christ* (Cambridge, 1972); P. Schäfer, *The History of the Jews in the Greco-Roman World* (London—New York, 2003), 105–106; M. H. Jensen, *Herod Antipas in Galilee: The Literary and Archaeological Sources*

on the Reign of Herod Antipas and its Socio-Economic Impact on Galilee (Tübingen, 2006).

18. "Younger Herod": Eusebius of Caesarea, *Ecclesiastical History* 1.9.1, 1.11.1. "King of the Judaeans": Josephus, *Judaean Antiquities* 14.14.4–5; idem, *Judaean War* 1.14.4; Schürer, *History of the Jewish People*, 1.281.

19. Eusebius of Caesarea, *Ecclesiastical History* 1.8.4–5.

20. A. Watson, *The Trial of Stephen: The First Christian Martyr* (Athens, Georgia, 2012), 46.

21. Compare *Matthew* 21:11, where he is "Jesus the prophet ... of Galilee"; and *John* 7:52, where he is derided as a (false) "prophet ... out of Galilee".

22. Stewart Penwell is not convinced that this is, exactly, an "ethnic slur". Consult S. Penwell, *Jesus the Samaritan: Ethnic Labeling in the Gospel of John* (Leiden, 2019), 14–17, here 16: "Bultmann is most likely correct ... that when Jesus is called a Samaritan he was presenting heretical (i.e. unacceptable) opinions."

23. *Acts* 11:26; E. Haenchen, *The Acts of the Apostles: A Commentary*, trans. H. Anderson and R. M. Wilson (Philadelphia, 1971), 371–72. The temporal indices in *Acts* 11:19 ("the persecution that took place") and *Acts* 12:1 ("about that time") may suggest a date circa 43 CE: Haenchen, *Acts of the Apostles*, 61–71. Note, too, that 'Christianity' (*Christianismos*) is put into circulation by Ignatius of Antioch in the early second century: T. Holland, *Dominion: How the Christian Revolution Remade the World* (New York, 2019), 120.

24. Consult the argumentive arc of S. Penwell, *Jesus the Samaritan: Ethnic Labeling in the Gospel of John* (Leiden, 2019).

25. The picture is, in fact, more complicated. The gospels contain many scenes outside Judaea in which Jesus' life is threatened. The Passion 'begins' in the first pages of the first gospel to be written, when certain Pharisees and Herodians conspire in Capernaum—a Galilean settlement—"against him, how to destroy him" (*Mark* 3:6). Thus, it seems that Jesus' peripateticism is determined by Herod's hostility in Galilee: Jensen, *Herod Antipas in Galilee*, 111–12.

26. Galilee and Peraea: Josephus, *Judaean Antiquities* 17.8.1. Exile in Gaul: Josephus, *Judaean Antiquities* 18.7.2; idem. *Judaean War* 2.9.6; Schürer, *History of the Jewish People*, 1:351–53; Schäfer, *History of the Jews in the Greco-Roman World*, 106.

27. F. Millar, "Reflections on the Trials of Jesus", *A Tribute to Geza Vermes: Essays on Jewish and Christian Literature and History*, ed. P. R. Davies and R. T. White (Sheffield, 1990), 368–69.

28. Here in the translation of Jensen, *Herod Antipas in Galilee*, 110. Compare *Mark* 6:14, "Jesus' name had become known".

29. Bruce, *New Testament History*, 25 (brothers' wives), 26 (nieces), 28 (niece and brother's wife). We can note, for instance, that Herod I's uncle married his niece

(Herod's sister), Salome—and that Herod later had this uncle (and brother-in-law) put to death, because he had slept with Herod's wife (his sister-in-law), Mariamme, when the "King of the Judeaeans" was in Syria: Schürer, *History of the Jewish People*, 1.298.

30. Josephus, *Judaean Antiquities* 18.136; *Matthew* 14:3–4; *Mark* 6:17–18; *Luke* 3:19–20; K. Aland, *Synopsis of the Four Gospels: Greek-English Edition of the Synopsis Quattuor Evangeliorum* (Stuttgart, 2003), 133 (no. 144); Schürer, *History of the Jewish People*, 1.344; and Jensen, *Herod Antipas in Galilee*, 96, 110–14.

31. Bruce, *New Testament History*, 28.

32. "Josephus explains the enmity between the two as being due above all to Antipas' fear of John's political influence on the people, while according to the New Testament, John was said to have denounced Antipas' unlawful marriage to Herodias. Both factors probably played a part": P. Schäfer, *The History of the Jews in the Greco-Roman World* (London—New York, 2003), 105.

33. It is worth noting, in light of Jesus' proclamation of the divine kingdom, that *Mark* colloquially calls Herod Antipas a king (*Mark* 6:14) and his tetrarchy a kingdom (*Mark* 6:23).

34. Josephus, *Judaean Antiquities* 18.119. Josephus and the gospels differ on the reason for John's beheading, but I tend to agree with Emil Schürer that their accounts are not unreconcilable: Schürer, *History of the Jewish People*, 1.345–48.

35. For Herod's "grief": *Matthew* 14:9; *Mark* 6:26. For the difficulty of correlating the gospels' unnamed "girl-child" (*korasion*) with Herodias' daughter Salome in Josephus: Schürer, *History of the Jewish People*, 1.348 note 28. And for Herod's *natalia*, which could be taken to mark his birthday or accession-day (as tetrarch): *Matthew* 14:6; *Mark* 6:21; Jensen, *Herod Antipas in Galilee*, 112 note 81.

36. M. Praz, *The Romantic Agony*, trans. A. Davidson (Oxford, 1933), 336–37.

37. R. Girard, *The Scapegoat*, trans. Y. Freccero (Baltimore, 1986), 130–31, 136.

38. C. à Lapide, *The Great Commentary of Cornelius à Lapide*, trans. T. W. Mossman, et al. (London, 1887–1890), 3.402.

39. *Matthew* 14:3–12; *Mark* 6:17–29; Aland, *Synopsis of the Four Gospels*, 133 (no. 144).

40. Though not much is said about Caiaphas in first-century texts, much can be inferred: R. Metzner, *Kaiphas. Der Hohepriester jenes Jahres. Geschichte und Deutung* (Leiden, 2010), 35–176.

41. Caiaphas elevated: Josephus, *Judaean Antiquities* 18.33–35. Caiaphas deposed: Josephus, *Judaean Antiquities* 18.95; Schürer, *History of the Jewish People*, 2.230.

42. R. Brown, *The Death of the Messiah: From Gethsemane to the Grave: A*

Commentary on the Passion Narratives in the Four Gospels (New York—London, 1994), 1.410.

43. Schürer, *History of the Jewish People*, 1.379–80.

44. Josephus, *Judaean Antiquities* 18.90–95; Schürer, *History of the Jewish People*, 1.379.

45. A. France, "The Procurator of Judea", *Tales from a Mother-of-Pearl Casket*, trans. H. Pène du Bois (New York, 1896), 26.

46. For a reconstructed text, translation, and level-headed interpretation: D. W. Chapman and E. J. Schnabel, *The Trial and Crucifixion of Jesus: Texts and Commentary* (Tübingen, 2015), 165–67.

47. H. K. Bond, *Pontius Pilate in History and Interpretation* (Cambridge, 1998), 12 note 62.

48. Schürer, *History of the Jewish People*, 1.383–87.

49. I am grateful to Talila Michaeli for a facsimile of the archaeological report, which I follow closely: S. Amorai-Stark, Y. Kalman, M. Hershkovitz, R. Chachy, G. Forster, and R. Porat, "An Inscribed Copper-Alloy Finger Ring from Herodium Depicting a Krater", *Israel Exploration Journal* 68, 2 (2018), 208–20.

50. P. Karasz, "Pontius Pilate's Name Is Found on 2,000-Year-Old Ring", *The New York Times* (20 November 2018); archived online at https://www.nytimes.com/2018/11/30/world/middleeast/pontius-pilate-ring.html; accessed on 9 June 2019.

51. Amorai-Stark, et al., "Inscribed Copper-Alloy Finger Ring", 216 note 15.

52. Tacitus, *Annals* 15.44.

53. Philo, *Embassy to Gaius* 299; Josephus, *Judaean War* 2.169.

54. Philo, *Embassy to Gaius* 178–224, here 188.

55. Ibid., 301–302.

56. Josephus, *Judaean Antiquities* 18.55, 59.

9. JUDAEAN PHILOSOPHIES AND CONFUSED JUDGES

1. Josephus, *Life of Josephus* 7–10.

2. Josephus, *Judaean War* 2.119.

3. The ordering of Pharisees–Sadducees–Essenes is consistent in Josephus' corpus: Josephus, *Life of Josephus* 10; idem, *Judaean War* 2.119; idem, *Judaean Antiquities* 13.171–73, 18.12–22 (note, though, that he inverts the order for rhetorical effect when he introduces the schema at *Judaean Antiquities* 18.11: Essenes–Sadducees–Pharisees). This is likely because he identifies as a Pharisee.

4. Josephus, *Life of Josephus* 12.

5. Epictetus, *Discourses* 1.15.2, 4. For the bold insistence by Epictetus' Stoic master,

Musonius Rufus, that philosophy is "a common obligation ... for men and women": R. M. Thorsteinsson, *Roman Christianity and Roman Stoicism: A Comparative Study of Ancient Morality* (Oxford, 2010), 49–51.

6. Josephus, *Life of Josephus* 11.
7. Josephus, *Judaean Antiquities* 18.9, 23.
8. Josephus, *Judaean War* 2.118.
9. Josephus, *Judaean Antiquities* 18.23.
10. Ibid., 18.23–25.
11. His epithet in *Mark* 3:19 (and *Matthew* 10:4), "Simon the Cananaean", likely stems from an Aramaic word for the "zealous". For more on which: A. Yarbro Collins, *Mark: A Commentary*, ed. H. W. Attridge (Minneapolis, 2007), 222–23.
12. A. Watson, *Jesus: A Profile* (Athens, Georgia, 1998), 72, 159 note 9.
13. M. Smith, "The Troublemakers", *The Cambridge History of Judaism, Volume Three: The Early Roman Period*, ed. W. Horbury, W. Davies, and J. Sturdy (Cambridge, 1999), 540: "The term '*zēlōtēs*' was long and widely used as an honorific designation of religious fanatics."
14. J. Schaper, "The Pharisees", *The Cambridge History of Judaism, Volume Three: The Early Roman Period*, ed. W. Horbury, W. Davies, and J. Sturdy (Cambridge, 1999), 404–405.
15. Cit. Schaper, "Pharisees", 420.
16. Schaper, "Pharisees", 420–21.
17. Schaper, "Pharisees", 409. A brilliant analysis is E. J. Bickerman, "The Chain of the Pharisaic Tradition", *Studies in Jewish and Christian History: A New Edition in English including The God of the Maccabees*, ed. A. Tropper (Leiden, 2007).
18. *Mark* 1:22. For Jesus' critique of "the tradition of the elders", compare *Mark* 7:1–23 and *Matthew* 15:1–9.
19. Eusebius of Caesarea, *Ecclesiastical History* 1.3.1.
20. B. de Spinoza, *Theological-Political Treatise*, ed. J. Israel, trans. M. Silverthorne and J. Israel (Cambridge, 2007), 41.
21. Jesus dines on three occasions with Pharisees in *Luke* (but only in *Luke*). Compare *Luke* 7:36, 11:37, and 14:1. Though it only becomes salient in late twentieth-century scholarship, the idea of a Pharisaic Jesus dates back to the seventeenth century, if not before: C. Facchini, "Jesus the Pharisee: Leon Modena, the Historical Jesus, and Renaissance Venice", *Journal for the Study of the Historical Jesus* 17, 1–2 (2019), 81–101.
22. *Luke* 14:1; Schaper, "Pharisees", 424–25.
23. G. Stemberger, "The Sadducees—Their History and Doctrines", *The Cambridge History of Judaism, Volume Three: The Early Roman Period*, ed. W. Horbury, W. Davies, and J. Sturdy (Cambridge, 1999), 428, 439–40.

24. Stemberger, "Sadducees", 428.

25. M. Goodman, *The Ruling Class of Judaea: The Origins of the Jewish Revolt against Rome A.D. 66–70* (Cambridge, 1987), 1–25.

26. Stemberger, "Sadducees", 434.

27. Pharisees and Sadducees: Stemberger, "Sadducees", 436. Denial of the resurrection: *Mark* 12:18; *Acts* 23:8; Stemberger, "Sadducees", 440–41.

28. Josephus, *Judaean Antiquities* 20.199.

29. Schaper, "Pharisees", 424–25.

30. Ibid., 425.

31. O. Betz, "The Essenes", *The Cambridge History of Judaism, Volume Three: The Early Roman Period*, ed. W. Horbury, W. Davies, and J. Sturdy (Cambridge, 1999), 453–54.

32. Jesus himself points this out, apropos of John, in *Luke* 7:33 and *Matthew* 11:18.

33. A further contrast is Jesus' practice of worshipping at the Temple, which is both reflected and confirmed by the first Christ-believers' decision to live in Jerusalem. The Essenes, on the contrary, seem to have "refused any contact" with Jerusalem and the Temple: P. Fredriksen, *When Christians Were Jews: The First Generation* (New Haven, 2019), 32.

34. Jesus' disciple: *Luke* 6:15; *Acts* 1:13. And Jesus himself: *John* 2:17.

35. Josephus, *Judaean War* 2.252–74.

36. Ibid., 2.264–65.

37. A. Watson, *The Trial of Jesus* (Athens, Georgia, 1995), 49. Compare D. R. Catchpole, *The Trial of Jesus: A Study in the Gospels and Jewish Historiography from 1770 to the Present Day* (Leiden, 1971), 126: "Jesus was no Zealot, nor was he close to the Zealots."

38. For more on this: Josephus, *Judaean War* 2.117–18; M. A. Brighton, *The Sicarii in Josephus's Judean War: Rhetorical Analysis and Historical Observations* (Atlanta, 2009), 2–11.

39. Josephus, *Judaean Antiquities* 18.63–64; Schürer, *History of the Jewish People*, 1.437; J. P. Meier, *A Marginal Jew: Rethinking the Historical Jesus, Volume One: The Roots of the Problem and the Person* (New Haven, 1991), 61.

40. *Acts* 21:38; Josephus, *Judaean War* 2.254–57; Eusebius, *Ecclesiastical History* 2.20.4–6; Brighton, *The Sicarii in Josephus's Judean War*, 53–62.

41. *Luke* 6:27–36; *Matthew* 5:38–48; K. Aland, *Synopsis of the Four Gospels: Greek-English Edition of the Synopsis Quattuor Evangeliorum* (Stuttgart, 2003), 67–68 (no. 80).

42. H. Bloom, *Jesus and Yahweh: The Names Divine* (New York, 2005), 18.

43. Quodvultdeus of Carthage, *Creedal Homilies* 1.6.13.

44. For *mirari*, see *Mark* 15:5; *Matthew* 27:14. And for *timere*, see *John* 19:8.

45. Watson, *Trial of Jesus*, 41.
46. Quodvultdeus of Carthage, *Creedal Homilies* 1.6.13.

10. JESUS AMONG THE BELIEVERS

1. *Matthew* 3:17; *Mark* 1:11; *Luke* 3:22; comparing *John* 1:32–34. Columnized in K. Aland, *Synopsis of the Four Gospels: Greek-English Edition of the Synopsis Quattuor Evangeliorum* (Stuttgart, 2003), 16 (no. 18).
2. J. Jeremias, *New Testament Theology: The Proclamation of Jesus* (New York, 1971), 69.
3. *Mark* 1:22, 27, and 2:10; Jeremias, *New Testament Theology*, 74.
4. J. Van Henten, "The First Testing of Jesus: A Rereading of Mark 1.12–13", *New Testament Studies* 45, 3 (1999), 349–66, here 363–64.
5. The necessity of the Q hypothesis is contested: P. Foster, "Is it Possible to Dispense with Q?" *Novum Testamentum* 45, 4 (2003), 313–37.
6. Other texts, such as *Matthew* 16:1, can be read in light of this: "Pharisees and Sadducees came, and *to tempt* (*peirazontes*) Jesus, they asked him to show them a sign from heaven." Compare *Mark* 8:11; *Luke* 11:16; *John* 6:30; Aland, *Synopsis of the Four Gospels*, 146 (no. 154).
7. Something like this is, of course, the literary conceit of a notable twentieth-century novel and film. The critical literature confirms it: G. H. Twelftree, *Jesus the Exorcist: A Contribution to the Study of the Historical Jesus* (Tübingen, 1993), 114–15.
8. J. Jeremias, *The Parables of Jesus*, trans. S. H. Hooke (London, 1954), 99. For later echoes of Jeremias' claim: J. Dupont, *Les tentations de Jésus au désert* (*Sine loco*: Desclée de Brouwer, 1968), 34–42, 70–72, 127–30; M. Hengel, *The Zealots: Investigations into the Jewish Freedom Movement in the Period from Herod I until 70 A.D.*, trans. D. Smith (Edinburgh, 1989), 308–309.
9. J. D. M. Derrett, *Law in the New Testament* (London, 1970), 264.
10. The meaning of this term is difficult and complex, but there is a strong narrative connection between Jesus' bold claims to authority and the expectation that he will die as a criminal. If his authority is 'scandalous', the threat of 'scandal' is immeasurably heightened by his humiliating death.
11. This is nicely observed more than once in R. M. Thorsteinsson, *Jesus as Philosopher: The Moral Sage in the Synoptic Gospels* (Oxford, 2018), 55: "Jesus ... cannot silence [his critics] or make them believe. Where no faith is present, no healing is possible ... Similarly, he cannot make the disciples fearless and he cannot make the authorities turn around. He has to be clever in his dealings with people, including appealing to the use and methods of reason"; and 109–10: "Jesus ... cannot have people say or do certain things without their

being ready to do so ... Jesus cannot (normally), for instance, heal people if there is no faith present. This means that, apart from performing miracles, he is very much dependent on methods of discourse and reason."

12. B. Pascal, *Pensées*, trans. A. J. Krailsheimer (London—New York, 1966), 97 (no. 209); idem, *Pensées*, ed. L. Brunschvicg (Paris, 1972), 273 (no. 599).

13. D. L. Dusenbury, *The Innocence of Pontius Pilate: How the Roman Trial of Jesus Shaped History* (London—New York, 2021), 209–10.

14. *Matthew* 12:22–30; *Mark* 3:22–27; *Luke* 11:14–23; Aland, *Synopsis of the Four Gospels*, 107 (no. 117). On the equivalence of 'Beelzebul' and 'Satan': Twelftree, *Jesus the Exorcist*, 104–106.

15. *Vulgate Bible. Volume VI: The New Testament*, ed. A. M. Kinney, intro. S. Edgar (Cambridge, Mass., 2013), 374–75.

16. Epictetus, *Discourses* 1.9.17; Thorsteinsson, *Jesus as Philosopher*, 122–23.

17. For the Graeco-Roman context of Jesus' warning against greed: A. J. Malherbe, "The Christianization of a *Topos* (Luke 12:13–34)", *Novum Testamentum* 38, 2 (1996), 123–35; T. D. Stegman, "Reading Luke 12:13–34 as an Elaboration of a Chreia: How Hermogenes of Tarsus Sheds Light on Luke's Gospel", *Novum Testamentum* 49, 4 (2007), 328–352.

18. Much more could be said on the office of 'divider' (*meristēs*) and the phenomenon of 'division' (*diamerismos*); but lexically, theoretically and symbolically, they are related.

19. One commentator calls this "an enigmatic ... retort from Jesus": Stegman, "Reading Luke 12:13–34 as an Elaboration of a Chreia", 335.

20. A non-canonical *comparandum* is *Gospel of Thomas* 72, which is cited by J. A. Fitzmyer, *The Gospel According to Luke (X–XXIV)* (New York, 1985), 968.

21. E. Haenchen, *The Acts of the Apostles: A Commentary*, trans. H. Anderson and R. M. Wilson (Philadelphia, 1971), 281–82.

22. For a fascinating reflection on the limits of translation, as such, in the Septuagint: E. Tov, "Did the Septuagint Translators Always Understand Their Hebrew Text?" *The Greek and Hebrew Bible: Collected Essays on the Septuagint* (Leiden—Cologne, 1999). For the Septuagint's significance for Christian origins: M. Müller, *The First Bible of the Church: A Plea for the Septuagint* (Sheffield, 1996); N. Fernández Marcos, *The Septuagint in Context: Introduction to the Greek Version of the Bible*, trans. W. G. E. Watson (Leiden—Cologne, 2000), 305–62. And for later Christian permutations on the Septuagint's origin (myths), and estimations of its authority: Fernández Marcos, *Septuagint in Context*, 191–301; A. Wasserstein and D. J. Wasserstein, *The Legend of the Septuagint: From Classical Antiquity to Today* (Cambridge, 2006), 95–173.

23. Compare *Exodus* 2:14; *Acts* 7:27. For the formative influence of the Septuagint on the gospels and *Acts*: Fernández Marcos, *Septuagint in Context*, 326–27, 332–

35; T. M. Law, *When God Spoke Greek: The Septuagint and the Making of the Christian Bible* (Oxford, 2013), 99–105. And for an argument on *Luke*'s use of the Septuagint: T. Muraoka, "Luke and the Septuagint", *Novum Testamentum* 54, 1 (2012), 13–15.

24. For a different formulation of the contrast with Moses: R. Girard, *The Scapegoat*, trans. Y. Freccero (Baltimore, 1986), 128–29.

25. For Spinoza's radical seventeenth-century formulation of this idea: B. de Spinoza, *Theological-Political Treatise*, ed. J. Israel, trans. M. Silverthorne and J. Israel (Cambridge, 2007), 63–64.

26. Even at the height of the Constantinian revolution, Eusebius holds that intelligent commentators realize that the reign of Christ is not "material" (*sōmatikōs*), but "mystical" (*mustikōs*): Eusebius of Caesarea, *Ecclesiastical History* 3.39.11–13.

27. Jeremias, *New Testament Theology*, 74.

11. JESUS AMONG THE LAWBREAKERS

1. I. Kant, *Religion within the Boundaries of Mere Reason, and Other Writings. Revised Edition*, ed. and trans. A. Wood and G. di Giovanni, rev. with intro. R. M. Adams (Cambridge, 2018), 188.

2. *John* 5:30, 8:15. A redactor can, of course, be hypothesized: E. Haenchen, *John 1: A Commentary on the Gospel of John Chapters 1–6*, ed. R. W. Funk with U. Busse, trans. R. W. Funk (Philadelphia, 1984), 253–54.

3. Eusebius of Caesarea, *Preparation for the Gospel* 11.19.

4. E. Haenchen, *John 2: A Commentary on the Gospel of John Chapters 7–21*, ed. R. W. Funk with U. Busse, trans. R. W. Funk (Philadelphia, 1984), 22.

5. B. M. Metzger, *A Textual Commentary on the Greek New Testament* (Stuttgart, 1994), 188; B. M. Metzger and B. D. Ehrman, *The Text of the New Testament: Its Transmission, Corruption, and Restoration* (Oxford, 2005), 319–20.

6. Metzger and Ehrman, *Text of the New Testament*, 87.

7. K. Aland and B. Aland, *The Text of the New Testament: An Introduction to the Critical Editions and to the Theory and Practice of Modern Textual Criticism*, trans. E. F. Rhodes (Leiden, 1989), 232, 307.

8. R. E. Brown, *The Gospel According to John (i–xii)* (New York, 1966), 335.

9. For a recent argument that this pericope, though not originally Johannine, first enters the "fourfold tradition" of the canonical gospels in *John* 8: C. Keith, "The Initial Location of the *Pericope Adulterae* in Fourfold Tradition", *Novum Testamentum* 51, 3 (2009), 209–31.

10. Jeremias, *Parables of Jesus*, 99.

11. As Richard Bauckham notes, the inscription on Jesus' cross—"King of the Judaeans"—is just a non-Judaean way of saying "King of Israel": R. Bauckham,

"Messianism According to the Gospel of John", *Challenging Perspectives on the Gospel of John*, ed. J. Lierman (Tübingen, 2006), 59–60.

12. The practice has a centuries-long cultic history in Europe: E. H. Kantorowicz, *Laudes Regiae: A Study in Liturgical Acclamations and Mediaeval Ruler Worship* (Berkeley, 1946).

13. *John* 6:6, 8:6. Note that the meaning of *peirazō* in *John* 6:5–6 is unquestionably to 'test' and not to 'lure into sin': Haenchen, *John 1*, 271.

14. Clement of Alexandria, *Exhortation 6*.

15. *John* 8:6; compare *Matthew* 12:10; *Mark* 3:2; *Luke* 6:7. Note, however, that the gospel-writers handle this hostility motif differently: J. A. Fitzmyer, *The Gospel According to Luke (I–IX)* (New York, 1981), 607.

16. Jesus is a rabbinic *iurisprudens* in the gospels, one who holds the *ius respondendi* on questions of divine law: Derrett, *Law in the New Testament*, 158–59.

17. A. Watson, *The Trial of Stephen: The First Christian Martyr* (Athens, Georgia, 2012), 103–106.

18. For the judicial significance of the moment when Pilate "*handed* Jesus *over* to be crucified": G. Agamben, *Pilate and Jesus*, trans. A. Kotsko (Stanford, 2015), 36, 47; D. L. Dusenbury, "The Judgment of Pontius Pilate: A Critique of Giorgio Agamben", *Journal of Law and Religion* 32, 2 (2017), 340–65, here 356–58.

19. Some of the earliest Christians seem to have called Jesus "the Just One". Compare *Acts* 3:14, 7:52, 22:14; and *James* 5:6. Cited by Watson, *Trial of Stephen*, 89.

20. Derrett, *Law in the New Testament*, 160.

21. Ibid., 177.

22. The first parallel is differently noted in G. Steiner, *Lessons of the Masters: The Charles Eliot Norton Lectures* (Cambridge, Mass., 2003), 33–34.

23. Plato, *Meno* 84c–85d. Socrates is jokingly said to have had a hand in editing one of Plato's dialogues, but he is still not pictured as writing it: Plato, *Theaetetus* 142d–143c, here 143c.

24. The argument that it is Jesus' act of writing, proving his literacy, which determines the place of this pericope within *John*, is made in C. Keith, *The Pericope Adulterae, the Gospel of John, and the Literacy of Jesus* (Leiden, 2009).

25. C. à Lapide, *The Great Commentary of Cornelius à Lapide*, trans. T. W. Mossman, et al. (London, 1887–1890), 5.294–95.

26. Derrett, *Law in the New Testament*, 177.

27. Ibid., 176. (My italics.)

28. Steiner, *Lessons of the Masters*, 33–34.

29. This is something that Johannine circle seems to share with Pauline thought— and Pauline influences on the gospels, including *John,* cannot be ruled out:

M. Müller, "Paul: The Oldest Witness to the Historical Jesus", *'Is This Not the Carpenter?' The Question of the Historicity of the Figure of Jesus*, ed. T. L. Thompson and T. S. Verenna (London, 2012), 118–21; G. van Kooten, "John's Counter-Symposium: 'The Continuation of Dialogue' in Christianity—A Contrapuntal Reading of John's Gospel and Plato's *Symposium*", *Intolerance, Polemics, and Debate in Antiquity: Politico-Cultural, Philosophical, and Religious Forms of Critical Conversation*, ed. G. van Kooten and J. van Ruiten (Leiden, 2019), 295–96.

30. Derrett, *Law in the New Testament*, 186. (My italics.)

31. A. Schopenhauer, *The World as Will and Representation, Volume 2*, trans. J. Norman, A. Welchman, C. Janaway (Cambridge, 2018), 569. (My italics.)

32. U. Luz, *Matthew 1–7: A Commentary*, ed. H. Koester, trans. J. E. Crouch (Minneapolis, 2007), 242–46, here 242: "[This *logion* is] not subject to tradition-history deconstruction ... and therefore may well come from [Jesus]."

33. For highly suggestive rabbinic sayings: Luz, *Matthew 1–7*, 245. And for a philosophical parallel: Epictetus, *Discourses* 2.18.15–21.

34. Lapide, *Great Commentary*, 5.293.

35. Z. M. Salih, "Sudan Woman Faces Death by Stoning for Adultery in First Case for a Decade", *The Guardian* (13 July 2022).

36. Augustine of Hippo, *Homilies on the Gospel of John* 33.6.

37. Augustine draws this out in his sermons on *John* 8: Augustine of Hippo, *Homilies on the Gospel of John* 33.5–6.

12. JESUS AMONG THE RULERS

1. *Mark* 12:17; compare *Matthew* 22:21; *Luke* 20:25. Columnized in K. Aland, *Synopsis of the Four Gospels: Greek-English Edition of the Synopsis Quattuor Evangeliorum* (Stuttgart, 2003), 245–46 (no. 280).

2. *Mark* 12:17; *Matthew* 22:22; *Luke* 20:26.

3. This *logion* is collected in the *Gospel of Thomas*—with one striking addition: "He said to them, 'Give Caesar's property to Caesar; give God's property to God; *and what is mine, give to me*'" (*Gospel of Thomas* 100).

4. *Mark* 11:27, 12:13; *Matthew* 21:45–46, 22:15; *Luke* 20:1, 19–20.

5. Josephus, *Judaean War* 2.117–18; M. Hengel, *The Zealots: Investigations into the Jewish Freedom Movement in the Period from Herod I until 70 A.D.*, trans. D. Smith (Edinburgh, 1989), 76–145. Judas' father, Ezekias, led a rebellion during the reign of Herod I. There may have been zealotic tendencies, but Ezekias' grievances and doctrines are unclear: E. Gabba, "The Social, Economic and Political History of Palestine 63 BCE–CE 70", *The Cambridge History of Judaism, Volume*

Three: The Early Roman Period, ed. W. Horbury, W. Davies, and J. Sturdy (Cambridge, 1999), 101–103, 129.

6. Josephus, *Judaean War* 7.323–24; Gabba, "Social, Economic and Political History of Palestine", 133, 166.

7. Josephus, *Judaean War* 7.410, 418–19.

8. For "Jesus is lord": *Romans* 10:9; *I Corinthians* 12:3. And for "Caesar is lord": *Martyrdom of Polycarp* 8.2.

9. Hengel, *Zealots*, 107 (citing a fragment from the Qumran caves).

10. "The circulation in Judaea of Roman *denarii* bearing the emperor's image could not be avoided ... for gold and silver coins were not minted in the province. But the copper coins manufactured in the country carried no human portrait in the time of Roman rule (as under the Herodians) but only the emperor's name and inoffensive emblems." E. Schürer, *The History of the Jewish People in the Age of Jesus Christ (175 B.C.–A.D. 135)*, rev. and ed. G. Vermes and F. Millar, with P. Vermes and M. Black (Edinburgh, 1973), 1.380.

11. Jerusalem Talmud, *Megillah* 3.2.

12. Hippolytus of Rome, *Refutation of All Heresies* 9.26.1–2. Compare the outrage reported in Josephus, *Judaean War* 2.169–74.

13. From the beginning, this pericope distanced Jesus and his cohort from the Zealots: A. Yarbro Collins, *Mark: A Commentary*, ed. H. W. Attridge (Minneapolis, 2007), 555.

14. R. M. Thorsteinsson, *Jesus as Philosopher: The Moral Sage in the Synoptic Gospels* (Oxford, 2018), 116 note 153.

15. J. A. Fitzmyer, *The Gospel According to Luke (X–XXIV)* (New York, 1985), 1296. Compare *Mark* 12:14; *Matthew* 22:17; *Luke* 20:22.

16. Josephus, *Judaean War* 2.118.

17. Hengel, *Zealots*, 107 (citing a fragment from the Qumran caves).

18. *Mark* 1:15 (kingdom of God); *Matthew* 4:17 (kingdom of heaven).

19. *Mark* 4:11 (kingdom of God); *Matthew* 13:11 (kingdom of heaven); *Luke* 8:10 (kingdom of God).

20. M. Zerwick and M. Grosvenor, *A Grammatical Analysis of the Greek New Testament* (Rome, 1981), 113.

21. *I Corinthians* 4:1–5 (mysteries of God); *I Timothy* 3:9 (mystery of faith); *Ephesians* 3:9 (economy of the mystery).

22. R. Girard, *The Scapegoat*, trans. Y. Freccero (Baltimore, 1986), 196–97.

23. *Matthew* 16:21–23; *Mark* 8:31–33; Aland, *Synopsis of the Four Gospels*, 151 (no. 159).

24. *Mark* 4:11; compare *Matthew* 13:11; *Luke* 8:10; Aland, *Synopsis of the Four Gospels*, 115 (no. 123).

25. *Matthew* 22:21; compare *Mark* 12:17; *Luke* 20:25; Aland, *Synopsis of the Four Gospels*, 246 (no. 280).

26. Jesus' rebuke to Peter: *Matthew* 16:21–23; *Mark* 8:31–33. Jesus' verdict on the census-tax: *Matthew* 22:21; compare *Mark* 12:17; *Luke* 20:25.

27. Compare *Matthew* 6:24; *Luke* 16:13; the partial parallel in *Gospel of Thomas* 47; and the (conjectural) source-text, *Q* 16:13, in *The Critical Edition of Q: Synopsis Including the Gospels of Matthew and Luke, Mark and Thomas*, ed. J. M. Robinson, P. Hoffmann, and J. S. Kloppenborg (Leuven, 2000), 462–63.

28. Josephus, *Judaean War* 2.122.

29. Seneca, *Moral Epistles* 31.10: Parem autem te deo pecunia non faciet; deus nihil habet.

30. D. J. Armitage, *Theories of Poverty in the World of the New Testament* (Tübingen, 2016).

31. Porphyry of Tyre, *Letter to Marcella* 14.

32. Compare *Matthew* 6:24; *Luke* 16:13; and the (conjectural) source-text, *Q* 16:13.

33. *Mark* 8:36; compare *Matthew* 16:26; *Luke* 9:25; Aland, *Synopsis of the Four Gospels*, 152 (no. 160).

34. *Mark* 8:37; compare *Matthew* 16:26; Aland, *Synopsis of the Four Gospels*, 152 (no. 160).

35. Pseudo-Jerome, *Commentary on Mark* 12.14.

36. Josephus, *Judaean War* 7.253–55; Gabba, "Social, Economic and Political History of Palestine", 133.

37. *Mark* 10:35–41; compare *Matthew* 20:20–24; *Luke* 22:24; Aland, *Synopsis of the Four Gospels*, 225–26 (no. 263).

13. *REALPOLITIK* AND THE TRANSCENDENT KINGDOM

1. *Matthew* 20:25–26; *Mark* 10:42–43; *Luke* 22:25–26; Columnized in K. Aland, *Synopsis of the Four Gospels: Greek-English Edition of the Synopsis Quattuor Evangeliorum* (Stuttgart, 2003), 226 (no. 263).

2. P. Veyne, *Bread and Circuses: Historical Sociology and Political Pluralism*, trans. B. Pearce, ed. O. Murray (London, 1990), 10–34.

3. There may be an echo here of the Graeco-Roman phenomenon of *amici principi*. And occurring as it does, in *John*, it can be read as a fore-echo of the "friend of Caesar" moment in the Roman trial of Jesus (*John* 19:12).

4. *Matthew* 11:7–9; compare *Luke* 7:24–26. In a similar vein, Jesus criticizes Judaean scribes who "like to walk around in *long robes*" (*Mark* 12:38; *Luke* 20:46).

5. The meaning of this *logion* is much contested: *Matthew* 11:12; compare *Luke* 16:16.

6. For *parabolē* as "dark saying": J. Jeremias, *The Parables of Jesus*, trans. S. H. Hooke (London, 1954), 14 note 21.

7. G. Steiner, *Lessons of the Masters: The Charles Eliot Norton Lectures* (Cambridge, Mass., 2003), 35, 160.

8. "Enigmatics": H. Bloom, *Jesus and Yahweh: The Names Divine* (New York, 2005), 10. Criminality and the parables: Jeremias, *Parables of Jesus*, 20–21.

9. The term has a history: C. Schmitt, *Political Romanticism*, trans. G. Oakes (Cambridge, Mass., 1991).

10. For more on this: Dusenbury, *Innocence of Pontius Pilate*, 238–47.

11. *Matthew* 11:7–9; compare *Luke* 7:24–26; Aland, *Synopsis of the Four Gospels*, 98–99 (no. 107).

12. *Luke* 12:57–59; compare *Matthew* 5:25–26; Aland, *Synopsis of the Four Gospels*, 187 (no. 206).

13. E. Auerbach, "Romanticism and Realism (1933)", *Time, History, and Literature: Selected Essays of Erich Auerbach*, ed. J. I. Porter, trans. J. O. Newman (Princeton, 2014), 156.

14. THE ACTION IN THE TEMPLE

1. In *Luke* 21:1, the scene is less dramatic; we read only that Jesus "looked up".

2. Josephus, *Judaean War* 1.152–54.

3. M. Zerwick and M. Grosvenor, *A Grammatical Analysis of the Greek New Testament* (Rome, 1981), 150.

4. *Luke* 12:59; *Matthew* 5:25–26. Columnized in K. Aland, *Synopsis of the Four Gospels: Greek-English Edition of the Synopsis Quattuor Evangeliorum* (Stuttgart, 2003), 187 (no. 206).

5. Nor is it his only act of honour for a woman in the last week of his life. See the scene in which a woman—to the horror of most onlookers—anoints Jesus with costly, aromatic substances in *Mark* 14:3–9. "What she has done", Jesus says, "will be told in remembrance of her" (*Mark* 14:9). This prediction holds true to the present day.

6. *Mark* 8:31–33; compare *Matthew* 16:21–23; Aland, *Synopsis of the Four Gospels*, 151 (no. 159).

7. *Luke* 12:59; *Matthew* 5:25–26; Aland, *Synopsis of the Four Gospels*, 187 (no. 206).

8. *Mark* 12:43–44; compare *Luke* 21:3–4; Aland, *Synopsis of the Four Gospels*, 254 (no. 286).

9. *Mark* 11:15, 12:41.

10. *John* 2:15–16, 8:12, 20.

11. In *Mark*, the Action in the Temple clearly takes place on Jesus' second day in

Jerusalem: *Mark* 11:11–12, 15–19. In *Matthew* and *Luke*, however, it appears to take place on his *first* day in the holy city: *Matthew* 21:10–12, 18; *Luke* 19:41, 45.

12. *Matthew* 21:12–15; *Mark* 11:15–18; *Luke* 19:45–48; Aland, *Synopsis of the Four Gospels*, 238–40 (nos. 273–74).

13. *John* 2:18–21; E. Haenchen, *John 1: A Commentary on the Gospel of John Chapters 1–6*, ed. R. W. Funk with U. Busse, trans. R. W. Funk (Philadelphia, 1984), 184–85.

14. *Mark* 11:17; compare *Zechariah* 14:21; *Isaiah* 56:7; *Jeremiah* 7:11; A. Yarbro Collins, *Mark: A Commentary*, ed. H. W. Attridge (Minneapolis, 2007), 529–32.

15. It is critical to note that Jesus' whip in *John 2* is a symbol of force; it is not a heavy lash. Further, Jesus "did not use" what Haenchen calls "a kind of whip" on the Temple merchants, but only "drove the animals out with it": Haenchen, *John 1*, 183. And what is this 'kind of whip'? *John* tells us that Jesus makes for himself, from materials at hand in the Temple's outer courts, a *phragellion ek schoiniōn*—a "light whip of cords" (*John* 2:15). The Greek *phragellion* derives from a Latin diminutive, *flagellum*, for 'light whip'; and the other Greek diminutive, *schoiniōn*, becomes "little cords" in the Rheims Translation, and "small cords" in the Authorized Version. These diminutives occur nowhere else in the gospels. Later in *John*, when Jesus is scourged, the gospel-writer selects a verb rooted in a different Greek term, *mastix*, for 'heavy whip' (*John* 19:1).

16. *Mark* 11:17 (*oikos proseuchēs*); *John* 2:16 (*oikon tou patros mou*); compare *Matthew* 21:13 and *Luke* 19:46; Aland, *Synopsis of the Four Gospels*, 238–39 (nos. 273).

17. *Mark* 11:17 (*spēlaion lēstōn*); *John* 2:16 (*oikon emporiou*). There may be a recollection, in *Mark*'s phrasing, of the Zealots' brutal occupation of the Temple: Yarbro Collins, *Mark*, 531.

18. *Matthew* 6:24; *Luke* 16:13; Aland, *Synopsis of the Four Gospels*, 58 (no. 66).

19. *Mark* 8:37; compare *Matthew* 16:26; Aland, *Synopsis of the Four Gospels*, 152 (no. 160).

20. *Mark* 12:41; compare *John* 8:20.

21. I am necessarily compressing, here, what I take to be the more complex logic of this scene.

22. *Mark* 12:44; *Luke* 21:4; Aland, *Synopsis of the Four Gospels*, 254 (no. 286). For sacrifice as a relic—and immersive reminder—of what Bataille calls "the intimate order": G. Bataille, *Theory of Religion*, trans. R. Hurley (New York, 1992), 27–57, here 52. And for a different, deep reflection on the theme of sacrifice: T. Eagleton, *Radical Sacrifice* (New Haven—London, 2018).

23. *John* 2:15–17; Haenchen, *John 1*, 184.

24. *Zechariah* 14:21; and in defence of this rendering of *Chananaios* as 'trader':

Yarbro Collins, *Mark*, 529. Note that I have transposed "on that day" from the end of the verse—in the Septuagint's Greek, and in Yarbro Collins's translation—to the beginning.

25. *Matthew* 22:15–22; *Mark* 12:13–17; *Luke* 20:20–26; Aland, *Synopsis of the Four Gospels*, 245–46 (no. 280).

26. *Mark* 12:17; compare *Matthew* 22:21; *Luke* 20:25; Aland, *Synopsis of the Four Gospels*, 246 (no. 280).

27. Compare *Matthew* 21:17–18, 23; *Mark* 11:19–20, 27. The chronology of *Luke* 20:1 is vaguer: "One day, as he was teaching the people in the Temple ..."

28. *Matthew* 27:11; *Mark* 15:2; *Luke* 23:3; *John* 18:33; Aland, *Synopsis of the Four Gospels*, 308 (no. 336).

29. *Matthew* 21:23; *Mark* 11:28; *Luke* 20:2; Aland, *Synopsis of the Four Gospels*, 241 (no. 276).

30. *Mark* 11:29; compare *Matthew* 21:24; *Luke* 20:3; Aland, *Synopsis of the Four Gospels*, 241 (no. 276).

31. *Mark* 11:33; compare *Matthew* 21:27; *Luke* 20:8; Aland, *Synopsis of the Four Gospels*, 241 (no. 276).

32. *Matthew* 21:25; *Mark* 11:30; *Luke* 20:4. A relevant contrast is made by the gospel-writer (not Jesus) at *John* 12:43, where we read that many "loved human glory (*doxan tōn anthrōpōn*) more than the glory that comes from God (*doxan tou theou*)".

15. THE INCIDENT WITH THE ALABASTER JAR

1. *Matthew* 24:1–2; *Mark* 13:1–2; *Luke* 21:5–6. Columnized in K. Aland, *Synopsis of the Four Gospels: Greek-English Edition of the Synopsis Quattuor Evangeliorum* (Stuttgart, 2003), 255 (no. 287).

2. *Matthew* 21:33–46; *Mark* 12:1–12; *Luke* 20:9–19; Aland, *Synopsis of the Four Gospels*, 242–44 (no. 278).

3. *Luke* 21:24 (*kairoi ethnōn*); or, "the time of the pagans": J. A. Fitzmyer, *The Gospel According to Luke (X–XXIV)* (New York, 1985), 1342, 1347.

4. *Mark* 12:12; compare *Matthew* 21:46; *Luke* 20:19; Aland, *Synopsis of the Four Gospels*, 244 (no. 278).

5. It is in a historical sense unfortunate that, at *Matthew* 27:25, the gospel-writer abandons the Marcan term 'crowd' (*ochlos*)—which he is content to keep in *Matthew* 21:46 and in much of *Matthew* 27—for the denser, more symbolic term 'people' (*laos*). In one of the most viciously misinterpreted lines of the New Testament, we therefore read: "Then *the people as a whole* answered, 'His blood be on us and on our children!'" (*Matthew* 27:25). There can be no remotely credible interpretation of this line which does not set out from the fact that

three times in the same scene, the gospel-writer calls this so-called 'people', merely, a 'crowd'. Compare *Matthew* 27:15 (*toi ochlōi*), 27:20 (*tous ochlous*), and 27:24 (*tou ochlou*). Note in particular *Matthew* 27:20 where we read that "the chief priests and the elders *persuaded the crowds* (*epeisan tous ochlous*) to ask ... to have Jesus killed". It is no sovereign people, in *Matthew* 27:25, which calls some sort of bloodguilt upon its children. The text of *Matthew* clearly shows it to be a 'crowd' gathered, and controlled, by the Temple elites. Further, Ulrich Luz's comment is illuminating: "Who in the LXX belongs to πᾶς ὁ λαός is determined in each case by the context." U. Luz, *Matthew 21–28: A Commentary*, ed. H. Koester, trans. J. E. Crouch (Minneapolis, 2005), 501.

6. *Mark* 15:15; compare *Matthew* 27:25–26; *Luke* 23:24–25; *John* 19:14–16; Aland, *Synopsis of the Four Gospels*, 314 (no. 341).

7. *Matthew* 27:20; *Mark* 15:11; *Luke* 23:13–18; and *John* 19:6. The first time the cry of "Crucify him!" is raised, what we read in *John* is that "*the chief priests and the police ... shouted, 'Crucify him!'*"

8. Prophet: *Matthew* 21:10–11. Christ-figure: *Matthew* 21:8–9; *Mark* 11:8–9; *Luke* 19:35–38; *John* 12:12–15; Aland, *Synopsis of the Four Gospels*, 235 (no. 269). Deranged or demon-inspired: *Mark* 3:21–23; *John* 10:20. Impostor: *Matthew* 27:62–63. Threat to the nation: *John* 11:47–48.

9. *Matthew* 26:1–5; *Mark* 14:1–2; *Luke* 22:1–2; *John* 11:45–57; Aland, *Synopsis of the Four Gospels*, 276 (no. 305).

10. *Mark* 14:48–49; compare *Matthew* 26:55–56; *Luke* 22:52–53; Aland, *Synopsis of the Four Gospels*, 300 (no. 331). There may be an echo of this in Jesus' statement to a high priest, Annas, in *John* 18:20: "I have spoken openly to the world; I have always taught in synagogues and in the Temple ... I have said nothing in secret."

11. For the precision of 'reconstruct', here, see *John* 2:18–22, 12:16, 13:28–29.

12. *Matthew* 26:14, 47; *Mark* 14:10, 43; *Luke* 22:3, 47.

13. *Matthew* 26:50. There may be an echo of this in *John* 13:27, where Jesus says to Judas: "Do quickly what you are going to do."

14. Celsus hints that more than one of Jesus' disciples betrayed him, writing: "He was betrayed by those whom he called disciples." Origen speculates that the pagan "called the one man, Judas, many disciples to make the charge seem more effective": Origen, *Against Celsus* 2.11.

15. Aristotle is one iconic Greek betrayer. He not only deserted his philosophical master, Plato, but satirized the Platonic doctrine of Ideas. Is it necessarily "an objection to *Plato*", asks Origen, "that, after listening to his teaching for twenty years, Aristotle deserted him"? Couldn't this volte-face be an objection to *Aristotle*? Origen presses the question. "Is it *possible* that ... Plato was right", he

asks, and that "Aristotle became wicked and ungrateful to his teacher"? Origen, *Against Celsus* 2.12.

16. *Mark* 14:10–11; compare *Matthew* 26:14–16; *Luke* 22:3–6; Aland, *Synopsis of the Four Gospels*, 279 (no. 307). For 'rabbi': *Matthew* 26:49; *Mark* 14:45.

17. *Matthew* 26:6; *Mark* 14:3; *Luke* 7:36, where the setting is simply a Pharisee's house; and *John* 12:1. I call Lazarus "the Dead Man" (who has been raised) to parallel Simon "the Leper" (who has been healed?). Consult, for instance, *John* 11:44 ("the dead man came out") and 12:1 ("raised from the dead"). In *John* 11:1, he is called "Lazarus of Bethany"; but after his revivification by Jesus (whatever we make of that), he is notorious as a man who had 'died'.

18. *Matthew* 26:6; *Mark* 14:3; *John* 11:18. Unique to *Luke* is Jesus' appearance in "a certain village", in the house of Martha who "had a sister named Mary": *Luke* 10:38–42. It is Mary who *anoints* Jesus' feet in *John* 12:3, who *sits* at his feet in *Luke* 10:39, like a disciple. For Bethany's proximity to Jerusalem: *John* 11:18; E. Haenchen, *John 2: A Commentary on the Gospel of John Chapters 7–21*, ed. R. W. Funk with U. Busse, trans. R. W. Funk (Philadelphia, 1984), 61.

19. *Matthew* 26:1–5; *Mark* 10:32–34, 14:1–2; *John* 11:7–8, 16, 45–57.

20. By placing the Incident with the Alabaster Jar in *Luke* 7, well before the Action in the Temple in *Luke* 19, the third gospel is the only outlier. Note in passing that the woman's vessel is one detail *Luke* shares with the other gospel-writers. The ointment with which Jesus is anointed is kept in "an alabaster jar" (*Luke* 7:37).

21. See *John* 11:54, though Bethany—in *John*—marks a stage on Jesus' return to Jerusalem.

22. *John* 11:2, 12:3; Haenchen, *John 2*, 56–57, 84.

23. *Mark* 14:3; *Matthew* 26:7; Aland, *Synopsis of the Four Gospels*, 277 (no. 306).

24. *Mark* 14:3 has "nard", and *John* 12:3 "pure nard". In *Matthew* 26:7 and *Luke* 7:37–38, the substance is unidentified. Alabaster jar: *Matthew* 26:7; *Mark* 14:3; *Luke* 7:37. Anointing of the head: *Matthew* 26:7; *Mark* 14:3; anointing of the feet: *Luke* 7:38; *John* 12:3. Poured out: *Matthew* 26:7; *Mark* 14:3; rubbed with hair: *Luke* 7:38; *John* 12:3.

25. *Luke* 7:38–39; J. A. Fitzmyer, *The Gospel According to Luke (I–IX)* (New York, 1981), 689.

26. *Matthew* 26:8; *Mark* 14:4; Aland, *Synopsis of the Four Gospels*, 277 (no. 306).

27. *Mark* 14:5; *John* 12:5; Aland, *Synopsis of the Four Gospels*, 277 (no. 306).

28. Three hundred denarii represents a common wage for 300 days' labour: Haenchen, *John 2*, 84 note 6. Thus, too, in *Luke*'s parallel scene of Jesus' anointing at table, the sum of 500 denarii represents 500 days' labour (*Luke* 7:41).

29. This is not only the argument of Judas in *John* 12:5, but of the Twelve in *Matthew* 26:9 and *Mark* 14:5.

30. *Mark* 12:42–44; compare *Luke* 21:2–4; Aland, *Synopsis of the Four Gospels*, 253–54 (no. 286).

31. *Mark* 14:7; compare *Matthew* 26:11; *John* 12:8; Aland, *Synopsis of the Four Gospels*, 278 (no. 306).

32. *Mark* 8:37; *Matthew* 16:26; compare *Luke* 9:25; Aland, *Synopsis of the Four Gospels*, 152 (no. 160).

33. Compare *Matthew* 26:6–16; *Mark* 14:3–11. The chronology of *John* 11:45–12:12, and 13:1–30, is much vaguer. We will recall that the conspiracy to kill Jesus in *Luke* 22:1–6 is not related to Jesus' anointing by "a sinner" in a Pharisee's house, in *Luke* 7:36–50.

34. *Mark* 14:11; compare *Luke* 22:5. The idea that Judas is given "thirty silver pieces" by the Temple authorities is unique to *Matthew* 26:15, 27:3–10. Judas' economic motive is only implicit in *John* 11:4–6, 12:26–30.

35. Steiner, *Lessons of the Masters*, 37.

36. Joseph's ordeal is reprised—with its redemptive conclusion—in *Acts* 7:9–16; E. Haenchen, *The Acts of the Apostles: A Commentary*, trans. H. Anderson and R. M. Wilson (Philadelphia, 1971), 279–80.

37. For more on 'Judeophobia' in antiquity: P. Schäfer, *Judeophobia: Attitudes toward the Jews in the Ancient World* (Cambridge, Mass., 1997).

38. R. Girard, *The Scapegoat*, trans. Y. Freccero (Baltimore, 1986), 105, 110.

39. *Pace* H. Bloom, *Jesus and Yahweh: The Names Divine* (New York, 2005), 22–24: "Judas Iscariot [is] ... a transparently malevolent fiction." Taking note of Bloom's further characterization: "[The] canonical New Testament ... is replete with misinformed hatred of the Jews, though composed almost entirely by Jews in flight from themselves, and desperate to ingratiate themselves with their Roman overlords."

40. Bion of Borysthenes, *Fragments* 35 = Stobaeus, *Florilegium* 3.10.37 = Theon, *Progymnasmata* 5. For more on Bion's life: Diogenes Laertius, *Lives of the Philosophers* 4.7.46–57; J. F. Kindstrand, *Bion of Borysthenes: A Collection of the Fragments with Introduction and Commentary* (Uppsala, 1976), 3–20.

41. For the sexual aspect of Bion's enslavement: Diogenes Laertius, *Lives of the Philosophers* 4.7.46; Kindstrand, *Bion of Borysthenes*, 7–8.

42. Sallust, *Jugurthine War* 8.2.

43. M. Bulgakov, *The Master and Margarita*, trans. with notes R. Pevear and L. Volokhonsky, foreword B. Fishman (London, 2016), 124.

16. JESUS THE GALILEAN

1. Following the reading *laois Israēl* (peoples of Israel), rather than the singular *laos* (people) attested by some manuscripts. The *laoi*, here, represent a "Hellenistic

interpretation" of the tribes of Israel: E. Haenchen, *The Acts of the Apostles: A Commentary*, trans. H. Anderson and R. M. Wilson (Philadelphia, 1971), 226–27.

2. E. Haenchen, *John 1: A Commentary on the Gospel of John Chapters 1–6*, ed. R. W. Funk with U. Busse, trans. R. W. Funk (Philadelphia, 1984), 117–18.

3. *Acts of the Apostles* 1:12–26 (reconstitution of the Twelve), 4:6 (high-priestly line).

4. *Acts* 4:25–26; *Psalm* 2:1–2; here in the translation of Haenchen, *Acts of the Apostles*, 225. For an echo of the same verses of *Psalm 2*, in the same translation, in *Revelation* 11: T. M. Law, *When God Spoke Greek: The Septuagint and the Making of the Christian Bible* (Oxford, 2013), 114–15.

5. G. Samuelsson, *Crucifixion in Antiquity: An Inquiry into the Background and Significance of the New Testament Terminology of Crucifixion* (Tübingen, 2013).

6. Compare *Matthew* 19:1–2 ("beyond the Jordan"); *Mark* 10:1 ("beyond the Jordan"); *Luke* 9:10 ("a city called Bethsaida"); and *John* 11:54 ("a town called Ephraim in the region near the wilderness").

7. Thus *Matthew* 27:38; *Mark* 15:27; compare *Luke* 23:33; *John* 19:18; K. Aland, *Synopsis of the Four Gospels: Greek-English Edition of the Synopsis Quattuor Evangeliorum* (Stuttgart, 2003), 317 (no. 344).

8. For the dry, rather than disparaging tone of this question: E. Haenchen, *John 2: A Commentary on the Gospel of John Chapters 7–21*, ed. R. W. Funk with U. Busse, trans. R. W. Funk (Philadelphia, 1984), 179.

9. S. Penwell, *Jesus the Samaritan: Ethnic Labeling in the Gospel of John* (Leiden, 2019), 97–98, 137, 174.

10. This is the consensus on Antipas' parentage, but for more on Herod I's parentage: B. Eckhardt, "'An Idumean, That Is, a Half-Jew': Hasmoneans and Herodians between Ancestry and Merit", *Jewish Identity and Politics between the Maccabees and Bar Kokhba: Groups, Normativity, and Rituals*, ed. B. Eckhardt (Leiden, 2012); and for more on Malthace: D. R. Schwartz, "Malthace, Archelaus, and Herod Antipas: Between Genealogy and Typology", *Jewish Identity and Politics between the Maccabees and Bar Kokhba: Groups, Normativity, and Rituals*, ed. B. Eckhardt (Leiden, 2012).

11. M. H. Jensen, *Herod Antipas in Galilee: The Literary and Archaeological Sources on the Reign of Herod Antipas and its Socio-Economic Impact on Galilee* (Tübingen, 2006), 116–17.

12. Ibid., 109. For 'deaconesses': "Joanna ... and Susanna ... provided (Greek *diēkonoun*, Latin *ministrabant*) for them out of their resources" (*Luke* 8:3). For Chuza's name: R. Bauckham, *Gospel Women: Studies of the Named Women in the Gospels* (Grand Rapids, 2002), 157.

13. The Greek *suntrophos* can mean foster-brother, and it is translated woodenly

as *conlactaneus* in the Latin New Testament. It nevertheless seems to picture Manaen as a "friend of the ruler" (*amicus principi*).

14. This is a politically intriguing tradition—but dubious, too: Haenchen, *John 2*, 167–68.

15. For Graeco-Roman *comparanda* to the miraculous birth-narratives in *Matthew* and *Luke*: M. D. Litwa, *How the Gospels Became History: Jesus and Mediterranean Myths* (New Haven—London, 2019), 86–95.

16. This dialect has been termed "Galilean Aramaic": M. Goodman, "Galilean Judaism and Judaean Judaism", *The Cambridge History of Judaism, Volume Three: The Early Roman Period*, ed. W. Horbury, W. D. Davies, and J. Sturdy (Cambridge, 1999), 600.

17. Or rather, "Jesus the Nazoraean"—on which: Haenchen, *John 2*, 192.

18. Note that this is not, however, "an uncontested tradition. 'There is no single tribe in Israel from which prophets have not arisen' (*Sukk.* 27b). Seder Olam Rabba 21 is a further generalization: 'There is no city in the land of Israel in which there has been no prophet'": Haenchen, *John 2*, 19.

19. S. Kierkegaard, *Either/Or, Part II*, ed. and trans. H. V. Hong and E. H. Hong (Princeton, 1990), 342.

17. JESUS THE REJECT

1. For a rich comment on this nude or lightly dressed figure: A. Yarbro Collins, *Mark: A Commentary*, ed. H. W. Attridge (Minneapolis, 2007), 688–95. For whatever reason, he is omitted by both *Matthew* and *Luke*: U. Luz, *Matthew 21–28: A Commentary*, ed. H. Koester, trans. J. E. Crouch (Minneapolis, 2005), 411.

2. E. Auerbach, *Mimesis: The Representation of Reality in Western Literature*, trans. W. R. Trask (Princeton, 2003), 41–42.

3. Ibid., 42. (My italics.) For an astute comment on Peter's Galilean accent: R. Girard, *The Scapegoat*, trans. Y. Freccero (Baltimore, 1986), 153–54.

4. Though *Mark* notes the fire, only *John* describes it as "a charcoal fire". See *Mark* 14:67; *John* 18:18. Columnized in K. Aland, *Synopsis of the Four Gospels: Greek-English Edition of the Synopsis Quattuor Evangeliorum* (Stuttgart, 2003), 306 (no. 333).

5. Auerbach, *Mimesis*, 41–43.

6. Girard, *Scapegoat*, 156.

7. Ibid., 105, 110.

8. Auerbach, *Mimesis*, 41–42.

9. Girard, *Scapegoat*, 154.

10. Yarbro Collins, *Mark: A Commentary*, 701.

11. For a nuanced comment and this translation of *Isaiah* 50:6 (lightly modified): Yarbro Collins, *Mark: A Commentary*, 705–707.

12. Or, rather, it can be read—as by Origen—in a realist fashion: Luz, *Matthew 21–28*, 419–20.

13. H. S. Reimarus, *The Goal of Jesus and His Disciples*, trans. G. W. Buchanan (Leiden, 1970), 126.

14. Here in Hans Dieter Betz's translation (typography lightly modified), and for more on this saying: H. D. Betz, *The Sermon on the Mount: A Commentary on the Sermon on the Mount, including the Sermon on the Plain (Matthew 5:3–7:27 and Luke 6:20–49)*, ed. A. Yarbro Collins (Minneapolis, 1995), 486–91. See, too: *Mark* 4:24; *Luke* 6:37–38; Aland, *Synopsis of the Four Gospels*, 60 (no. 68).

15. *Matthew* 5:7–10; Betz, *Sermon on the Mount*, 132–46.

16. For Caiaphas in *Luke–Acts* (and for Annas): *Acts* 4:5–6; E. Haenchen, *The Acts of the Apostles: A Commentary*, trans. H. Anderson and R. M. Wilson (Philadelphia, 1971), 216; H. Conzelmann, *Acts of the Apostles: A Commentary on the Acts of the Apostles*, trans. J. Limburg, A. T. Kraabel, and D. H. Juel, ed. E. J. Epp and C. R Matthews (Philadelphia, 1987), 32.

17. "One can call him an incomparable victim without any sentimental piety or suspect emotion": Girard, *Scapegoat*, 126.

18. I note in passing that *Luke* 22:35–38, where Jesus urges his disciples to buy swords (of huge interest to Reimarus and epigones), and then says that "two swords" are enough (of huge interest to medieval political theologians), seems to me to be a Lucan narrative device (whatever its origins) to account for the presence of swords *at all* in Gethsemane (when Jesus' disciples did not carry them earlier in the gospels), and for the presence of *so few* swords in Gethsemane (indicated by this one, impulsive act of violence).

19. *Luke* 22:66–71; Aland, *Synopsis of the Four Gospels*, 303–305 (no. 332).

20. *Luke* 20:3; compare *Mark* 11:29; *Matthew* 21:24; Aland, *Synopsis of the Four Gospels*, 241 (no. 276).

21. For more on Jesus' practice of counter-questioning: B. J. Koet, "Counter-Questions in the Gospel of Luke: An Assessment", *Asking Questions in Biblical Texts*, ed. B. J. Koet and A. L. H. M. van Wieringen (Leuven—Paris, 2022 (forthcoming)).

22. M. Foucault, *Lectures on the Will to Know: Lectures at the Collège de France, 1970–1971*, ed. D. Defert, et al., trans. G. Burchell (New York, 2013).

23. *Luke* 22:37; compare *Isaiah* 53:12; Aland, *Synopsis of the Four Gospels*, 289 (no. 316).

24. Later in the book, Paul emphasizes that Jesus called him *Saoul* and spoke to him in Aramaic (*Acts* 26:14). For more on which: Haenchen, *Acts of the Apostles*, 74–75, 685.

25. Paul is a functionary of the courts within the literary horizons of *Luke–Acts*. Many commentators deny the historicity of this tradition: Conzelmann, *Acts of the Apostles*, 71.

26. For the earliest traditions of Paul's death in Rome: D. L. Eastman, *Paul the Martyr: The Cult of the Apostle in the Latin West* (Atlanta, 2011), 15–20.

27. Compare this to the anxiety voiced by the secretary (*grammateus*) of Ephesus, temple-state of Artemis, in *Acts* 19:35–40; Haenchen, *Acts of the Apostles*, 575–76; Conzelmann, *Acts of the Apostles*, 166.

28. I have in mind, here, Jean-Jacques Rousseau's theory of "national religions": D. L. Dusenbury, *The Innocence of Pontius Pilate: How the Roman Trial of Jesus Shaped History* (London—New York, 2021), 239–47.

29. A brilliant new study of Christianization "from below" in northern Europe is S. Orlinski, "The Unwitting Apostles of the North: Human Trafficking and Christianization in the Viking Age", *Viking-Age Slavery*, ed. M. Toplak, H. Østhus, and R. Simek (Vienna, 2021). And for a rich evocation of the long-vanished medieval Christian kingdom of Nubia, see F.-X. Fauvelle, *The Golden Rhinoceros: Histories of the African Middle Ages*, trans. T. Tice (Princeton, 2018), 29–43.

18. BLASPHEMY AND MAJESTY

1. A. Watson, *The Trial of Jesus* (Athens, Georgia, 1995), 72. (My italics.)

2. D. L. Dusenbury, *The Innocence of Pontius Pilate: How the Roman Trial of Jesus Shaped History* (London—New York, 2021), 121–24.

3. This charge is first made in the first pages of the first gospel to be written: "It is blasphemy!" (*Mark* 2:7). It is worth noting that the scribes sitting in Jesus' house in Capernaum (*Mark* 2:1) only formulate this objection "in their hearts" (*en tais kardiais, Mark* 2:6). But, in the gospels, the heart is where our thoughts are most revealing.

4. *Blasphēmia* is catalogued, too, in a parallel text, *Matthew* 15:18–20. Columnized in K. Aland, *Synopsis of the Four Gospels: Greek-English Edition of the Synopsis Quattuor Evangeliorum* (Stuttgart, 2003), 143 (no. 150).

5. Compare *Matthew* 26:65–67; *Mark* 14:64–65; *Luke* 22:63–64; *John* 18:19–24; *Acts* 23:1–5.

6. R. A. Bauman, *Impietas in Principem: A Study of Treason against the Roman Emperor with Special Reference to the First Century A.D.* (Munich, 1974), 1–24, 71–108.

7. Dusenbury, *Innocence of Pontius Pilate*, 10–11, 165–66.

8. Josephus, *Judaean War* 2.169–77; Philo, *Embassy to Gaius* 299–305; J. E. Taylor, "Pontius Pilate and the Imperial Cult in Roman Judaea", *New Testament Studies*

52 (2002), 555–82; P. Schäfer, *The History of the Jews in the Greco-Roman World* (London—New York, 2003), 110–11.

9. *Mark* 8:31–9:1; compare *Matthew* 16:21–28; *Luke* 9:22–27; Aland, *Synopsis of the Four Gospels*, 151–52 (nos. 159–60).

10. *Mark* 9:30–32; compare *Matthew* 17:23–23; *Luke* 9:43–45; Aland, *Synopsis of the Four Gospels*, 157 (no. 164).

11. *Mark* 10:32–34; compare *Matthew* 20:17–19; *Luke* 18:31–34; Aland, *Synopsis of the Four Gospels*, 224–25 (no. 262).

12. *Psalm* 2:1–2 (Septuagint); *Acts of the Apostles* 4:25–26. For a philosophical comment on this text: R. Girard, *The Scapegoat*, trans. Y. Freccero (Baltimore, 1989), 107–108.

13. *Mark* 9:30–32; compare *Matthew* 17:23–23; *Luke* 9:43–45; Aland, *Synopsis of the Four Gospels*, 157 (no. 164).

14. *Mark* 8:31–33; *Matthew* 16:21–23; compare *Luke* 9:22; Aland, *Synopsis of the Four Gospels*, 151 (no. 159).

15. *Mark* 9:30–32; compare *Matthew* 17:23–23; *Luke* 9:43–45; Aland, *Synopsis of the Four Gospels*, 157 (no. 164).

16. *Mark* 8:31–33; *Matthew* 16:21–23; compare *Luke* 9:22; Aland, *Synopsis of the Four Gospels*, 151 (no. 159).

17. Dusenbury, *Innocence of Pontius Pilate*, 241–45.

18. Compare *Mark* 9:30–32; *John* 15:18–19.

19. *Matthew* 12:7, which cites *Hosea* 6:6. Note that *Hosea* 6:6 is cited, too, by Jesus in *Matthew* 9:13. For more on which: U. Luz, *Matthew 8–20: A Commentary*, ed. H. Koester, trans. J. E. Crouch (Minneapolis, 2001), 33–35, 181–83. And compare *Mark* 12:33–34, where one of Jesus' interlocutors—a scribe who is "not far from the kingdom of God"—says that the injunction to love is "more important than all whole burnt offerings and sacrifices".

20. Julian the Apostate stresses that sacrifice is an immemorial practice which pagans and Judaeans have in common—and Christians have abandoned: G. G. Stroumsa, "From Abraham's Religion to the Abrahamic Religions", *Historia Religionum* 3 (2011), 11–22, here 17. For more on which, consult his highly illuminating study: G. G. Stroumsa, *The End of Sacrifice: Religious Transformations in Late Antiquity*, trans. S. Emanuel (Chicago, 2009).

19. JESUS THE CONVICT

1. *Matthew* 27:11; *Mark* 15:2; *Luke* 23:3; compare *John* 18:37. Columnized in K. Aland, *Synopsis of the Four Gospels: Greek-English Edition of the Synopsis Quattuor Evangeliorum* (Stuttgart, 2003), 309 (no. 336).

2. S. Krzhizhanovsky, *The Letter Killers Club*, trans. J. Turnbull and N. Formozov (New York, 2012), 47–51, esp. 50–51.

3. For the peculiarity of Jesus' silence vis-à-vis the ancient "noble death" genre: A. Yarbro Collins, *Mark: A Commentary*, ed. H. W. Attridge (Minneapolis, 2007), 636.

4. *Mark* 15:14; compare *Matthew* 27:23 and *Luke* 23:22.

5. "Systematic suspicion of the Gospels never yields interesting results": R. Girard, *The Scapegoat*, trans. Y. Freccero (Baltimore, 1989), 107.

6. B. Pascal, *Pensées*, trans. A. J. Krailsheimer (London—New York, 1966), 112 (no. 271); idem, *Pensées*, ed. L. Brunschvicg (Paris, 1972), 240 (no. 545). (Translation modified.)

7. *Matthew* 26:63–66; *Mark* 14:60–64; *Luke* 22:67–71; Aland, *Synopsis of the Four Gospels*, 304–305 (no. 332).

8. Compare *Matthew* 27:18; *Mark* 15:10; *Luke* 23:4–5; and *John* 18:29–31, 19:4–7.

9. Compare *Matthew* 27:15–16, 20; *Mark* 15:11, 15; *Luke* 23:13, 18; and *John* 18:38, 19:6–7.

10. Compare *Matthew* 27:16; *Mark* 15:7; *Luke* 23:19; and *John* 18:40. For this convict's name: R. E. Moses, "Jesus Barabbas, a Nominal Messiah? Text and History in Matthew 27.16–17", *New Testament Studies* 58 (2011), 43–56, here 56.

11. Compare *Matthew* 27:15–17; *Mark* 15:6–9; *Luke* 23:18–20; and *John* 18:38–40.

12. Compare *Matthew* 27:20–23; *Mark* 15:11–14; *Luke* 23:13, 18–23; and *John* 18:40, 19:6–7.

13. Compare *Matthew* 27:22–23; *Mark* 15:12–14; *Luke* 23:13–16, 20–23; and *John* 19:4–6.

14. Compare *Matthew* 27:24–26; *Mark* 15:15; *Luke* 23:23–25; and *John* 19:12–16.

15. Philo, *Embassy to Gaius* 299–306; Josephus, *Judaean War* 2.169–74; E. Schürer, *The History of the Jewish People in the Age of Jesus Christ (175 B.C.–A.D. 135)*, rev. and ed. G. Vermes and F. Millar, with P. Vermes and M. Black (Edinburgh, 1973), 1.384–86.

16. Compare *Matthew* 27:27–31; *Mark* 15:16–20; *Luke* 23:16, 22 (in *Luke* the judicial brutality is centred on the Herod trial, at *Luke* 23:11; the Roman torture of Jesus is elided but may be echoed in Pilate's determination to "have Jesus flogged"); and *John* 19:1–5.

17. Compare *Matthew* 27:37; *Mark* 15:26; *Luke* 23:38; *John* 19:19; Aland, *Synopsis of the Four Gospels*, 317 (no. 344).

18. *Matthew* 27:3–10; compare *Acts* 1:16–19.

19. "Pilate did not dream by day; he understood that if he did not convict Christ, he would be no friend of the emperor—and he condemned him": S. Kierkegaard,

Søren Kierkegaard's Journals and Papers, Volume 1, ed. and trans. H. V. Hong and E. H. Hong (Bloomington, 1967), 139.

20. Dusenbury, *Innocence of Pontius Pilate*, 133–40.

21. Ibid., xxii–xxiii, 34–35, 61–64.

22. For confirmation of this reading: U. Luz, *Matthew 21–28: A Commentary*, ed. H. Koester, trans. J. E. Crouch (Minneapolis, 2005), 500.

23. Or rather, no one but Nils Runeberg, a twentieth-century Swedish heretic in one of Jorge Luis Borges' fictions: J. L. Borges, "Three Versions of Judas", *Labyrinths: Selected Stories and Other Writings*, ed. D. A. Yates and J. E. Irby (New York, 1964).

24. *Mark* 7:6 and *Matthew* 15:7–8, citing *Isaiah* 29:13; Aland, *Synopsis of the Four Gospels*, 142 (no. 150).

25. *Matthew* 23:27–28. Note that the parallels in *Luke* 11:37–51 are set earlier in Jesus' prophetic life.

26. *Mark* 7:6 and *Matthew* 15:7–8, citing *Isaiah* 29:13; Aland, *Synopsis of the Four Gospels*, 142 (no. 150).

27. *Matthew* 23:1, 24:1.

28. For more on which: D. Pevarello, "Criticism of Verbosity in Ancient Philosophical and Early Christian Writings: Jesus' Critique of the 'Polylogia' of Pagan Prayers (Matthew 6:7) in its Graeco-Roman Context", *Religio-Philosophical Discourses in the Mediterranean World: From Plato, through Jesus, to Late Antiquity*, ed. A. Klostergaard Petersen and G. van Kooten (Leiden, 2017).

29. *Matthew* 23:29–36; compare *Luke* 11:45–52.

30. B. de Spinoza, *Theological-Political Treatise*, ed. J. Israel, trans. M. Silverthorne and J. Israel (Cambridge, 2007), 31; idem, *Tractatus Theologico-Politicus. Traité Théologico-Politique*, Latin ed. F. Akkerman, French trans. J. Lagrée and P.-F. Moreau (Paris, 1999), 120–23.

31. Plato, *Apology* 39c–e; A. J. Droge, "'That Unpredictable Little Beast': Traces of an Other Socrates", *Reading Religions in the Ancient World*, ed. D. E. Aune and R. D. Young (Leiden, 2007), 62.

32. "Of course, with 'children' Matthew is not thinking of a curse hanging over countless generations of Israel": U. Luz, *Matthew 21–28: A Commentary*, ed. H. Koester, trans. J. E. Crouch (Minneapolis, 2005), 502–503.

33. Compare *Mark* 13:14; *Luke* 21:21; Aland, *Synopsis of the Four Gospels*, 258–59 (no. 290).

20. "WHAT IS TRUTH?"

1. Clement of Alexandria, *Exhortation* 6.

2. *John* 1:17, 10:34, 19:7.

3. G. Agamben, *Karman: A Brief Treatise on Action, Guilt, and Gesture*, trans. A. Kotsko (Stanford, 2018), 1–5.

4. For a very ancient tradition of a *later* Roman trial—a trial of two of Jesus' cousins—in which his mystical kingdom is not felt to be a political threat: D. L. Dusenbury, *The Innocence of Pontius Pilate: How the Roman Trial of Jesus Shaped History* (London—New York, 2021), 49–53.

5. "The seating of a judge upon the *sella* was a necessary formality without which his words had no validity": E. Schürer, *The History of the Jewish People in the Age of Jesus Christ (175 B.C.–A.D. 135)*, rev. and ed. G. Vermes and F. Millar, with P. Vermes and M. Black (Edinburgh, 1973) 1.339 note 7.

6. M. Zerwick, *A Grammatical Analysis of the Greek New Testament* (Rome, 1981), 341.

7. Origen, *Against Celsus* 2.34. For more on this passage: J. G. Cook, *The Interpretation of the New Testament in Greco-Roman Paganism* (Tübingen, 2000), 52–53.

8. E. J. Bickerman, "Utilitas Crucis", *Studies in Jewish and Christian History: A New Edition in English including The God of the Maccabees*, ed. A. Tropper (Leiden, 2007), 2.778.

9. Or rather, "Jesus the Nazoraean"—on which: E. Haenchen, *John 2: A Commentary on the Gospel of John Chapters 7–21*, ed. R. W. Funk with U. Busse, trans. R. W. Funk (Philadelphia, 1984), 192.

10. I. Kant, *Religion within the Boundaries of Mere Reason, and Other Writings. Revised Edition*, ed. and trans. A. Wood and G. di Giovanni, rev. with intro. R. M. Adams (Cambridge, 2018), 154; idem, *Die Religion innerhalb der Grenzen der blossen Vernunft. Die Metaphysik der Sitten* (Berlin, 1914), 125.

11. B. de Spinoza, *Theological-Political Treatise*, ed. J. Israel, trans. M. Silverthorne and J. Israel (Cambridge, 2007), 103; idem, *Tractatus Theologico-Politicus. Traité Théologico-Politique*, Latin ed. F. Akkerman, French trans. J. Lagrée and P.-F. Moreau (Paris, 1999), 290–92.

12. T. Engberg-Pedersen, *John and Philosophy: A New Reading of the Fourth Gospel* (Oxford, 2017), 313: "[The writer of *John*] fully belonged to (Jewish-Hellenistic) Greco-Roman literary culture in the same way as, for instance, Philo of Alexandria."

13. Francis Bacon—a practiced barrister, and ultimately Lord Chancellor of England—detects a flash of "Giddinesse" in Pilate's question, which inspires the first sentence his *Essayes*: "What is Truth; said jesting Pilate; And would not stay for an Answer." F. Bacon, *The Essayes or Counsels, Civill and Morall*, ed. with comm. M. Kiernan (Cambridge, Mass., 1985), 7. The young Aldous Huxley is clearly impressed: A. Huxley, *Jesting Pilate* (London, 1926).

14. F. Nietzsche, "The Antichrist. Curse upon Christianity", in *The Case of Wagner. Twilight of the Idols. The Antichrist. Ecce Homo. Dionysus Dithyrambs. Nietzsche*

Contra Wagner, ed. G. Colli and M. Montinari, trans. A. Del Caro, C. Diethe, et al. (Stanford, 2021), 182.

15. Augustine, *Tractates on the Gospel of John 112–24. Tractates on the First Epistle of John*, trans. J. W. Rettig (Washington, D.C., 1995), 25 (translation modified); idem, *In Ioannis Evangelium Tractatus CXXIV*, ed. D. Radbodus Willems (Turnhout, 1954), 646.

21. DEATH AND PARADISE

1. E. Auerbach, *Mimesis: The Representation of Reality in Western Literature*, trans. W. R. Trask (Princeton, 2003), 43–44.

2. *Matthew* 27:38; *Mark* 15:27; *Luke* 23:33; *John* 18; K. Aland, *Synopsis of the Four Gospels: Greek-English Edition of the Synopsis Quattuor Evangeliorum* (Stuttgart, 2003), 316–17 (no. 344).

3. J. A. Fitzmyer, *The Gospel According to Luke (X–XXIV)* (New York, 1985), 1508.

4. This is his unmistakable logic in, for instance, *Matthew* 21:40–41; *Mark* 12:9; *Luke* 20:15–16; Aland, *Synopsis of the Four Gospels*, 243 (no. 278).

5. F. Nietzsche, *The Case of Wagner. Twilight of the Idols. The Antichrist. Ecce Homo. Dionysus Dithyrambs. Nietzsche Contra Wagner*, ed. G. Colli and M. Montinari, trans. A. Del Caro, C. Diethe, et al. (Stanford, 2021), 171: "Even today, a life *such as this* is possible, even essential for *certain* humans: genuine, original Christianity is possible at all times."

6. I read Nietzsche's gloss on *Luke* 23:43, in section 35, as a continuation of this thought in section 34: Nietzsche, *The Antichrist*, 167.

7. Nietzsche, *The Antichrist*, 162.

8. S. Noble, *The Kitāb al-Manfaʿa of Abdallāh ibn al-Fadl al-Antākī: Critical Edition, Translation and Commentary* (doctoral thesis of the Katholieke Universiteit Leuven, defended on 20 April 2022), 108, 221.

9. Kant, *Religion within the Boundaries of Mere Reason*, 186–87; idem, *Die Religion innerhalb der Grenzen der blossen Vernunft*, 159–61.

10. B. de. Spinoza, *Theological-Political Treatise*, ed. J. Israel, trans. M. Silverthorne and J. Israel (Cambridge, 2007), xviii and note ("supreme philosopher"), 176 (*I John* 4:7–8), 180–81 (Jesus' sayings and *I John* 4:7–8).

11. For the context and meaning of which: R. M. Thorsteinsson, *Roman Christianity and Roman Stoicism: A Comparative Study of Ancient Moratlity* (Oxford, 2010), 27–39 (love in Seneca), 43–54 (love in Musonius Rufus), 58–70 (love in Epictetus), and 92–104 (love in Paul).

12. Noting that Kristeva thematizes, rather, a Christian ennoblement of suffering: J. Kristeva, *This Incredible Need to Believe*, trans. B. B. Brahic (New York, 2011), 84–90.

BIBLIOGRAPHY

Premodern works

Note. I have relied on the editions and translations listed below. Translations of Greek and Latin texts are rarely my own, but they have throughout been compared to the originals, and often modified. The same is true of biblical texts. I mainly draw on the *Second Edition of the Revised Standard Version* reprinted in Kurt Aland's *Synopsis of the Four Gospels* (Stuttgart, 2013), and the *New Revised Standard Version in The Book of Common Prayer ... According to the use of The Episcopal Church* (New York, 2007). But they, too, have been compared to the originals and often modified. I cite the fourteenth-century Wycliffe New Testament, the sixteenth-century Douay-Rheims Translation, and the seventeenth-century Authorized Version where I prefer their wordings.

Aristotle, *Rhetoric*	*The "Art" of Rhetoric*. Greek with trans. J. H. Freese. Cambridge, Mass., 1926.
Augustine of Hippo, *Homilies on the Gospel of John*	(i) *In Iohannis Evangelium tractatus CXXIV*. Ed. R. Willems. Turnhout, 1954. (ii) *In Joannis Evangelium tractatus CXXIV*. Ed. J.-P. Migne. Paris, 1902. (iii) *Homilies on the Gospel of John*. Trans. J. Gibb and J. Innes. Ed. P. Schaff. New York, 1888.
Augustine of Hippo, *On Christian Doctrine*	*City of God and Christian Doctrine*. Ed. P. Schaff. New York, 1890.

BIBLIOGRAPHY

Augustine of Hippo, *The City of God against the Pagans*

(i) *La cité de Dieu.* Ed. B. Dombart and A. Kalb. French trans. G. Combès. Annot. G. Bardy. Paris, 1959–1960. 5 vols.
(ii) *The City of God against the Pagans.*

Bion of Borysthenes, *Fragments*

Bion of Borysthenes: A Collection of the Fragments. Ed. and comm. J. F. Kindstrand. Uppsala, 1976.

Cassius Dio, *Roman History*

Roman History V. Greek with trans. E. Cary. London, 1955.

Cicero, *On Ends*

De Finibus Bonorum et Malorum. Latin with trans. H. Rackham. London, 1931.

Clement of Alexandria, *Exhortation*

The Exhortation to the Greeks. The Rich Man's Salvation. And the Fragment of an Address Entitled, To the Newly Baptized. Greek with trans. G. W. Butterworth. Cambridge, Mass., 1960.

Clement of Alexandria, *Miscellanies*

Stromateis, Books One to Three. Trans. J. Ferguson. Washington, D.C., 1991.

Diogenes Laertius, *Lives of the Philosophers*

Lives of Eminent Philosophers in Two Volumes. Greek with trans. R. D. Hicks. Cambridge, Mass., 1959.

Dio of Prusa, *Orations*

Dio Chrysostom IV. Discourses XXXVII–LX. Greek with trans. H. L. Crosby. London, 1962.

Epictetus, *Discourses*

(i) *The Discourses as Reported by Arrian, The Manual, and Fragments ... Volume I. Discourses Books I and II.* Greek with trans. W. A. Oldfather. Cambridge, Mass., 1956.
(ii) Idem. *The Discourses as Reported by Arrian, The Manual, and Fragments ... Volume II. Discourses Books III and IV. The*

BIBLIOGRAPHY

Enchiridion. Greek with trans. W. A. Oldfather. Cambridge, Mass., 1952.

Eusebius of Caesarea, *Demonstration of the Gospel* — *Die Demonstratio Evangelica.* Ed. I. Heikel. Leipzig, 1913.

Eusebius of Caesarea, *Ecclesiastical History* — *The Ecclesiastical History, Volume I.* Greek with trans. K. Lake. Cambridge, Mass., 1926.

Eusebius of Caesarea, *Preparation for the Gospel* — *Die Praeparatio Evangelica, Teil 2. Die Bücher XI bis XV. Register.* Ed. K. Mras. Berlin, 1983.

Gospel of Peter — (i) *The Apocryphal Gospels.* Trans. S. Gathercole. London, 2021.
(ii) J. K. Elliott. *The Apocryphal New Testament: A Collection of Apocryphal Christian Literature in an English Translation based on M. R. James.* Oxford, 1993.

Gospel of Thomas — (i) *The Apocryphal Gospels.* Trans. S. Gathercole. London, 2021.
(ii) *The Fifth Gospel. New Edition.* Trans. H.-G. Bethge, et al. London—New York, 2011.

Hippolytus of Rome, *Refutation of All Heresies* — *Refutation of All Heresies.* Greek with trans. M. D. Litwa. Atlanta, 2016.

Homer, *Iliad* — *The Iliad.* Greek with trans. A. T. Murray. London—New York, 1928.

Irenaeus of Lyon, *Against Heresies* — *The Apostolic Fathers with Justin Martyr and Irenaeus.* Ed. P. Schaff. New York, 1886.

Jerome, *Commentary on Titus* — *Commentaries on Galatians, Titus, and Philemon.* Trans. T. P. Scheck. Notre Dame, 2010.

BIBLIOGRAPHY

Jerome, *On Illustrious Men*   *On Illustrious Men.* Trans. T. P. Halton. Washington, D.C., 2000.

Jerusalem Talmud, *Megillah*   *The Talmud of the Land of Israel: A Preliminary Translation and Explanation. Volume 19: Megillah.* Trans. J. Neusner. Chicago, 1987.

Josephus, *Against Apion*   *Against Apion.* Trans. with comm. J. M. G. Barclay. Leiden, 2007.

Josephus, *Judaean Antiquities*   *Jewish Antiquities.* Greek with trans. H. St. J. Thackeray, R. Marcus, A. Wikgren, and L. Feldman. Cambridge, Mass., 1957–1965. 6 vols.

Josephus, *Judaean War*   *Judean War 2. Translation and Commentary.* Trans. S. Mason with H. Chapman. Leiden, 2008.

Josephus, *Life of Josephus*   *Life of Josephus.* Trans. with comm. S. Mason. Leiden, 2003.

Justin the Philosopher, *First Apology*   (i) *Apologie pour les chrétiens.* Greek with French trans. and annot. C. Munier. Paris, 2006.
(ii) *Saint Justin Martyr.* Trans. T. Falls. Washington, D.C., 1948.

Lactantius, *Deaths of the Persecutors*   (i) *Liber de Mortibus persecutorum.* Ed. J.-P. Migne. Paris, 1844.
(ii) *The Minor Works.* Trans. M. F. McDonald. Washington, D.C., 1965.

Lactantius, *Divine Institutes*   (i) *Divinarum institutionum libri septem Fasc. 3, Libri V et VI.* Ed. E. Heck and A. Wlosok. Berlin, 2009.
(ii) *Divine Institutes.* Trans. with notes A. Bowen and P. Garnsey. Liverpool, 2003.

	(ii) *The Divine Institutes, Books I–VII*. Trans. M. F. McDonald. Washington, D.C., 1964.
Letter of Mara bar Sarapion	*Spicilegium Syriacum: Containing Remains of Bardesan, Meliton, Ambrose and Mara bar Serapion*. Ed. with English trans. and notes W. Cureton. London, 1855.
Livy, *History of Rome*	*Livy VI. Books XXIII–XXV*. Latin with trans. F. G. Moore. London, 1940.
Lucian of Samosata, *The Death of Peregrinus*	*Lucian, Volume V*. Greek with trans. A. M. Harmon. Cambridge, Mass., 1936.
Martyrdom of Polycarp	*The Apostolic Fathers II. The Shepherd of Hermas. The Martyrdom of Polycarp. The Epistle to Diognetus*. Greek with trans. K. Lake. Cambridge, Mass., 1965.
Minucius Felix, *Octavius*	*Tertullian. Apology—De Spectaculis. Minucius Felix*. Latin with trans. T. R. Glover and G. H. Rendall with W. C. A. Kerr. Cambridge, Mass., 1977.
Nemesius of Emesa, *On Human Nature*	*De Natura Hominis*. Ed. M. Morani. Leipzig, 1987.
Origen, *Against Celsus*	(i) *Contra Celsum libri VIII*. Ed M. Marcovich. Leiden, 2001. (ii) *Contra Celsum*. Trans. with notes H. Chadwick. Cambridge, 1980.
Philo, *Embassy to Gaius*	*The Embassy to Gaius*. Greek with trans. F. H. Colson. Cambridge, Mass., 1971.
Philo, *On the Decalogue*	*Philo, Volume VII*. Greek with trans. F. H. Colson. Cambridge, Mass., 1998.
Philostratus, *Life of Apollonius*	*The Life of Apollonius of Tyana ... in Two Volumes*. Greek with trans. F. C. Conybeare. Cambridge, Mass., 1989.

BIBLIOGRAPHY

Plato, *Apology*   *Euthyphro. Apology. Crito. Phaedo. Phaedrus.* Greek with trans. H.N. Fowler. London, 1971.

Plato, *Crito*   Ibid.

Plato, *Meno*   *Laches. Protagoras. Meno. Euthydemus.* Greek with trans. W. R. M. Lamb. London, 1924.

Plato, *Phaedo*   *Euthyphro. Apology. Crito. Phaedo. Phaedrus.* Greek with trans. H.N. Fowler. London, 1971.

Plato, *Republic*   *The Republic, Books I–V.* Greek with trans. P. Shorey. Cambridge, Mass., 1937.

Plato, *Theaetetus*   *Theaetetus. Sophist.* Greek with trans. H. N. Fowler. London, 1967.

Pliny the Younger, *Letters*   *Letters and Panegyricus.* Latin with trans. B. Radice. London, 1969. 2 vols.

Plutarch, *Life of Alexander*   *Lives VII. Demosthenes and Cicero, Alexander and Caesar.* Greek with trans. B. Perrin. Cambridge, Mass., 1967.

Plutarch, *Life of Marcellus*   *Lives V. Agesilaus and Pompey, Pelopidas and Marcellus.* Greek with trans. B. Perrin. Cambridge, Mass., 1955.

Porphyry of Tyre, *Letter to Marcella*   *Letter to His Wife Marcella concerning the Life of Philosophy and the Ascent to the Gods.* Trans. A. Zimmern. Grand Rapids, 1986.

Porphyry of Tyre, *On Abstinence from Killing Animals*   *On Abstinence from Killing Animals.* Trans. G. Clark. London—New York, 2000.

Pseudo-Jerome, *Commentary on Mark*   (i) *Expositio evangelii secundum Marcum.* Ed. M. Cahill. Turnhout, 1997. (ii) *The First Commentary on Mark.* Trans. with notes M. Cahill. Oxford, 1998.

BIBLIOGRAPHY

Quodvultdeus of Carthage, *Creedal Homilies*

(i) *Quodvultdeus Carthaginiensis Opera tributa*. Ed. R. Braun. Turnhout, 1976.

(ii) *The Creedal Homilies: Conversion in Fifth-Century North Africa*. Trans. with comm. T. M. Finn. Mahwah, New Jersey, 2004.

Sallust, *Jugurthine War*

The War with Catiline. The War with Jugurtha. Latin with trans. J. C. Rolfe. Rev. J. T. Ramsey. Cambridge, Mass., 2013.

Seneca, *Moral Epistles*

Ad Lucilium Epistulae Morales. Latin with trans. R. M. Gummere. London—New York, 1920.

Septuagint

(i) *Septuaginta. Id est Vetus Testamentum graece iuxta LXX interpretes*. Ed. A. Rahlfs. Stuttgart, 1979.

(ii) *The Old Testament in Greek according to the Text of Codex Vaticanus, Supplemented from Other Uncial Manuscripts, with a Critical Apparatus Containing the Variants of the Chief Ancient Authorities for the Text of the Septuagint. Volume 1*. Ed. A. E. Brooke and N. McLean. Cambridge, 2009.

Socrates Scholasticus, *Ecclesiastical History*

The Ecclesiastical History of Socrates. London, 1853.

Suetonius, *Lives of the Twelve Caesars*

Suetonius. Latin with trans. J. C. Rolfe. London, 1913–14. 2 vols.

Tacitus, *Annals*

The Annals. Books XIII–XVI. Latin with trans. J. Jackson. London, 1981.

Tatian of Adiabene, *Oration to the Greeks*

Oratio ad Graecos and Fragments. Greek with trans. M. Whittaker. Oxford, 1982.

Tertullian of Carthage, *Apology*

Tertullian. Apology—De Spectaculis. Minucius Felix. Latin with trans. T. R. Glover and G.

BIBLIOGRAPHY

H. Rendall with W. C. A. Kerr. Cambridge, Mass., 1977.

Modern works

Agamben, G. *The Time That Remains: A Commentary on the Letter to the Romans.* Trans. P. Dailey. Stanford, 2005.

———, *The Highest Poverty: Monastic Rules and Form-of-Life.* Trans. A. Kotsko. Stanford, 2013.

———, *Pilato e Gesù.* Rome, 2014.

———, *Pilate and Jesus.* Trans. A. Kotsko. Stanford, 2015.

———, *Karman: A Brief Treatise on Action, Guilt, and Gesture.* Trans. A. Kotsko. Stanford, 2018.

Aland, K. *Synopsis of the Four Gospels: Greek-English Edition of the Synopsis Quattuor Evangeliorum. On the Basis of the Greek Text of the Nestle-Aland 27th Edition… Fifteenth Edition.* Stuttgart, 2003.

Aland, K., and B. Aland. *The Text of the New Testament: An Introduction to the Critical Editions and to the Theory and Practice of Modern Textual Criticism.* Trans. E. F. Rhodes. Leiden, 1989.

Alon, I. *Socrates in Medieval Arabic Literature.* Leiden—Jerusalem, 1991.

Amorai-Stark, S., Y. Kalman, M. Hershkovitz, R. Chachy, G. Forster, and R. Porat. "An Inscribed Copper-Alloy Finger Ring from Herodium Depicting a Krater." *Israel Exploration Journal* 68, 2 (2018), 208–20.

Armitage, D. J. *Theories of Poverty in the World of the New Testament.* (Wissenschaftliche Untersuchungen zum Neuen Testament 423.) Tübingen, 2016.

Aslan, R. *Zealot: The Life and Times of Jesus of Nazareth.* New York, 2013.

Auerbach, E. *Mimesis: The Representation of Reality in Western Literature.* Trans. W. R. Trask. Princeton, 2003.

———, *Time, History, and Literature: Selected Essays of Erich Auerbach.* Ed. J. I. Porter. Trans. J. O. Newman. Princeton, 2014.

Bacon, F. *The Essayes or Counsels, Civill and Morall.* Ed. with comm. M. Kiernan. Cambridge, Mass., 1985.

Bahrdt, C. F. *System der moralischen Religion zur endlichen Beruhigung für Zweifler und Denker. Allen Christen und Nichtchristen lesbar.* Berlin, 1790.

Barker, J. W. *Tatian's Diatessaron: Composition, Redaction, Recension, and Reception.* (Oxford Early Christian Studies.) Oxford, 2022.

BIBLIOGRAPHY

Barnes, T. D. "Sossianus Hierocles and the Antecedents of the 'Great Persecution'." *Harvard Studies in Classical Philology* 80 (1976), 239–52.

Bataille, G. *Theory of Religion*. Trans. R. Hurley. New York, 1992.

Bauckham, R. *Gospel Women: Studies of the Named Women in the Gospels*. Grand Rapids, 2002.

———, "Messianism According to the Gospel of John." *Challenging Perspectives on the Gospel of John*. (Wissenschaftliche Untersuchungen zum Neuen Testament 219.) Ed. J. Lierman. Tübingen, 2006.

Bauman, R. A. *Impietas in Principem: A Study of Treason against the Roman Emperor with Special Reference to the First Century A.D.* Munich, 1974.

Bayle, P. *A Philosophical Commentary on These Words of the Gospel, Luke 14.23, "Compel Them to Come In, That My House May Be Full"*. (Natural Law and Enlightenment Classics.) Ed. J. Kilcullen and C. Kukathas. Indianapolis, 2005.

Bekken, P. J. *The Lawsuit Motif in John's Gospel from New Perspectives: Jesus Christ, Crucified Criminal and Emperor of the World*. (Supplements to Novum Testamentum 158.) Leiden, 2015.

Bentham, J. *Not Paul, but Jesus. Volume III: Doctrine*. London, 2013.

Berchman, R. M. *Porphyry against the Christians*. (Studies in Platonism, Neoplatonism, and the Platonic Tradition 1.) Leiden, 2005.

Betz, H. D. "Jesus and the Cynics: Survey and Analysis of a Hypothesis." *The Journal of Religion* 74, 4 (1994), 453–75.

———, *The Sermon on the Mount: A Commentary on the Sermon on the Mount, including the Sermon on the Plain (Matthew 5:3–7:27 and Luke 6:20–49)*. (Hermeneia.) Ed. A. Yarbro Collins. Minneapolis, 1995.

Betz, O. "The Essenes." *The Cambridge History of Judaism, Volume Three: The Early Roman Period*. Ed. W. Horbury, W. Davies, and J. Sturdy. Cambridge, 1999.

Bickerman, E. J. "The Chain of the Pharisaic Tradition." *Studies in Jewish and Christian History: A New Edition in English including The God of the Maccabees*. (Ancient Judaism and Early Christianity 68, 1–2.) Ed. A. Tropper. Leiden, 2007.

———, "The Name of Christians." *Studies in Jewish and Christian History: A New Edition in English including The God of the Maccabees*. (Ancient Judaism and Early Christianity 68,1–2.) Ed. A. Tropper. Leiden, 2007.

————, "Utilitas Crucis." *Studies in Jewish and Christian History: A New Edition in English including The God of the Maccabees*. (Ancient Judaism and Early Christianity 68,1–2.) Ed. A. Tropper. Leiden, 2007.

Blake, W. "The Everlasting Gospel." *Blake's Poetry and Designs*. (A Norton Critical Edition.) Ed. M. L. Johnson and J. E. Grant. New York—London, 1979.

Bloch, E. *Atheism in Christianity: The Religion of the Exodus and the Kingdom*. Trans. J. T. Swann. London, 2009.

Bloom, H. *Jesus and Yahweh: The Names Divine*. New York, 2005.

Bond, H. K. *Pontius Pilate in History and Interpretation*. (Society for New Testament Studies—Monograph Series 100.) Cambridge, 1998.

————, "Dating the Death of Jesus: Memory and the Religious Imagination." *New Testament Studies* 59 (2013), 461–75.

Borges, J. L. "Three Versions of Judas." *Labyrinths: Selected Stories and Other Writings*. Ed. D. A. Yates and J. E. Irby. New York, 1964.

Bosworth, A. S. *Conquest and Empire: The Reign of Alexander the Great*. Cambridge, 1988.

Bovon, F. *The Emergence of Christianity: Collected Studies III*. (Wissenschaftliche Untersuchungen zum Neuen Testament 319.) Ed. L. Drake. Tübingen, 2013.

Bremmer, J. N. "Lucian on Peregrinus and Alexander of Abonuteichnos: A Sceptical View of Two Religious Entrepreneurs." *Beyond Priesthood: Religious Entrepreneurs and Innovators in the Roman Empire*. Ed. R. L. Gordon, G. Petridou, and J. Rüpke. Berlin, 2017.

————, "Dying for the Community: From Euripides' *Erechtheus* to the Gospel of John." *Sōtēria: Salvation in Early Christianity and Antiquity. Festschrift in Honour of Cilliers Breytenbach*. (Novum Testamentum Supplements 175.) Ed. D. du Toit, C. Gerber, and C. Zimmermann. Leiden, 2019.

Brent, A. *The Imperial Cult and the Development of Church Order: Concepts and Images of Authority in Paganism and Early Christianity before the Age of Cyprian*. Leiden, 1999.

Brighton, M. A. *The Sicarii in Josephus's Judean War: Rhetorical Analysis and Historical Observations*. (Early Judaism and Its Literature 27.) Atlanta, 2009.

BIBLIOGRAPHY

Brown, R. *The Death of the Messiah: From Gethsemane to the Grave: A Commentary on the Passion Narratives in the Four Gospels*. New York—London, 1994. 2 vols.

———, *The Gospel According to John (i–xii)*. New York, 1966.

Bruce, F. F. *New Testament History*. New York, 1980.

Bulgakov, M. *The Master and Margarita*. Trans. with notes R. Pevear and L. Volokhonsky. Foreword B. Fishman. London, 2016.

Bultmann, R. *Primitive Christianity in its Contemporary Setting*. Trans. R. H. Fuller. New York, 1956 (reprinted 1965).

———, *The History of the Synoptic Tradition*. Trans. J. Marsh. Oxford, 1972.

Busine, A. *Paroles d'Apollon. Pratiques et traditions oraculaires dans l'Antiquité tardive (IIe–VIe siècles)*. (Religions in the Graeco-Roman World 156.) Leiden, 2005.

Carleton Paget, J. N. "The Jew of Celsus and *Adversus Judaeos* Literature." *Zeitschrift für Antikes Christentum* 21, 2 (2017), 201–42.

Catchpole, D. R. *The Trial of Jesus: A Study in the Gospels and Jewish Historiography from 1770 to the Present Day*. (Studia Post-Biblica 18.) Leiden, 1971.

Chapman, D. W., and E. J. Schnabel. *The Trial and Crucifixion of Jesus: Texts and Commentary*. (Wissenschaftliche Untersuchungen zum Neuen Testament 344.) Tübingen, 2015.

Charles-Daubert, F. "*L'Esprit* de Spinosa et les *Traités des trois imposteurs*: rappel des différentes familles et de leurs principales caractéristiques." *Heterodoxy, Spinozism, and Free Thought in Early-Eighteenth-Century Europe: Studies on the Traité des Trois Imposteurs*. (Archives Internationales d'Histoire des Idées 148.) Ed. S. Berti, F. Charles-Daubert, and R. H. Popkin. Dordrecht, 1996.

Conzelmann, H. *Acts of the Apostles: A Commentary on the Acts of the Apostles*. (Hermeneia.) Trans. J. Limburg, A. T. Kraabel, and D. H. Juel. Ed. E. J. Epp and C. R Matthews. Philadelphia, 1987.

Cook, J. G. *The Interpretation of the New Testament in Greco-Roman Paganism*. Tübingen, 2000.

———, *The Interpretation of the Old Testament in Greco-Roman Paganism*. (Studien und Texte zu Antike und Christentum 23.) Tübingen, 2004.

BIBLIOGRAPHY

Crawford, M. R. *The Eusebian Canon Tables: Ordering Textual Knowledge in Late Antiquity.* (Oxford Early Christian Studies.) Oxford, 2019.

Critical Edition of Q: Synopsis including the Gospels of Matthew and Luke, Mark and Thomas with ... Translations of Q and Thomas. (Hermeneia.) Ed. J. M. Robinson, P. Hoffmann, and J. S. Kloppenborg. Leuven, 2000.

Cullmann, O. *The State in the New Testament.* New York, 1956.

———, *The Johannine Circle.* Trans. J. Bowden. Philadelphia, 1976.

Darr, J. A. *Herod the Fox: Audience Criticism and Lukan Characterization.* (Journal for the Study of the New Testament Supplement Series 163.) Sheffield, 1998.

De Jonge, H. J. "Joseph Scaliger's Historical Criticism of the New Testament." *Novum Testamentum* 38, 2 (1996), 176–93.

Denzinger, H., ed. *Enchiridion Symbolorum definitionem et declarationem de rebus fidei et morum.* Rev. A. Schönmetzer. Barcelona, 1963.

DePalma Digeser, E. *A Threat to Public Piety: Christians, Platonists, and the Great Persecution.* Ithaca, New York, 2012.

Derrett, J. D. M. *Law in the New Testament.* London, 1970.

Desideri, P. "City and Country in Dio." *Dio Chrysostom: Politics, Letters, and Philosophy.* Ed. S. Swain. Oxford, 2000.

deSilva, D. A. *The Jewish Teachers of Jesus, James, and Jude: What Earliest Christianity Learned from the Apocrypha and Pseudepigrapha.* Oxford, 2012.

Dibelius, M. *From Tradition to Gospel.* Trans. B. L. Woolf. Cambridge, 1982.

Dihle, A. *Die Goldene Regel. Eine Einführung in die Geschichte der antiken und frühchristlichen Vulgärethik.* (Studienhefte zur Altertumswissenschaft 7.) Göttingen, 1962.

Döring, K. *Exemplum Socratis: Studien zur Sokratesnachwirkung in der kynisch-stoischen Popularphilosophie der frühen Kaiserzeit und im frühen Christentum.* (Hermes-Einzelschriften 42.) Wiesbaden, 1979.

Dormeyer, D. *The New Testament among the Writings of Antiquity.* Trans. R. Kossov. Sheffield, 1998.

Droge, A. J. "'That Unpredictable Little Beast': Traces of an Other Socrates." *Reading Religions in the Ancient World.* (Novum Testamentum Supplements 125.) Ed. D. E. Aune and R. D. Young. Leiden, 2007.

BIBLIOGRAPHY

Dupont, J. *Les tentations de Jésus au désert.* (Studia Neotestamentica 4.) *Sine loco*: Desclée de Brouwer, 1968.

Dusenbury, D. L. *Platonic Legislations: An Essay on Legal Critique in Ancient Greece.* Cham, 2017.

———, "The Judgment of Pontius Pilate: A Critique of Giorgio Agamben." *Journal of Law and Religion* 32, 2 (2017), 340–65.

———, "'A World like a Russian Novel': The Trials of Socrates and Jesus." *TLS. The Times Literary Supplement* (10 April 2020), 21.

———, *The Innocence of Pontius Pilate: How the Roman Trial of Jesus Shaped History.* London—New York, 2021.

———, "A Choice, and Not a Law: The Role of Virginity in Foucault's Thinking." *TLS. The Times Literary Supplement* (16 July 2021). Archived online at https://www.the-tls.co.uk/articles/history-of-sexuality-volume-four-michel-foucault-book-review-d-l-dusenbury/. Accessed on 7 August 2022.

Dyck, C. "1793." *The Cambridge Kant Lexicon.* Ed. J. Wuerth. Cambridge, 2021.

Eckhardt, B. "'An Idumean, That Is, a Half-Jew': Hasmoneans and Herodians between Ancestry and Merit." *Jewish Identity and Politics between the Maccabees and Bar Kokhba: Groups, Normativity, and Rituals.* Ed. B. Eckhardt. Leiden, 2012.

Eagleton, T. "Lunging, Flailing, Mispunching." *London Review of Books* 28, 20 (2006), 32–34.

———, *Radical Sacrifice.* New Haven—London, 2018.

Eastman, D. L. *Paul the Martyr: The Cult of the Apostle in the Latin West.* (Writings from the Greco-Roman World Supplement Series 4.) Atlanta, 2011.

Eisler, R. *The Messiah Jesus and John the Baptist according the Flavius Josephus' Recently Rediscovered 'Capture of Jerusalem' and the Other Jewish and Christian Sources.* Trans. A. H. Krappe. New York, 1931.

Engberg-Pedersen, T. *John and Philosophy: A New Reading of the Fourth Gospel.* Oxford, 2017.

Facchini, C. "Jesus the Pharisee: Leon Modena, the Historical Jesus, and Renaissance Venice." *Journal for the Study of the Historical Jesus* 17, 1–2 (2019), 81–101.

Fauvelle, F.-X. *The Golden Rhinoceros: Histories of the African Middle Ages.* Trans. T. Tice. Princeton, 2018.

Fernández Marcos, N. *The Septuagint in Context: Introduction to the Greek Version of the Bible.* Trans. W. G. E. Watson. Leiden—Cologne, 2000.

Fitzmyer, J. A. *The Gospel According to Luke (I–IX).* New York, 1981.

———, *The Gospel According to Luke (X–XXIV).* New York, 1985.

Flusser, D., with R. S. Notley. *The Sage from Galilee: Rediscovering Jesus' Genius.* Grand Rapids, 2007.

Fornari, G. *Dionysus, Christ, and the Death of God. Volume 1, The Great Mediations of the Classical World.* East Lansing, Michigan, 2021.

———, *Dionysus, Christ, and the Death of God. Volume 2, Christianity and Modernity.* East Lansing, Michigan, 2021.

Foster, P. "Is it Possible to Dispense with Q?" *Novum Testamentum* 45, 4 (2003), 313–37.

Foucault, M. *Fearless Speech.* (Semiotext(e) Foreign Agents.) Ed. J. Pearson. Los Angeles, 2001.

———, *Lectures on the Will to Know: Lectures at the Collège de France, 1970–1971.* Ed. D. Defert, et al. Trans. G. Burchell. New York, 2013.

———, *Confessions of the Flesh. The History of Sexuality, Volume 4.* Ed. F. Gros. Trans. R. Hurley. New York, 2021.

France, A. "The Procurator of Judea." *Tales from a Mother-of-Pearl Casket.* Trans. H. Pène du Bois. New York, 1896.

Fredriksen, P. *When Christians Were Jews: The First Generation.* New Haven, 2019.

Frend, W. H. C. "Prelude to the Great Persecution: The Propaganda War." *Journal of Ecclesiastical History* 38 (1987), 1–18.

Freyne, S. *Galilee, Jesus and the Gospels: Literary Approaches and Historical Investigations.* Philadelphia, 1988.

———, *Galilee and Gospel: Collected Essays.* (Wissenschaftliche Untersuchungen zum Neuen Testament 125.) Tübingen, 2000.

———, *Jesus, a Jewish Galilean: A New Reading of the Jesus-Story.* New York—London, 2004.

Gabba, E. "The Social, Economic and Political History of Palestine 63 BCE–CE 70." *The Cambridge History of Judaism, Volume Three: The Early*

Roman Period. Ed. W. Horbury, W. Davies, and J. Sturdy. Cambridge, 1999.

Gathercole, S. "Christians According to Second-Century Philosophers." *Religio-Philosophical Discourses in the Mediterranean World: From Plato, through Jesus, to Late Antiquity.* Ed. A. Klostergaard Petersen and G. van Kooten. Leiden, 2017.

Girard, R. *The Scapegoat.* Trans. Y. Freccero. Baltimore, 1989.

———, *I See Satan Fall Like Lightning.* Trans. J. G. Williams. Maryknoll, New York, 2001.

Glück, L. *Poems 1962–2012.* New York, 2012.

Goldmann, L. *The Hidden God: A Study of Tragic Vision in the Pensées of Pascal and the Tragedies of Racine.* Trans. P. Thody. London—New York, 2016.

Goodman, M. *The Ruling Class of Judaea: The Origins of the Jewish Revolt against Rome A.D. 66–70.* Cambridge, 1987.

———, "Galilean Judaism and Judaean Judaism." *The Cambridge History of Judaism, Volume Three: The Early Roman Period.* Ed. W. Horbury, W. D. Davies, and J. Sturdy. Cambridge, 1999.

Gradel, I. *Emperor Worship and Roman Religion.* (Oxford Classical Monographs.) Oxford, 2002.

Griswold, E. "Is This the End of Christianity in the Middle East?" *The New York Times Magazine* (22 July 2015). Archived online at https://www.nytimes.com/2015/07/26/magazine/is-this-the-end-of-christianity-in-the-middle-east.html. Accessed on 1 August 2022.

Groetsch, U. *Hermann Samuel Reimarus (1694–1768): Classicist, Hebraist, Enlightenment Radical in Disguise.* (Studies in Intellectual History 237.) Leiden, 2015.

Gurtner, D. M. "Water and Blood and Matthew 27:49: A Johannine Reading in the Matthean Passion Narrative?" *Studies on the Text of the New Testament and Early Christianity.* (New Testament Tools, Studies and Documents 50.) Ed. D. M. Gurtner, J. Hernández, and P. Foster. Leiden, 2015.

Haenchen, E. *The Acts of the Apostles: A Commentary.* Trans. H. Anderson and R. M. Wilson. Philadelphia, 1971.

———, *John 1: A Commentary on the Gospel of John Chapters 1–6.*

BIBLIOGRAPHY

(Hermeneia.) Ed. R. W. Funk with U. Busse. Trans. R. W. Funk. Philadelphia, 1984.

⸻, *John 2: A Commentary on the Gospel of John Chapters 7–21.* (Hermeneia.) Ed. R. W. Funk with U. Busse. Trans. R. W. Funk. Philadelphia, 1984.

Hägg, T. "The Gospels: From Sayings to a Full Life." *The Art of Biography in Antiquity.* Cambridge, 2012.

Halper, Y. *Jewish Socratic Questions in an Age without Plato: Permitting and Forbidding Open Inquiry in 12–15th Century Europe and North Africa.* Leiden, 2021.

Harrington, J. M. *The Lukan Passion Narrative: The Markan Material in Luke 22,54–23,25. A Historical Survey: 1891–1997.* Leiden, 2000.

Hengel, M. *The Zealots: Investigations into the Jewish Freedom Movement in the Period from Herod I until 70 A.D.* Trans. D. Smith. Edinburgh, 1989.

Hine, H. M. "Seneca and Paul: The First Two Thousand Years." *Paul and Seneca in Dialogue.* (Ancient Philosophy and Religion 2.) Ed. J. R. Dodson and D. E. Briones. Leiden, 2017.

Hoehner, H. W. *Herod Antipas: A Contemporary of Jesus Christ.* (Society for New Testament Studies Monograph Series 17.) Cambridge, 1972.

Hoeren, T. "Präjakobiner in Deutschland. Carl Friedrich Bahrdt (1740–1792)." *Zeitschrift für Religions- und Geistesgeschichte* 47 (1995), 55–72.

Hoffmann, P., T. Hieke, and U. Bauer. *Synoptic Concordance. A Greek Concordance to the First Three Gospels in Synoptic Arrangement, statistically evaluated, including occurrences in Acts.* Berlin—New York, 2000. 4 vols.

Holland, T. *Dominion: How the Christian Revolution Remade the World.* New York, 2019.

Horbury, W. "Christ as Brigand in Ancient Anti-Christian Polemic." *Jesus and the Politics of His Day.* Ed. E. Bammel and C. F. D. Moule. Cambridge, 1984.

⸻, "The New Testament and Rabbinic Study—an Historical Sketch." *The New Testament and Rabbinic Literature.* (Supplements to the Journal for the Study of Judaism 136.) Ed. R. Bieringer, F. García Martínez, D. Pollefeyt, and P. Tomson. Leiden, 2010.

Hubbard, J. M. "Does Justin Argue with Jews? Reconsidering the Relevance of Philo." *Vigiliae Christianae* (forthcoming).

BIBLIOGRAPHY

Huttunen, N. "Epictetus' Views on Christians: A Closed Case Revisited." *Religio-Philosophical Discourses in the Mediterranean World: From Plato, through Jesus, to Late Antiquity.* Ed. A. Klostergaard Petersen and G. van Kooten. Leiden, 2017.

Huxley, A. *Jesting Pilate.* London, 1926.

Jantsch, T. "Salvation and the Fate of Jesus in Luke–Acts." *Sōtēria: Salvation in Early Christianity and Antiquity. Festschrift in Honour of Cilliers Breytenbach.* (Novum Testamentum Supplements 175.) Ed. D. du Toit, C. Gerber, and C. Zimmermann. Leiden, 2019.

Jenkins, P. *The Next Christendom: The Coming of Global Christianity.* Oxford, 2011.

Jensen, M. H. *Herod Antipas in Galilee: The Literary and Archaeological Sources on the Reign of Herod Antipas and its Socio-Economic Impact on Galilee.* (Wissenschaftliche Untersuchungen zum Neuen Testament 215.) Tübingen, 2006.

Jeremias, J. *The Parables of Jesus.* Trans. S. H. Hooke. London, 1954.

———, *New Testament Theology: The Proclamation of Jesus.* New York, 1971.

Jervis, L. A. "Suffering for the Reign of God: The Persecution of Disciples in Q." *Novum Testamentum* 44, 4 (2002), 313–32.

Johansson, K. *The Birds in the Iliad: Identities, Interactions and Functions.* (Gothenburg Studies in History 2.) Gothenburg, 2012.

Johnson, A. P. "Philosophy, Hellenicity, Law: Porphyry on Origen, Again." *The Journal of Hellenic Studies* 132 (2012), 55–69.

Kaminska, B. A. "*Christus Medicus* and Beyond: The Thaumaturgic Power of Christ and Medical Metaphors in the Premodern Netherlands." *Images of Miraculous Healing in the Early Modern Netherlands.* (Brill's Studies on Art, Art History, and Intellectual History 58.) Leiden, 2021.

Kant, I. *Die Religion innerhalb der Grenzen der blossen Vernunft. Die Metaphysik der Sitten.* (Kant's gesammelte Schriften 6.) Berlin, 1914.

———, *Religion within the Boundaries of Mere Reason, and Other Writings. Revised Edition.* Ed. and trans. A. Wood and G. di Giovanni. Rev. with intro. R. M. Adams. Cambridge, 2018.

Kantorowicz, E. H. *Laudes Regiae: A Study in Liturgical Acclamations and Mediaeval Ruler Worship.* (University of California Publications in History 33.) Berkeley, 1946.

BIBLIOGRAPHY

Karamanolis, G. *The Philosophy of Early Christianity.* (Ancient Philosophies.) London—New York, 2021.

Karasz, P. "Pontius Pilate's Name Is Found on 2,000-Year-Old Ring." *The New York Times* (20 November 2018). Archived online at https://www.nytimes.com/2018/11/30/world/middleeast/pontius-pilate-ring.html. Accessed on 9 June 2019.

Kasher, A. "Polemic and Apologetic Methods of Writing in *Contra Apionem.*" *Josephus' Contra Apionem: Studies in its Character and Context with a Latin Concordance to the Portion Missing in Greek.* (Arbeiten zur Geschichte des antiken Judentums und des Urchristentums 34.) Ed. L. H. Feldman and J. R. Levison. Leiden—Cologne, 1996.

Keith, C. "The Initial Location of the *Pericope Adulterae* in Fourfold Tradition." *Novum Testamentum* 51, 3 (2009), 209–31.

———, *The Pericope Adulterae, the Gospel of John, and the Literacy of Jesus.* (New Testament Tools, Studies and Documents 38.) Leiden, 2009.

Kierkegaard, S. *Søren Kierkegaard's Journals and Papers, Volume 1.* Ed. and trans. H. V. Hong and E. H. Hong. Bloomington, 1967.

———, *Either/Or, Part II.* (Kierkegaard's Writings 4.) Ed. and trans. H. V. Hong and E. H. Hong. Princeton, 1990.

Kindstrand, J. F. *Bion of Borysthenes: A Collection of the Fragments with Introduction and Commentary.* Ed. and comm. J. F. Kindstrand. Uppsala, 1976.

Kinzig, W. "Pagans and the Bible." *The New Cambridge History of the Bible: From the Beginnings to 600.* Ed. J. Carleton Paget and J. Schaper. Cambridge, 2013.

Klein, D. *Hermann Samuel Reimarus (1694–1768).* (Beiträge zur historischen Theologie 145.) Tübingen, 2009.

Knipp, D. *'Christus Medicus' in der frühchristlichen Sarkophagskulptur. Ikonographische Studien zur Sepulkralkunst des späten vierten Jahrhunderts.* (Vigiliae Christianae Supplements 37.) Leiden, 1998.

Koet, B. J. "Counter-Questions in the Gospel of Luke: An Assessment." *Asking Questions in Biblical Texts.* (Contributions to Biblical Exegesis and Theology.) Ed. B. J. Koet and A. L. H. M. van Wieringen. Leuven—Paris, 2022 (forthcoming).

Kristeva, J. *This Incredible Need to Believe.* Trans. B. B. Brahic. New York, 2011.

BIBLIOGRAPHY

Krzhizhanovsky, S. *The Letter Killers Club*. Trans. J. Turnbull and N. Formozov. New York, 2012.

Kuehn, M. "Kant's Jesus." *Kant's Religion within the Boundaries of Mere Reason*. Ed. G. Michalson. Cambridge, 2014.

Lampe, K. *The Birth of Hedonism: The Cyrenaic Philosophers and Pleasure as a Way of Life*. Princeton, 2015.

Lapide, C. à. *The Great Commentary of Cornelius à Lapide*. Trans. T. W. Mossman, et al. London, 1887–1890. 6 vols.

Laupot, E. "Tacitus' Fragment 2: The Anti-Roman Movement of the *Christiani* and the Nazoreans." *Vigiliae Christianae* 54, 3 (2000), 233–47.

Law, T. M. *When God Spoke Greek: The Septuagint and the Making of the Christian Bible*. Oxford, 2013.

Lepers, P. "Noblest of Men, Great Egoist or Idiot? Nietzsche on Jesus." *Nietzsche und die Reformation*. Ed. H. Heit and A. Urs Sommer. Berlin, 2020.

Lierman, J. "The Mosaic Pattern of John's Christology." *Challenging Perspectives on the Gospel of John*. Ed. J. Lierman. (Wissenschaftliche Untersuchungen zum Neuen Testament 219.) Tübingen, 2006.

Lieu, J. *Christian Identity in the Jewish and Graeco-Roman World*. Oxford, 2004.

Litwa, M. D. *Iesus Deus: The Early Christian Depiction of Jesus as a Mediterranean God*. Minneapolis, 2014.

———, *How the Gospels Became History: Jesus and Mediterranean Myths*. New Haven—London, 2019.

Lohse, E. *Colossians and Philemon: A Commentary on the Epistles to the Colossians and to Philemon*. (Hermeneia.) Ed. H. Koester. Trans. W. R. Poehlmann and R. J. Karris. Philadelphia, 1971.

Luz, U. *Matthew 8–20: A Commentary*. (Hermeneia.) Ed. H. Koester. Trans. J. E. Crouch. Minneapolis, 2001.

———, *Matthew 21–28: A Commentary*. (Hermeneia.) Ed. H. Koester. Trans. J. E. Crouch. Minneapolis, 2005.

———, *Matthew 1–7: A Commentary*. (Hermeneia.) Ed. H. Koester. Trans. J. E. Crouch. Minneapolis, 2007.

Magny, A. *Porphyry in Fragments: Reception of an Anti-Christian Text in Late Antiquity*. London—New York, 2014.

BIBLIOGRAPHY

Malherbe, A. J. "The Christianization of a *Topos* (Luke 12:13–34)." *Novum Testamentum* 38, 2 (1996), 123–35.

———, *Light from the Gentiles: Hellenistic Philosophy and Early Christianity; Collected Essays, 1959–2012. Volume 1.* (Supplements to Novum Testamentum 150.) Ed. C. R. Holladay, J. T. Fitzgerald, G. E. Sterling, and J. W. Thompson. Leiden, 2014.

Marshak, A. K. "Rise of the Idumeans: Ethnicity and Politics in Herod's Judea." *Jewish Identity and Politics between the Maccabees and Bar Kokhba: Groups, Normativity, and Rituals.* Ed. B. Eckhardt. Leiden, 2012.

Matthews, C. R. *Philip, Apostle and Evangelist: Configurations of a Tradition.* (Supplements to Novum Testamentum 105.) Leiden, 2002.

McKechnie, P. "Judaean Embassies and Cases before Roman Emperors, AD 44–66." *Journal of Theological Studies* (N.S.) 56, 2 (2005), 339–61.

Meier, J. P. *A Marginal Jew: Rethinking the Historical Jesus, Volume 1: The Roots of the Problem and the Person.* New Haven, 1991.

———, *A Marginal Jew: Rethinking the Historical Jesus, Volume 3: Companions and Competitors.* New York—London, 2001.

Merleau-Ponty, M. *Nature: Course Notes from the Collège de France.* Ed. D. Séglard. Trans. R. Vallier. Evanston, Illinois, 2003.

Metzger, B. M. *A Textual Commentary on the Greek New Testament.* London—New York, 1975.

Metzger B. M., and B. D. Ehrman. *The Text of the New Testament: Its Transmission, Corruption, and Restoration.* Oxford, 2005.

Metzner, R. *Kaiphas. Der Hohepriester jenes Jahres. Geschichte und Deutung.* (Ancient Judaism and Early Christianity 75.) Leiden, 2010.

Millar, F. "Reflections on the Trials of Jesus." *A Tribute to Geza Vermes: Essays on Jewish and Christian Literature and History.* (Journal for the Study of the Old Testament Supplement Series 100.) Ed. P. R. Davies and R. T. White. Sheffield, 1990.

———, *The Roman Near East, 31 BC–AD 33.* Cambridge, Mass., 1993.

Mitchell, M. M. "Origen, Celsus and Lucian on the 'Dénouement of the Drama' of the Gospels." *Reading Religions in the Ancient World.* (Novum Testamentum Supplements 125.) Ed. D. E. Aune and R. D. Young. Leiden, 2007.

Moorhead, J. "The Word *modernus*." *Latomus* 65, 2 (2006), 425–33.

BIBLIOGRAPHY

Moses, R. E. "Jesus Barabbas, a Nominal Messiah? Text and History in Matthew 27.16–17." *New Testament Studies* 58 (2011), 43–56.

Müller, M. *The First Bible of the Church: A Plea for the Septuagint.* (Journal for the Study of the Old Testament Supplement Series 206.) Sheffield, 1996.

———, "Paul: The Oldest Witness to the Historical Jesus." *'Is This Not the Carpenter?' The Question of the Historicity of the Figure of Jesus.* Ed. T. L. Thompson and T. S. Verenna. (Copenhagen International Seminar.) London, 2012.

———, *The Expression 'Son of Man' and the Development of Christology: A History of Interpretation.* (Copenhagen International Seminar.) New York—London, 2014.

Muraoka, T. "Luke and the Septuagint." *Novum Testamentum* 54, 1 (2012), 13–15.

Mussies, G. *Dio Chrysostom and the New Testament: Collected Parallels.* (Studia ad Corpus Hellenisticum Novi Testamenti 2.) Leiden, 1972.

Nabokov, V. *Bend Sinister.* New York, 1990.

———, *Glory.* Trans. D. Nabokov. London, 2012.

New English Bible: The Apocrypha. Oxford—Cambridge, 1970.

Nicolotti, A. *From the Mandylion of Edessa to the Shroud of Turin: The Metamorphosis and Manipulation of a Legend.* (Art and Material Culture in Medieval and Renaissance Europe 1.) Leiden, 2014.

Niehoff, M. R. *Jewish Exegesis and Homeric Scholarship in Alexandria.* Cambridge, 2011.

———, "A Jewish Critique of Christianity from Second-Century Alexandria: Revisiting the Jew Mentioned in *Contra Celsum*." *Journal of Early Christian Studies* 21, 2 (2013), 151–75.

Nietzsche, F. *Menschliches, Allzumenschliches. Zweiter Band. Nachgelassene Fragmente. Frühling 1878 bis November 1879.* (Kritische Gesamtausgabe 4.3.) Ed. G. Colli and M. Montinari. Berlin, 1967.

———, *Friedrich Nietzsche Briefe. Januar 1887–Januar 1889.* (Nietzsche Briefwechsel: Kritische Gesamtausgabe 3,5.) Ed. G. Colli and M. Montinari with H. Anania-Hess. Berlin—New York, 1984.

———, *Der Fall Wagner. Götzen-Dämmerung. Der Antichrist. Ecce homo.*

BIBLIOGRAPHY

Dionysos-Dithyramben. Nietzsche contra Wagner. (Kritische Studienausgabe 6.) Ed. G. Colli and M. Montinari. Berlin—New York, 1988.

———, *Menschliches, Allzumenschliches I und II.* (Kritische Studienausgabe 2.) Ed. G. Colli and M. Montinari. Berlin—New York, 1988.

———, *Human, All Too Human.* Trans. R. J. Hollingdale. Cambridge, 1996.

———, *The Case of Wagner. Twilight of the Idols. The Antichrist. Ecce Homo. Dionysus Dithyrambs. Nietzsche Contra Wagner.* (The Complete Works of Friedrich Nietzsche.) Ed. G. Colli and M. Montinari. Trans. A. Del Caro, C. Diethe, et al. Stanford, 2021.

Noble, S. *The Kitāb al-Manfaʿa of Abdallāh ibn al-Fadl al-Antākī: Critical Edition, Translation and Commentary.* Doctoral thesis of the Katholieke Universiteit Leuven. Defended on 20 April 2022.

Nothaft, C. P. E. *Dating the Passion: The Life of Jesus and the Emergence of Scientific Chronology (200–1600).* (Time, Astronomy, and Calendars 1.) Leiden, 2012.

Orlinski, S. "The Unwitting Apostles of the North: Human Trafficking and Christianization in the Viking Age." *Viking-Age Slavery.* Ed. M. Toplak, H. Østhus, and R. Simek. Vienna, 2021.

Pascal, B. *Pensées.* Ed. L. Brunschvicg. Paris, 1972.

Pascal, B. *Pensées.* Trans. A. J. Krailsheimer. London—New York, 1966.

Pelikan, J. *Jesus through the Centuries: His Place in the History of Culture.* New Haven, 1985.

Penwell, S. *Jesus the Samaritan: Ethnic Labeling in the Gospel of John.* (Biblical Interpretation Series 170.) Leiden, 2019.

Petersen, W. L. "Tatian the Assyrian." *A Companion to Second-Century Christian "Heretics".* (Supplements to Vigiliae Christianae 76.) Ed. A. Marjanen and P. Luomanen. Leiden, 2005.

Pevarello, D. "Criticism of Verbosity in Ancient Philosophical and Early Christian Writings: Jesus' Critique of the 'Polylogia' of Pagan Prayers (Matthew 6:7) in its Graeco-Roman Context." *Religio-Philosophical Discourses in the Mediterranean World: From Plato, through Jesus, to Late Antiquity.* Ed. A. Klostergaard Petersen and G. van Kooten. Leiden, 2017.

BIBLIOGRAPHY

Pines, S. *An Arabic Version of the Testimonium Flavianum and its Implications.* Jerusalem, 1971.

———, "Spinoza's *Tractatus Theologico-Politicus*, Maimonides and Kant." *Studies in the History of Jewish Thought.* (The Collected Works of Shlomo Pines 5.) Ed. W. Z. Harvey and M. Idel. Jerusalem, 1997.

Plátová, J. "The Text of Mark 10:29–30 in Quis dives salvetur? by Clement of Alexandria." *The Process of Authority: The Dynamics in Transmission and Reception of Canonical Texts.* Ed. J. Dušek and J. Roskovec. Berlin, 2016.

Pokorný, P. "Jesus as the Ever-Living Lawgiver in the *Letter* of Mara bar Sarapion." *The Letter of Mara bar Sarapion in Context.* (Culture and History of the Ancient Near East 58.) Ed. A. Merz and T. Tieleman. Leiden, 2012.

Popkin, R. H. "Spinoza and the *Three Imposters*." *The Third Force in Seventeenth-Century Thought.* (Brill's Studies in Intellectual History 22). Leiden, 1992.

Potter, D. *Prophets and Emperors: Human and Divine Authority from Augustus to Theodosius.* Cambridge, Mass., 1994.

Pound, E. *Collected Early Poems of Ezra Pound.* Ed. M. J. King. Intro. L. L. Martz. New York, 1976.

———, *The Cantos of Ezra Pound.* New York, 1993.

Praz, M. *The Romantic Agony.* Trans. A. Davidson. Oxford, 1933.

Reimarus, H. S. *The Goal of Jesus and His Disciples.* Trans. G. W. Buchanan. Leiden, 1970.

———, *Reimarus: Fragments.* Ed. C. H. Talbert. Trans. R. S. Fraser. London, 1971.

Ridings, D. *The Attic Moses: The Dependency Theme in Some Early Christian Writers.* Gothenburg, 1995.

Rives, J. "Human Sacrifice among Pagans and Christians." *Journal of Roman Studies* 85 (1995), 65–85.

Rowlands, J. "Jesus and the Wings of Yhwh. Bird Imagery in the Lament over Jerusalem (Matt 23:37–39; Luke 13:34–35)." *Novum Testamentum* 61 (2019), 115–36.

Salih, Z. M. "Sudan Woman Faces Death by Stoning for Adultery in First Case for a Decade." *The Guardian* (13 July 2022). Archived online at

BIBLIOGRAPHY

https://www.theguardian.com/global-development/2022/jul/13/sudan-woman-faces-death-by-stoning-for-adultery-in-first-case-for-a-decade. Accessed on 13 July 2022.

Samuelsson, G. *Crucifixion in Antiquity: An Inquiry into the Background and Significance of the New Testament Terminology of Crucifixion.* (Wissenschaftliche Untersuchungen zum Neuen Testament 310.) Tübingen, 2013.

Schäfer, P. *Judeophobia: Attitudes toward the Jews in the Ancient World.* Cambridge, Mass., 1997.

———, *The History of the Jews in the Greco-Roman World.* London—New York, 2003.

Schaper, J. "The Pharisees." *The Cambridge History of Judaism, Volume Three: The Early Roman Period.* Ed. W. Horbury, W. Davies, and J. Sturdy. Cambridge, 1999.

Scheid, J. *The Gods, the State, and the Individual: Reflections on Civic Religion in Rome.* Trans. C. Ando. Philadelphia, 2015.

Schiavone, A. *Pontius Pilate: Deciphering a Memory.* New York—London, 2017.

Schmidt, T. C. "Calculating December 25 as the Birth of Jesus in Hippolytus' *Canon* and *Chronicon*." *Vigiliae Christianae* 69, 5 (2015), 542–63.

Schmitt, C. *Political Romanticism.* (Studies in Contemporary German Social Thought.) Trans. G. Oakes. Cambridge, Mass., 1991.

Schopenhauer, A. *The World as Will and Representation, Volume 2.* (The Cambridge Edition of the Works of Schopenhauer.) Trans. J. Norman, A. Welchman, and C. Janaway. Cambridge, 2018.

Schürer, E. *The History of the Jewish People in the Age of Jesus Christ (175 B.C.–A.D. 135).* Rev. and ed. G. Vermes and F. Millar, with P. Vermes and M. Black. Edinburgh, 1973. 2 vols.

Schwartz, D. R. "Malthace, Archelaus, and Herod Antipas: Between Genealogy and Typology." *Jewish Identity and Politics between the Maccabees and Bar Kokhba: Groups, Normativity, and Rituals.* Ed. B. Eckhardt. Leiden, 2012.

Sebeok, T., and J. Umiker-Sebeok. "'You Know My Method'." *The Sign of*

BIBLIOGRAPHY

Three: Dupin, Holmes, Peirce. Ed. U. Eco and T. Sebeok. Bloomington, 1983.

Shaw, B. D. "The Myth of the Neronian Persecution." *The Journal of Roman Studies* 105 (2015), 73–100.

Slings, S. R. *Critical Notes on Plato's Politeia.* (Mnemosyne 267.) Ed. G. Boter and J. van Ophuijsen. Leiden, 2005.

Smith, M. "The Troublemakers." *The Cambridge History of Judaism, Volume Three: The Early Roman Period.* Ed. W. Horbury, W. Davies, and J. Sturdy. Cambridge, 1999.

Spinoza, B. de. *Tractatus Theologico-Politicus. Traité Théologico-Politique.* (Œuvres 3.) Latin ed. F. Akkerman. French trans. J. Lagrée and P.-F. Moreau. Paris, 1999.

———, *Theological-Political Treatise.* Ed. J. Israel. Trans. M. Silverthorne and J. Israel. Cambridge, 2007.

Stegman, T. D. "Reading Luke 12:13–34 as an Elaboration of a Chreia: How Hermogenes of Tarsus Sheds Light on Luke's Gospel." *Novum Testamentum* 49, 4 (2007), 328–352.

Steiner, G. "The Scandal of Revelation." *Salgamundi* 98–99 (1993), 42–70.

———, "Two Suppers." *Salgamundi* 108 (1995), 33–61.

———, *Lessons of the Masters: The Charles Eliot Norton Lectures.* Cambridge, Mass., 2003.

Stemberger, G. "The Sadducees—Their History and Doctrines." *The Cambridge History of Judaism, Volume Three: The Early Roman Period.* Ed. W. Horbury, W. Davies, and J. Sturdy. Cambridge, 1999.

Sterling, G. "*Mors philosophi*: The Death of Jesus in Luke." *The Harvard Theological Review* 94, 4 (2001), 383–402.

Stern, M. *Greek and Latin Authors on Jews and Judaism. Volume One: From Herodotus to Plutarch.* Jerusalem, 1976.

———, *Greek and Latin Authors on Jews and Judaism. Volume Two: From Tacitus to Simplicius.* Jerusalem, 1980.

———, *Greek and Latin Authors on Jews and Judaism. Volume Three: Appendixes and Indexes.* Jerusalem, 1984.

Stroumsa, G. G. "From Anti-Judaism to Antisemitism in Early Christianity?" *Contra Iudaeos: Ancient and Medieval Polemics between Christians and Jews.* Ed. O. Limor and G. G. Stroumsa. Tübingen, 1996.

BIBLIOGRAPHY

————, *Barbarian Philosophy: The Religious Revolution of Early Christianity.* (Wissenschaftliche Untersuchungen zum Neuen Testament 112.) Tübingen, 1999.

————, *The End of Sacrifice: Religious Transformations in Late Antiquity.* Trans. S. Emanuel. Chicago, 2009.

————, "From Abraham's Religion to the Abrahamic Religions." *Historia Religionum* 3 (2011), 11–22.

————, "Christ's Laughter: Docetic Origins Reconsidered." *The Crucible of Religion in Late Antiquity.* (Studien und Texte zu Antike und Christentum 124.) Tübingen, 2021.

————, "Reading Origen in Jerusalem." *Tablet Magazine* (26 July 2021). Archived online at https://www.tabletmag.com/sections/history/articles/reading-origen-in-jerusalem. Accessed on 28 June 2022.

Sturch, R. L. "The Πατρίς of Jesus." *The Journal of Theological Studies* (N.S.) 28, 1 (1977), 94–96.

Subin, A. D. *Accidental Gods: On Men Unwittingly Turned Divine.* London, 2021.

Sugirtharajah, R. S. *Jesus in Asia.* Cambridge, Mass., 2018.

Tanaseanu-Döbler, I. "The Logos in Amelius' Fragment on the Gospel of John and Plutarch's *De Iside.*" *Plutarch and the New Testament in Their Religio-Philosophical Contexts: Bridging Discourses in the World of the Early Roman Empire.* (Brill's Plutarch Studies 9.) Ed. R. Hirsch-Luipold. Leiden, 2022.

Taubes, J. *Occidental Eschatology.* Trans. D. Ratmoko. Stanford, 2009.

Taylor, J. E. "Pontius Pilate and the Imperial Cult in Roman Judaea." *New Testament Studies* 52 (2002), 555–82.

Thom, J. C. "Cleanthes' *Hymn to Zeus* and Early Christian Literature." *Antiquity and Humanity: Essays on Ancient Religion and Philosophy. Presented to Hans Dieter Betz on His Seventieth Birthday.* Ed. A. Yarbro Collins and M. Mitchell. Tübingen, 2001.

————, "Wisdom in the Wisdom of Solomon and Cleanthes' *Hymn to Zeus.*" *Septuagint and Reception: Essays prepared for the Association for the Study of the Septuagint in South Africa.* (Supplements to the Vetus Testamentum 127.) Ed. J. Cook. Leiden, 2009.

————, "God the Saviour in Greco-Roman Popular Philosophy." *Sōtēria:*

BIBLIOGRAPHY

Salvation in Early Christianity and Antiquity. Festschrift in Honour of Cilliers Breytenbach. (Novum Testamentum Supplements 175.) Ed. D. du Toit, C. Gerber, and C. Zimmermann. Leiden, 2019.

Thorsteinsson, R. M. *Roman Christianity and Roman Stoicism: A Comparative Study of Ancient Morality.* Oxford, 2010.

———, *Jesus as Philosopher: The Moral Sage in the Synoptic Gospels.* Oxford, 2018.

Tov, E. "Did the Septuagint Translators Always Understand Their Hebrew Text?" *The Greek and Hebrew Bible: Collected Essays on the Septuagint.* (Supplements to Vetus Testamentum 72.) Leiden—Cologne, 1999.

Trobisch, D. *The First Edition of the New Testament.* Oxford, 2000.

Twelftree, G. H. *Jesus the Exorcist: A Contribution to the Study of the Historical Jesus.* (Wissenschaftliche Untersuchungen zum Neuen Testament 54.) Tübingen, 1993.

van den Broek, R. *Gnostic Religion in Antiquity.* Cambridge, 2013.

van Henten, J. W. "The First Testing of Jesus: A Rereading of Mark 1.12–13." *New Testament Studies* 45, 3 (1999), 349–66.

———, "Jewish Martyrdom and Jesus' Death." *Deutungen des Todes Jesu im Neuen Testament.* Ed. J. Frey and J. Schröter. Tübingen, 2012.

van Kooten, G. H. "The 'True Light which Enlightens Everyone' (*John* 1:9): John, *Genesis*, The Platonic Notion of the 'True, Noetic Light', and the Allegory of the Cave in Plato's *Republic*." *The Creation of Heaven and Earth: Re-interpretations of Genesis i in the Context of Judaism, Ancient Philosophy, Christianity, and Modern Physics.* Ed. G. H. van Kooten. Leiden, 2005.

———, "The Last Days of Socrates and Christ: *Euthyphro, Apology, Crito,* and *Phaedo* Read in Counterpoint with John's Gospel." *Religio-Philosophical Discourses in the Mediterranean World: From Plato, through Jesus, to Late Antiquity.* Ed. A. Klostergaard Petersen and G. van Kooten. Leiden, 2017.

———, "John's Counter-Symposium: 'The Continuation of Dialogue' in Christianity—A Contrapuntal Reading of John's Gospel and Plato's *Symposium*." *Intolerance, Polemics, and Debate in Antiquity: Politico-Cultural, Philosophical, and Religious Forms of Critical Conversation.* Ed. G. van Kooten and J. van Ruiten. Leiden, 2019.

———, "Christ and Hermes: A Religio-Historical Comparison of the Johannine Christ-Logos with the God Hermes in Greek Mythology and Philosophy." *Im Gespräch mit C. F. Georg Heinrici. Beiträge zwischen Theologie und Religionswissenschaft.* Ed. M. Frenschkowski and L. Seehausen. Tübingen, 2021.

Van Voorst, R. E. "Jesus Tradition in Classical and Jewish Writings." *Handbook for the Study of the Historical Jesus.* Ed. T. Holmén and S. E. Porter. Leiden, 2011.

Varner, W. "On the Trail of Trypho: Two Fragmentary Jewish-Christian Dialogues from the Ancient Church." *Christian Origins and Hellenistic Judaism: Social and Literary Contexts for the New Testament.* (Texts and Editions for New Testament Study 10.) Ed. S. E. Porter and A. Pitts. Leiden, 2013.

Vermes, G. *Jesus the Jew: A Historian's Reading of the Gospels.* Philadelphia, 1981.

———, *Jesus: Nativity—Passion—Resurrection.* London, 2008.

Versnel, H. S. "Making Sense of Jesus' Death: The Pagan Contribution." *Deutungen des Todes Jesu im Neuen Testament.* Ed. J. Frey and J. Schröter. Tübingen, 2012.

Veyne, P. *Bread and Circuses: Historical Sociology and Political Pluralism.* Trans. B. Pearce. Ed. O. Murray. London, 1990.

Vulgate Bible. Volume VI: The New Testament. (Dumbarton Oaks Medieval Library 21.) Ed. A. M. Kinney. Intro. S. Edgar. Cambridge, Mass., 2013.

Wajdenbaum, P. "The Books of the Maccabees and Polybius." *The Bible and Hellenism: Greek Influence on Jewish and Early Christian Literature.* (Copenhagen International Seminar.) Ed. T. L. Thompson and P. Wajdenbaum. London—New York, 2014.

Wasserstein, A., and D. J. Wasserstein. *The Legend of the Septuagint: From Classical Antiquity to Today.* Cambridge, 2006.

Watson, A. *The Trial of Jesus.* Athens, Georgia, 1995.

———, *Jesus: A Profile.* Athens, Georgia, 1998.

———, *The Trial of Stephen: The First Christian Martyr.* Athens, Georgia, 2012.

Weiss, J. *Die Predigt Jesu vom Reiche Gottes.* Göttingen, 1892.

BIBLIOGRAPHY

Wetstein, J. J. Ἡ Καινὴ Διαθήκη. *Novum Testamentum Graecum editionis receptae cum lectionibus variantibus … Tomus I. Continens quatuor Evangelia*. Amsterdam, 1751.

Wintour, P. "Persecution of Christians 'Coming Close to Genocide' in Middle East." *The Guardian* (2 May 2019). Archived online at https://www.theguardian.com/world/2019/may/02/persecution-driving-christians-out-of-middle-east-report. Accessed on 5 June 2019.

Wittgenstein, L. *Vermischte Bemerkungen—Culture and Value*. Ed. G. H. von Wright with H. Nyman. Rev. A. Pichler. Trans. P. Winch. Oxford, 1980.

Wycliffe, J. *The Wycliffe New Testament (1388)*. Ed. W. R. Cooper. London, 2002.

Yarbro Collins, A. *Mark: A Commentary*. (Hermeneia.) Ed. H. W. Attridge. Minneapolis, 2007.

Young, J. *Friedrich Nietzsche: A Philosophical Biography*. Cambridge, 2010.

Zaas, P. "'Every Signal Worth Reading': Jesus and Jewish Sectarians in Mark." *Reading Religions in the Ancient World*. (Novum Testamentum Supplements 125.) Ed. D. E. Aune and R. D. Young. Leiden, 2007.

Zerwick, M., and M. Grosvenor. *A Grammatical Analysis of the Greek New Testament*. Rome, 1981.

INDEX

Note: Page numbers followed by "*n*" refer to notes.

INDEX

INDEX

INDEX

INDEX

INDEX

Mammon, 127, 128

Manaen (courtier), 161–62, 266*n*13

Mara bar Sarapion (philosopher), 66–67, 69–70, 199

views on Judaeans, 72–73

marauder-Jesus theory, 25

Mariyam. *See* Mary

Mark, 11, 12, 15, 41–42, 99

Caiaphas, 165–69, 175–76

copper coins, 139–41

details on Jesus' death, 43–45

"house of prayer", 143–45

Jesus as a Galilean, 162–63

Jesus' arrest, 149–51

Judaean elites' resolution, 151–52

on Pilate, 190–94

Mark (11), 142–43

Mark (12), 142

Mark (14), 166

Mark (15), 41–42, 150

Mark (2), 99

Mary (Jesus' mother), 13, 65, 153, 242*n*6

Matthew, 41, 42, 49, 100

critique of religious culture, 209

Judaean elites' resolution, 151–52

'mercy' and 'sacrifice', 185–86

on Pilate, 194–200

Realpolitik principle, 136–38

Temple aristocracy, 154–55

Matthew (23), 196–97

Matthew (27), 150, 195–97, 199

Caiaphas, 175–76

Mediterranean cities, 68

Meleager (philosopher), 21

Menander (dramatist), 16

'mercy', 185–86

Merleau-Ponty, Maurice, 41, 42–3

Millar, Fergus, 66–67, 83

Mimesis (Auerbach), 59

Mosaic law, 117

Moses, 3, 91, 105

Mosollamos (archer), 51–52

Muhammad, 6, 106

"mysteries of God", 125

"mystery of faith", 125

Nazarenes, 13

Nazareth, 12, 21, 226*n*9

New Testament, 125, 159, 222*n*11, 224*n*2

Nicodemus (disciple), 204

Nietzsche, Friedrich, 3, 4, 6–7, 10, 33–35, 67, 140–41, 210, 234*n*22

Orations (Dio), 13–14, 68

Origen (philosopher), 48–49, 62, 74, 237*n*30, 245*n*54

'pagan' philosophy, 23

parrhēsia, 61

Pascal, Blaise, 42, 47, 66, 102, 190, 237*n*24

Passion, 58, 65

Passover, 60, 160, 191–92

INDEX

INDEX

INDEX

Wölfenbuttel (library), 37–38

"Wölfenbuttel fragmentarist" (Kant), 37

Zealot doctrine, 123, 257*n*5

Zealot-Jesus theory, 25, 93, 169

Zealots, 90, 92–93, 123–24, 145–46

Zechariah (prophet), 146, 261*n*24